THE NOT-QUITE STATES OF AMERICA

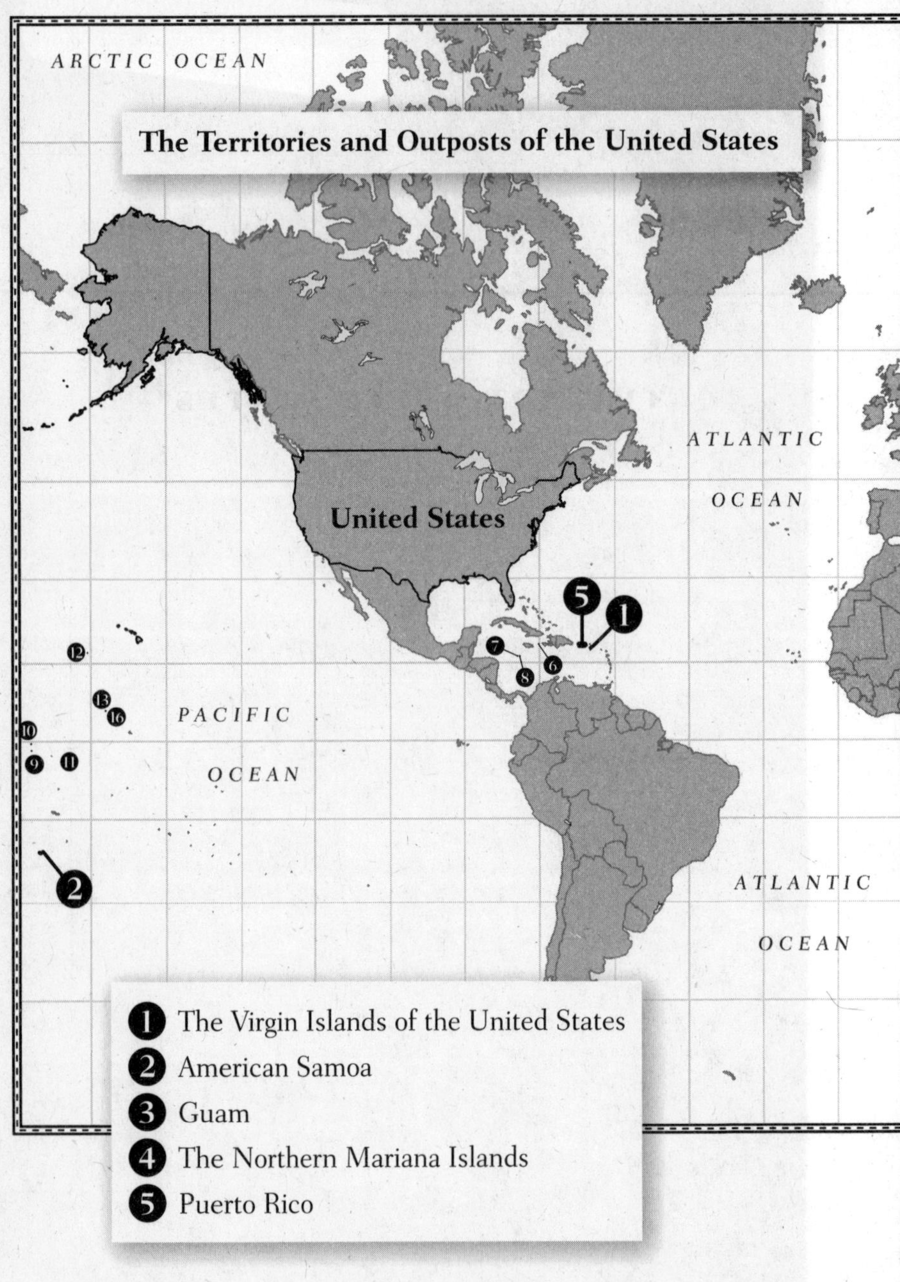
ARCTIC OCEAN
The Territories and Outposts of the United States
United States
ATLANTIC OCEAN
PACIFIC OCEAN
ATLANTIC OCEAN
1 The Virgin Islands of the United States
2 American Samoa
3 Guam
4 The Northern Mariana Islands
5 Puerto Rico

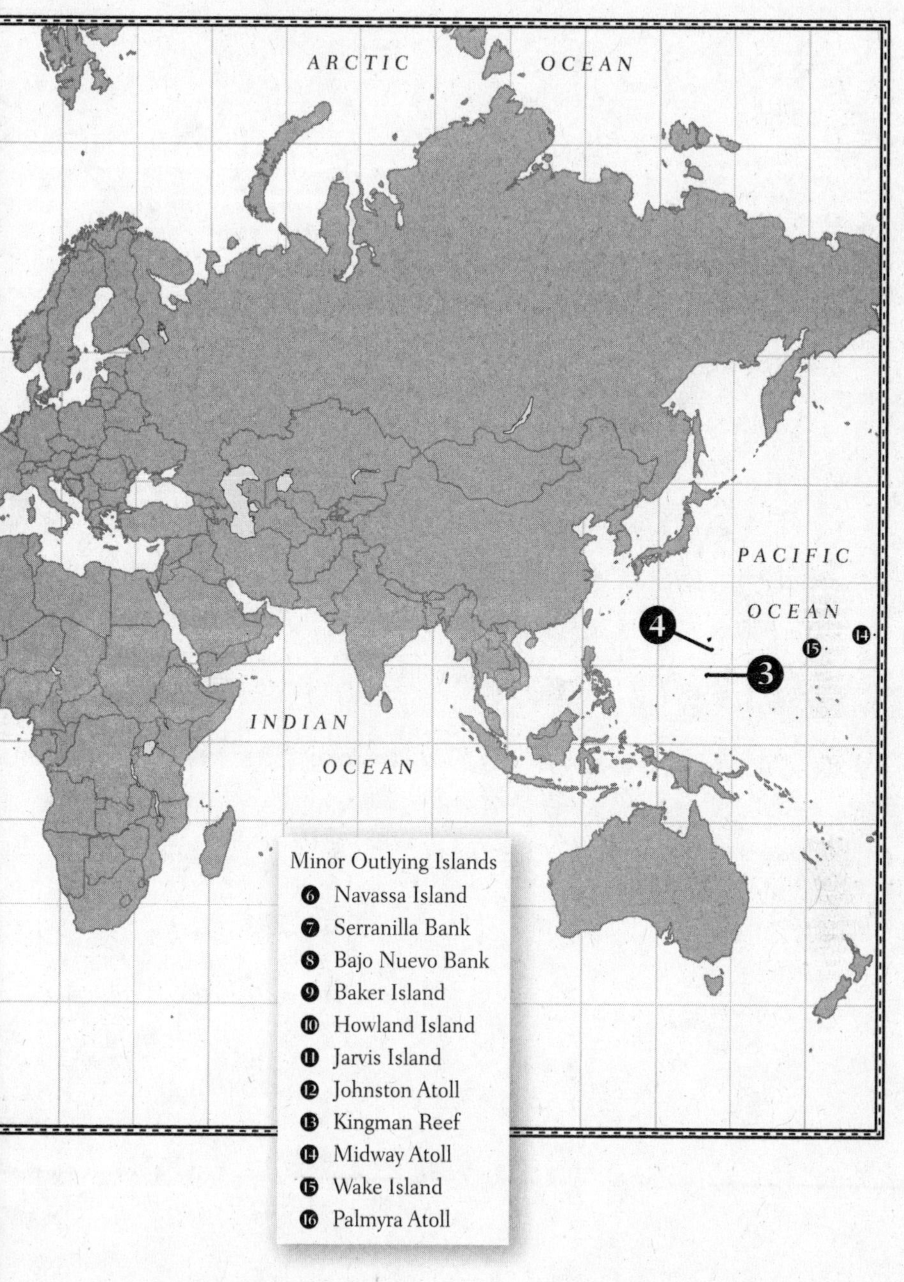

ARCTIC
OCEAN
PACIFIC
OCEAN
INDIAN
OCEAN
4
3
15
14
Minor Outlying Islands
6 Navassa Island
7 Serranilla Bank
8 Bajo Nuevo Bank
9 Baker Island
10 Howland Island
11 Jarvis Island
12 Johnston Atoll
13 Kingman Reef
14 Midway Atoll
15 Wake Island
16 Palmyra Atoll

THE NOT-QUITE STATES OF AMERICA

Dispatches from the Territories and Other Far-Flung Outposts of the USA

Doug Mack

W. W. NORTON & COMPANY
Independent Publishers Since 1923
NEW YORK LONDON

Printed in the United States of America
First Edition

For information about permission to reproduce selections from this book,
write to Permissions, W. W. Norton & Company, Inc.,
500 Fifth Avenue, New York, NY 10110

For information about special discounts for bulk purchases, please contact
W. W. Norton Special Sales at specialsales@wwnorton.com
or 800-233-4830

Manufacturing by Quad Graphics Fairfield
Book design by Brian Mulligan
Production manager: Louise Mattarelliano

Library of Congress Cataloging-in-Publication Data

Names: Mack, Doug, author.
Title: The Not-Quite States of America : Dispatches from the Territories and Other Far-Flung Outposts of the USA / Doug Mack.
Description: First edition. | New York : W. W. Norton & Company, 2017. | Includes bibliographical references and index.
Identifiers: LCCN 2016029476 | ISBN 9780393247602 (hardcover)
Subjects: LCSH: Mack, Doug—Travel. | United States—Territories and possessions—History. | United States—Insular possessions—History. | United States—Territories and possessions—Description and travel. | United States—Insular possessions—Description and travel.
Classification: LCC F965 .M33 2017 | DDC 909/.0971273—dc23 LC record available at https://lccn.loc.gov/2016029476

W. W. Norton & Company, Inc.
500 Fifth Avenue, New York, N.Y. 10110
www.wwnorton.com

W. W. Norton & Company Ltd.
15 Carlisle Street, London W1D 3BS

1 2 3 4 5 6 7 8 9 0

For Maren

CONTENTS

INTRODUCTION

I've always believed the disorienting sense of arrival in a new place to be one of the great joys of travel. This, however, was a whole new level of confusion.

On a clear January evening, I had boarded an airplane in Miami and flown across the sea. As we descended from the clouds, well after dark, I gazed down at the capital city, a tight cluster of low buildings and palmy treetops surrounding a broad harbor full of sailboats, their mast lights a swaying constellation against the darkened waters. The urban grid, traced by streetlights, was compact and orderly at the waterfront before tangling into a jumble of narrow lanes marching up a steep wooded hillside. It was one part pastoral tropics, one part humming city; I was instantly smitten.

We landed and taxied to the gate, and I turned on my cell phone to review my instructions from Verizon. All calls would incur international roaming charges, they said, but text messages, emails, and Internet use were all considered domestic. If I was talking, I was abroad; if I was typing, I was still in the United States—a neat, physics-defying party trick. I texted my wife, Maren, to confirm my safe arrival, then read the headlines on the *New York Times* website, which automatically redirected me to the international edition. When I clicked over to a local news site, the top stories were about dengue fever fears, the results of a regatta, and an area skier who was making final preparations for the Winter Olympics, where she would represent her tiny-but-proud national team.

I disembarked and instinctively looked for the sign to customs, but there was no customs—not on the way in, though there would be on the way out: paperwork, passport check, the whole gauntlet.

The owner of the guesthouse where I was staying met me at baggage claim, a burly guy named Ronnie Lockhart. He was grizzled and outwardly gruff but with a low-key kindness; think of your stereotype of a retired cop. As we headed into town, I noted that traffic drove on the left, like the British, but the cars were American, with steering wheels on the left. This was a combination I didn't know existed anywhere in the world, and it was a perpetual struggle not to yell out to Ronnie that he was driving on the wrong side of the road.

We wound past branches of Banco Popular and Scotiabank, past a U.S. National Guard recruiting storefront. The buildings were low-slung, with red-tile hipped roofs and large, louvered windows, and every surface fading and peeling in that inevitable tropical way. The streets were called Moravian Highway and Kronprindsens Gade and Espaniol and Rue de Saint-Barthélemy and Main Street. American flags twisted in the breeze outside all the official-looking buildings, but there were also quite a few Danish flags in places of prominence, and flashes of the green-gold-red stripes of Ethiopia on retaining-wall murals and café awnings. Outside the local cricket grounds, a billboard for a cell phone company showed a player in all-white regalia, with the tagline, "No drifters, no yips, no ducks. Basically, straight-up."

A couple of blocks later, a well-kept baseball stadium advertised upcoming appearances by Major League stars.

Everywhere, there were signals that I was in my homeland.

Everywhere, there were signals that I was not.

The sign at the airport had read WELCOME TO SAINT THOMAS, US VIRGIN ISLANDS. I was still in the USA, but far from the states.

• • • • •

FROM THIRTEEN original colonies, as every schoolkid knows, the USA has become a nation of fifty proud states. So pleasingly, conclusively round, that number. So tidily those rows of stars fit on the flag, as though geopolitical destiny were dictated by graphic-design convenience. But despite what we advertise on our flag, despite what it says right there in our name, the United States of America is not merely a nation of states but also—legally and officially—of those scattered shards of earth and populace that make up our outposts far from the North American continent: the territories of the Virgin Islands of the United States, American Samoa, Guam, the Northern Mariana Islands, and Puerto Rico, along with the uninhabited Minor Outlying Islands.

They have U.S. national parks and American Legion posts and U.S. post offices—just a standard first-class stamp gets your mail there; it's all the same country. Their millions of citizens earn American dollars and pay into Social Security and Medicare and serve in the U.S. military at impressively high rates. They participate in the Scripps Howard National Spelling Bee and receive Pell grants and play Little League baseball and have 4-H Clubs and serve as United States ambassadors. They pledge allegiance to the American flag, even if Old Glory hasn't made room for them.

Yet for the average resident of the states (lowercase *s*—because States would be the whole nation), the territories are all but forgotten. They're extant but inconsequential, vestiges from another era whose ongoing existence is a cultural curiosity, like Tab soda or professional mini golf. They flicker into our consciousness here and there—an offbeat news story, a friend's tropical-island vacation photos, a passing reference in the fine print of a governmental form—and for a moment we think, *Oh, right . . . we have territories*. Then, just as quickly, they disappear from our minds once more.

"Nobody knows in America, Puerto Rico's in America!" goes a line in *West Side Story*, the musical that may be the primary entry point for many Americans' knowledge of the territories. But in the classic patriotic songbook, they get no mention—America the beautiful stretches from sea to shining sea, not across the seas—just as they're absent from the maps in television weather forecasts and magazine infographics and classroom walls, even though Alaska and Hawaii typically sneak in with their "not to scale" boxes.

The territories are not part of our conception of ourselves. Picture the archetypal Americans across the eras—indigenous peoples and bewigged Founding Fathers and wilderness homesteaders and slaves and miners and cowboys and world-war-winning soldiers and factory workers and opportunity-seeking immigrants and outer-ring-suburb dwellers—and you are almost certainly imagining their natural habitat to be, implicitly, the *states*. Search the classic tales of the American Road Trip, that keystone of the country's literary canon, and you'll find, among others, Alexis de Tocqueville on the trail of *Democracy in America*, from Boston to Green Bay (which was then part of the Northwest Territory) to the Gulf of Mexico; Mark Twain traipsing across the West and to the then–Kingdom of Hawaii in *Roughing It*; and Sal Paradise and Dean Moriarty bopping from coast to coast and into Mexico in Jack Kerouac's *On the Road*. But none of the most famous journeys "in search of America," as they are inevitably framed, have included the present-day territories, the *not-quite* states.

For that matter, no sitting American president has visited all five inhabited territories. Lyndon B. Johnson holds the lead, with three; he was also the last president to visit American Samoa, in 1967. No sitting president has ever been to the Northern Mariana Islands.

• • • • •

UNTIL VERY RECENTLY, I couldn't even list the territories, let alone tell you anything about them. And if there's anyone with no excuse for this, it's me, a travel writer with a college degree in—*ahem*—American studies.

My obsession with Americana runs deep, pulsing through my childhood in Minneapolis, when my parents read me *Travels with Charley* and *How Many Miles to Galena?* at bedtime (two more American Road Trip books with no love for the territories). For my fifth birthday, I asked Mom and Dad to take me to Mickey's Diner, a Saint Paul institution of neon and chrome and short-order cooks. I'd never been before but thought it looked like my kind of place. I ate French toast and a crusty biker gave me a dollar. It's one of my earliest memories, and a scene I've long thought embodies the United States at its egalitarian finest: the wide-eyed preschooler and the burly Harley-rider, bonding over greasy food.

Years later, at Carleton College, amid the prairies and cornfields of southern Minnesota, I channeled this fascination into actual academics. I could rattle off esoteric facts (about the states) and hold forth for hours on history and culture (of the states) and tell you the name of just about every capital (of the states). I graduated with the self-satisfied confidence of the newly diplomaed: *I am a Credentialed Expert on All Things American.*

When I started out as a writer, my gaze turned overseas. I filed stories from Rome, from Ecuador, from a tiny Icelandic island. I was ever on the lookout for Americana and how it translated abroad—I can recommend the diner in Paris, but must warn you away from Tex-Mex in Berlin—but also prided myself as someone with a certain worldliness, a better-than-average understanding of how the European Union functioned, the politics of Costa Rica, the rising role of Chinese industry on the African continent.

Yet in all this time, it never occurred to me, Mr. American Studies Guy, Mr. Globally Aware Travel Writer, that there was more of my very own country to consider. Parts of the USA about which I was not just fairly ignorant but almost wholly unaware. Places I could not reliably find on a map, within a thousand miles or even, in some cases, within the correct hemisphere.

And then one day I encountered what I now think of as the Quarters of Destiny.

Zoom in on a three-story, slightly shabby brick apartment building in south Minneapolis, on a blustery Saturday morning in November. In a basement unit, Maren and I stand by our kitchen table with a glass jar full of pocket change. It's laundry day, and our attire shows it: she in yoga pants, I in tattered soccer shorts. Her shoulder-grazing chestnut hair is pulled back in a ponytail and her blue-green eyes are alight as we prepare to crank through our to-do list, beginning with sorting out the quarters from the jar. Most were destined for the washers and dryers down the hall, but if we were lucky, we'd find one or two state quarters to add to Maren's collection, which by now filled most of a cardboard portfolio with a cover awash in a collage featuring George Washington and the Statue of Liberty. On this day, we found one—Montana from the Philadelphia Mint—and after Maren placed it in the proper spot, we took a moment to admire the rest of the nearly complete lineup of silvery disks, arranged in chronological order of admission, from Delaware (1787) to Hawaii (1959).

Past Hawaii, I noticed, there were more quarters. I'm sure I'd seen them before, but they never registered. I pointed them out to Maren.

"Yeah!" She grinned. "The territories."

"Oh, right," I said. "We have territories."

I plucked the coins from the portfolio. The designs bore mottoes in wholly unfamiliar languages and objects that I couldn't identify—briefly interesting, but we had laundry to do, so I put the quarters back and promptly forgot about them.

A few days later, Maren saw a news article about a vast tropical paradise of a U.S. national park, all primeval jungles and comely beaches and sapphire waters. The photos conjured escapist daydreams as the winds of early onset winter bent the trees outside our window. It was the second-least-visited of all national parks (even fewer people visit a park in remote Alaska, which is much less appealing to a Minnesotan in November), and it was called the National Park of American Samoa.

Oh, yeah, I thought. *American Samoa. That's one of those mysterious places on the quarters.*

"I want to go there," Maren said, adding, "What's the deal with the territories, anyway?"

I laughed but then realized I couldn't answer the question. I had no idea why or how the United States controlled them, why they weren't states, who lived there, what life was like there. I couldn't name the first thing about local cultural traditions, attire, public transportation, what the billboards advertised, what the air smelled like . . . none of that.

And it suddenly *bugged* me that I didn't know. This was supposed to be my area of expertise. I looked at the quarters again and read the vital stats listed on a small flap in the portfolio. Here was the primer I'd never gotten in college:

Puerto Rico

Status designation: Commonwealth.

Year it officially became part of the United States: 1898.

Capital: San Juan.

Population: About 3.5 million.

Quarter at first glance: A lovely view of the turret of a stone fort overlooking the sea, with a tropical-looking flower hovering off to the side, and the words "Isla del Encanto" embossed in the sky.

Guam

Status designation: Organized, unincorporated territory.

Year it officially became part of the United States: 1898.

Capital: Hagåtña.

Population: About 165,000.

Quarter at first glance: An outline of the island, with a spray of bumps representing what I assumed were mountains, plus an outrigger sailboat and mushroom-looking thing that might have been a drum. Inscription on the coin: "Guahan I Tanó ManChamorro."

U.S. Virgin Islands

Status designation: Organized, unincorporated territory.

Year it officially became part of the United States: 1917.

Capital: Charlotte Amalie

Population: About 105,000.

Quarter at first glance: Three small islands, a cluster of shaggy-headed palm trees, and a smallish bird perched on a branch blooming with largish flowers that are surely colorful and enchantingly tropical in real life. Motto: "United in Pride and Hope."

American Samoa

Status designation: Unorganized, unincorporated territory.

Year it officially became part of the United States: 1900.

Capital: Pago Pago.

Population: About 55,000.

Quarter at first glance: A beach with palm trees and, hmm . . . maybe an aerial view of the Roman Colosseum, or a traditional bowl of some kind? Also, something that looked a bit like a broom and some kind of traditional staff-type thing. Above the bowl, there was text reading, "Samoa Muamua Le Atua."

Northern Mariana Islands

Status designation: Commonwealth.

Year it officially became part of the United States: 1976.

Capital: Saipan.

Population: About 54,000.

Quarter at first glance: A seaside tableau featuring a beach, another of those mushroom-drum things like on Guam's quarter, another outrigger sailboat, three small palm trees, two soaring birds, and a lei-like garland forming a half wreath along the bottom. No words.

I started to do a bit more research and learned that in addition to the quarter-worthy territories, there are eleven puny bits of earth—islands, atolls, banks, rocky outcroppings—that are part of the United States' "insular areas," which is to say the places that aren't states or federal districts (like the District of Columbia) but still fall under American sovereignty (though some are also claimed by other nations). These far-flung specks of unpeopled land are grouped together as the Minor Outlying Islands. There are three in the Caribbean: Navassa Island, Serranilla Bank, and Bajo Nuevo Bank; and eight in the Pacific: Baker Island, Howland Island, Jarvis Island, Johnston Atoll, Kingman Reef, Midway Atoll, Wake Island, and Palmyra Atoll. All have an official population of zero, although some have nonpermanent populations at military installations or scientific research stations.

If your head is already spinning a bit, well, so was mine.

• • • • •

My mental picture of those quarter-enshrined places was a hybrid of my own broad-brush stereotypes of both American culture and tropical locales. Marching bands on surfboards. Roadside diners whose blue plate specials were served in hollowed-out pineapples. Baseball fields in rain-forest clearings. Highways lined with palm trees and strip malls of the Swiss Family Robinson school of design, with monkeys drolly swinging from the ceiling at Foot Locker and dolphins frolicking in the food-court fountain and mall cops wearing leis. Norman Rockwell in a bikini.

Obviously, that wasn't right. Obviously, I had no clue.

I trekked to the bookstore in search of a history of the territories, or anything related to the subject, and found nothing at all. I searched Amazon, and the first page of results for "U.S. territories" was filled with coin-collecting portfolios like Maren's, plus sheets of stickers. I went to the Minneapolis Central Library, the main repository of information in a city routinely ranked among the nation's most well-read places, and found only obscure congressional bills. Nothing about the territories collectively, and the handful of books about the individual territories were difficult to track down because they were split up in different parts of the library, categorized not with United States history but with their surrounding region of the world. The U.S. Virgin Islands, for example, were grouped with the rest of the Caribbean, though aside from travel guides, there were only two books about the territory. On the same shelf, there were more volumes about the infamous Captain Morgan.

But once I started finding information, the intrigue made it worth the wait.

One day, I typed "Guam" into Google. That's all—Guam. I had intended to get a quick overview of its history, but I got distracted by the present, in the form of the Google News headlines, of which there were three:

GUAM LURING RUSSIAN TOURIST DOLLARS THANKS TO VISA WAIVER

From the *Moscow Times.*

US PLANS FOR GUAM MISSILE BASE SEEN AS COUNTERING STRENGTH OF CHINA

From the *South China Morning Post.*

DEAD MICE UPDATE:
TINY ASSASSINS DROPPED ON GUAM AGAIN

From National Public Radio. The dead mice had been stuffed full of acetaminophen—Tylenol—and dropped from helicopters into the jungle as poison to control the brown tree snake population. *Again*. Evidently it had worked previously. (How many snakes *were* there?)

So here you had an island that was at once overflowing with tourists from around the world, infested with jungle snakes with a taste for over-the-counter painkillers, and also served as the front line for keeping the world's rising superpower in check. And that was just the news from a random Tuesday.

Clearly, this was a place worth getting to know more.

The history, along with that of the other territories, turned out to be even more fascinating, with mixed-up histories of conquest and corrupt governors who sounded like Victorian-era literature villains come to life, all pith helmets and extravagant mustaches and diabolical plots. In various territories, there were pirates and bloody fights for independence and hippie dropouts and eccentric millionaires who lived in castles.

It also seemed that, right around the turn of the twentieth century, the territories *were* part of the national mythology and the everyday conversation. "I have recently been traveling over a large part of the United States," wrote Benjamin Kidd in the *Atlantic,* in December 1898. "On this subject of [overseas] expansion I talked with the people generally. It was impossible to avoid." It was one of the focal points of the 1900 presidential election, between Republican William McKinley and Democrat William Jennings Bryan.

A century or so ago, Americans didn't just know about the territories but *cared* about them, *argued* about them. But what changed? How and why did they disappear from the national conversation? Was there a compelling reason why they mattered for the present-day USA, or were they just remnants of a long-past historical moment?

As I kept reading, I became more baffled—and obsessed.

And more than once I also thought, *Well,* that's *messed up*.

For instance, there was the fact that residents of the territories cannot vote for president, because they're shut out of the Electoral College. Americans who live in any other nation on earth can vote absentee back in the states; even American astronauts in the International Space Station can vote for president. But Americans whose official address is in the territories—American soil—cannot, a fact that would seem to be at odds with the very ideals of our democracy.

They can, however, *run* for president—John McCain was born in the Panama Canal Zone back when it was part of the USA. (In other words, in the 2008 election, there *was* a candidate who was not born in the states—but, contrary to the swirling conspiracy theories, it wasn't Barack Obama.) They can also vote in the presidential primaries and be delegates at the political parties' national conventions. The governor of Puerto Rico spoke at the Republican National Convention in 2012, followed a few minutes later by a family band from American Samoa.

There was also a major asterisk when it came to congressional representation. Like the states, territories elect representatives to serve them in Washington, D.C. They have offices on the Hill, participate in committee discussions, do many of the things other congresspeople do. Except that they don't—can't—vote on any bills, which is to say they can't do the most important thing that congresspeople do. (Washington, D.C., gets three electoral votes but has a similar congressional setup.)

There was layer upon topsy-turvy layer of weirdness in the history, in the politics, in the present-day life. I'm a sucker for far-flung quirk, and here, it seemed, I'd hit the jackpot.

It's a big, wonderful, crazy place, this country of ours, and I love it. I love it precisely because it's such a diverse, enigmatic, ever-evolving patchwork, one you could spend a lifetime trying to understand. And the only way to do that, really, is to get out there and see it.

• • • • •

ON HIS DEATHBED, in 1936, King George V of Great Britain asked, "How is the empire?" His domain, of course, spanned truly across the globe—India, Hong Kong, Gibraltar, Bermuda, the list goes on, the sun never set. Our modern American outposts are not nearly as numerous or as populated as our onetime rulers were in their heyday,* but it's still curious that our holdings have no cohesive, collective reputation. If any of our leaders asked, "How is the empire?" the most likely public response would be, "We don't *have* an empire."

Yet today, with a population of nearly four million people, the U.S. territories are more than ten times larger than the pres-

* The sun does set on the American empire, by the way. Connect the farthest-west point, Guam, with the farthest-east point, the U.S. Virgin Islands, and you've gone less than halfway around the world. Time-zone-wise, they're fourteen hours apart. So in June, the sun never sets on the American Empire; in December, it does, every day.

ent-day colonial outposts of the British Empire. They're larger, in fact, than the remaining colonies of all the old-fashioned imperial dominions—Britain, Spain, France, Denmark, Belgium, the Netherlands, and so on—combined.

I wanted to answer King George's question for my own nation. I wanted to meet the people, eat the food, sniff the air, experience everyday life in all its joy and tragedy and poetry and banality. So I packed my bag with sunscreen and, as a talisman, a red-white-and-blue-checkered shirt. And I set off on a journey that would lead me from traditional villages to modern metropolises to lost-world jungles, more than thirty-one thousand miles, crossing the equator and the International Date Line but never changing currency or getting a visa. An altogether different sort of all-American Road Trip.

A VERY BRIEF NOTE ON THE TERRITORIES AND THEIR VARIOUS DESIGNATIONS

BEFORE HITTING THE ROAD, LET'S ESTABLISH SOME of the key terms used to categorize the territories:

1. All territories are either ***organized*** or ***unorganized***, which has to do with whether or not they've passed an Organic Act, which is essentially a territorial constitution.
2. The territories are also either ***incorporated*** or ***unincorporated***, which describes whether or not a place is considered fully part of (incorporated with) the United States and all of its federal laws. Unincorporated means that some, but not all, of the U.S. Constitution applies, that Congress has ultimate oversight and veto power over everything, and that the place is neither on equal terms with the states nor officially on the path to statehood. All inhabited territories are unincorporated.

Guam and the U.S. Virgin Islands are ***organized unincorporated*** territories.

Puerto Rico and the Northern Mariana Islands are officially ***commonwealths***, not territories at all—theoretically, commonwealths have a bit more local autonomy, though there's much debate about the real-world distinction between the two designations. For all practical purposes, commonwealths are just another form of organized unincorporated territories (and so, for the most part, I'm using "territories" as a catch-all term, including the commonwealths).

American Samoa and most Minor Outlying Islands are ***unorganized***, ***unincorporated*** territories.

Then there's Palmyra Atoll, which is a thousand miles south of Hawaii, and is ***unorganized*** but ***incorporated***. From a legal standpoint, this five-square-mile atoll with no permanent population has more constitutional rights than any inhabited territory. If that seems a bit unexpected, well, we're just getting started.

THE NOT-QUITE STATES OF AMERICA

Chapter 1

THE EMPIRE'S NEW CLOTHES

The Virgin Islands of the United States

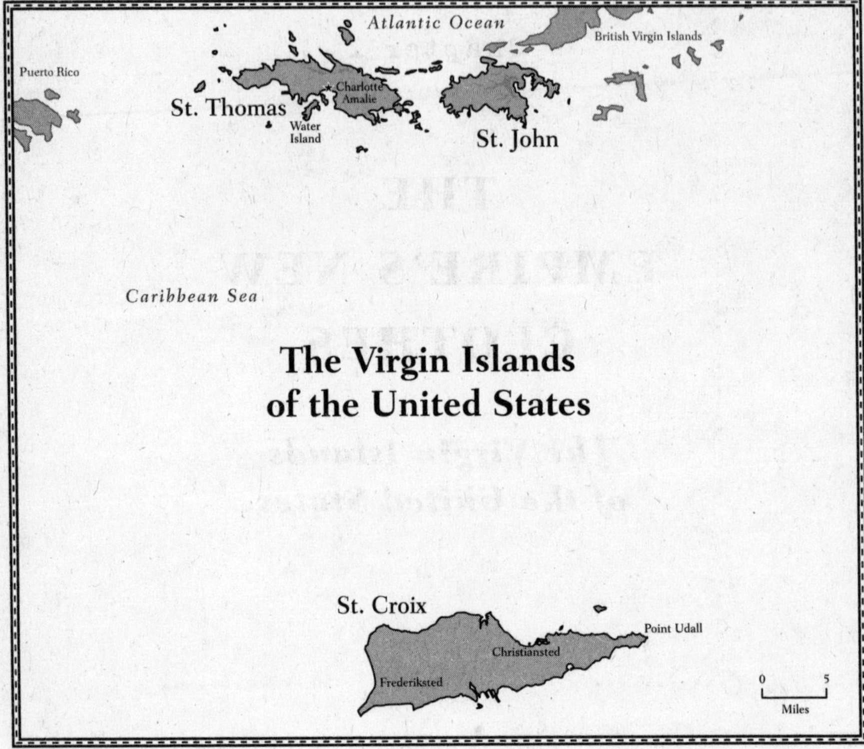
Atlantic Ocean
British Virgin Islands
Puerto Rico
Charlotte Amalie
St. Thomas
Water Island
St. John
Caribbean Sea
The Virgin Islands of the United States
St. Croix
Point Udall
Christiansted
Frederiksted
0
5
Miles

By the time I got to the rum bar in the rain forest, the beer-drinking pigs were already sloshed. The bartender had cut them off. I was crushed, deprived of that obscure but potent strain of the American Dream: *If you work hard, someday you will be able to buy cans of beer at a jungle bar and give them to pigs in a pen out back. They will grasp the cans in their capacious mouths, bite them open, chug the contents, and spit out the crushed aluminum with rapturous grins, while you think,* This is a magnificent country.

The bar, a palm-roofed, open-sided hut called the Montpellier Domino Club, was up a lonely, hilly road tunneled by trees and cratered with potholes; it was about four miles inland from the town of Frederiksted, on the west side of Saint Croix, the largest of the four U.S. Virgin Islands.

The pigs were large, state-fair-sized, and had a loutish charm as they lunged for the cans, front legs up on the edge of their pens, keening. Their thirst is so prodigious that some years ago they switched over to nonalcoholic beer on doctor's orders, after too many piglets were born with fetal alcohol syndrome. Yet the corpulent porkers sometimes overdo it even on O'Doul's, all that cheered-on chugging tiring them out. Like today, when a cruise ship was in port in Frederiksted and the tourist vans kept coming and coming.

"They're done—we've had enough excitement for the day," the bar's owner, Norma, a stout Trinidadian of middle years, told me when I arrived around four p.m.

I settled onto a stool at the bar, a small three-sided affair with a worn wood countertop, and dried palm fronds beckoned lazily from the ceiling. On the far wall behind the bar, a shelf held more types of rum than I knew existed, most of them Cruzan, the island's pride. There was seating for perhaps fifteen around the bar, but right now there were just three other patrons, who had all moved down from the mainland USA decades ago. There was Leon, wearing a coral polo shirt and rimless glasses, and who I took to be a retired business executive; Ray, whose calculator watch and unkempt hair telegraphed *science teacher*; and Linda, a woman I couldn't quite read aside from noting her intense gaze and the incongruity of the chartreuse bike helmet she was wearing while sitting at the bar.

They were clearly regulars, their conversation suffused with a jocular familiarity that can only be earned through many hours and many drinks together.

Leon: "I should leave soon to get to Home Depot and repot my orchids before it gets dark."

Ray: "When's your orchid show in Florida?"

Leon: "Next month. You should tag along. There'll be plenty of ladies there."

The topics caromed unhurriedly: the state of local property values, the surprisingly high quality of the bar's johnny cakes (a fried flatbread, dense and delicious), and the need—oft-stated but never acted upon—to head home for the day. The three bartenders chimed in as conversational equals; there were two young women and Norma, who held court with an easygoing charisma from a folding chair in the center of the bar area.

All in all, it was the sort of take-a-load-off-you're-with-friends atmosphere you'd find at any corner dive bar in the states. As if to prove the workaday nature of the place, and defying all jungle-rum-bar logic, Ray and Linda were drinking cans of Old Milwaukee. In foam cozies. Which they'd brought from home.

Of course, I thought. *That makes sense.*

And the thing is, I meant it. Everything about this place had a certain offbeat logic, in keeping with the rhythms of life here. I'd been in the U.S. Virgin Islands for more than a week now and had come to expect these sorts of pairings, to smile and nod and appreciate the multiverse of possibilities.

• • • • •

WHEN I FIRST arrived in Charlotte Amalie, Saint Thomas—the territory's capital and commercial center, with 18,500 residents—my disorientation was so profound that I could feel my gray matter pulsing. All those mixed messages, from my phone to the street names to the American cars driving British-style, on the left. I took it all in, wide-eyed, enchanted.

I was staying at a guesthouse called the Crystal Palace, a cardinal-red Spanish Colonial manor midway up one of Charlotte Amalie's three hills. It was the longtime family home of the proprietor, Ronnie Lockhart, a fifth-generation Saint Thomian; his grandfather, he said, had designed the territorial flag. The house had a distinct feel of fading grandeur, particularly the third-floor living room, with its oil paintings of sailing ships and a rack of Panama hats that looked like they hadn't been touched for decades. The living room was open to a tiled porch, where I lingered the first morning, eating a bowl of Frosted Flakes, the town and the harbor laid out before me.

The waterfront was just three blocks away and seemed so close that I could reach out and touch it—nudge the crowds of tourists walking along its edge, pick up the massive yachts at anchor, including the white and gleaming and wedge-like iShip, designed by (and for) Steve Jobs. The low-angled sunlight pumped up the already-saturated colors: the red-tile rooftops, the lush green hills, the azure acreage of placid sea. I texted photos to Maren as fast as I could take them, while Ronnie watched, entertained by my awe.

At the mouth of the harbor bulged smallish Hassel Island, and the larger, two-square-mile Water Island, population 182. The latter is the runt of the four official U.S. Virgin Islands, which also include Saint Thomas, population fifty-one thousand and the governmental and commercial center; Saint John, three miles east, with about four thousand people and the National Park of the Virgin Islands; and Saint Croix, forty miles south, home to roughly fifty thousand residents and twice the land area of Saint Thomas. Along with the British Virgin Islands, just a few miles north and east of Saint John, these are the northwestern points of the Lesser Antilles, the chain of hilly, inkblot landmasses curving along the eastern edge of the Caribbean.

Between the Crystal Palace and the harbor was a grid of narrow lanes and low-slung historic buildings outlined in white trim. To either side, more of the same, and, on some of the more vertiginous inclines, steps replaced streets on the most direct route up the hill. The city beckoned: *Come on down, Doug! You can wander for hours! Meander for days! Explore for—*

"You won't be goin' *anywhere* except where I tell you," Ronnie said. "Go another way and they're probably gonna take your wallet and maybe shoot you." He pointed out the one acceptable route for the short walk to the harbor as he leaned over the edge of the porch, his gaze narrowing. I sighed heavily, recalling the crime warnings I'd read before my trip. I'd tried hard not to get too anxious about them, particularly since, inevitably, one of the key anecdotes dated to before I was born, the 1972 mass shooting at the Fountain Valley Golf Course on Saint Croix, which targeted tourists and left eight people dead. Even now, I knew, the USVI had one of the highest murder rates on the planet. But I'd been clinging to tourist denial, in the thrall of the tropical landscape and centuries-old streetscape.

"Last year, they killed somebody during Night Out Against Crime in Frenchtown," Ronnie said, meeting my alarmed gaze. Satisfied that I understood his point, he looked back down at the town.

"And *that* is a real problem," he growled. I looked down, expecting to see some menacing figure, but he was gesturing to the rooftops of Main Street, a block inland from the waterfront and lined with duty-free shops in historic buildings. Above the red tile danced a green inflatable arm-waver, that kitschy icon of car-sales lots.

"They wouldn't have that at Colonial Williamsburg, and they shouldn't have it here!" Ronnie said. He stared hard at the arm-waver, clearly hoping today would be the day he mastered telekinesis.

Two other guests ambled onto the porch, a middle-aged couple from Denmark, and then a third, also Danish. This was a funny coincidence, I said out loud, which was met with a quartet of blank stares.

"We get a *lot* of Danes here," Ronnie said, in the same tone that someone at Disney World might say, *We get a* lot *of families.*

Before 1917, these islands were known as the Danish West Indies. This much I knew from my research. I hadn't understood, though, that modern-day Danes come here by the planeful, including regular charter flights from Copenhagen to Charlotte Amalie, as one of my breakfast companions, Anne, now explained. They spread out across the islands to see the sites that are part of their history but no longer part of their homeland, the forts and edifices preserved and docent-staffed by a country with no claim to this specific history.

Anne turned out to be the president of the Danish West Indies Historical Society; she was studious and chic in blue-framed glasses. The topic turned to history and I showed her the books I had in the messenger bag at my feet. I pulled them out and one by one, and she dismissed each as inferior, with a small, shy wince. Then she talked me into buying her own book for $55.

Ronnie stood idly at the edge of the porch, chuckling at my conversation with Anne and glaring at the arm-waver. Finally, he looked up with a smirk and said, "*She* respects history."

• • • • •

From a narrowly focused American perspective, the most important event in the history of the Danish West Indies may have been the arrival on Saint Croix, in 1765, of a pale, redheaded boy of eight or ten years old (the record is inconclusive) named Alexander, and his subsequent coming-of-age in Christiansted, the island's largest town. His was an inauspicious beginning: born out of wedlock on the Caribbean island of Nevis to a Scottish immigrant mother, who died three years after they arrived on Saint Croix, leaving her two sons orphaned.

But young Alexander was a sharp-witted autodidact, and in 1772 he wrote a newspaper essay that so impressed local leaders that they raised funds to send him to college in the British colonies in North America. He continued to thrive and soon he was a household name: Alexander Hamilton.

It's amusing to imagine him, or any other Founding Father, wandering the present-day streets of the U.S. Virgin Islands (or, if you're a local, "the USVI" or, most frequently, just "the VI"). The Danish colonial architecture would feel familiar enough, and I do enjoy picturing Benjamin Franklin's reaction to the iShip. But I suspect they'd all be taken aback by the fact that these islands are now part of the United States but not actual states, and not on any path to statehood—a setup that, politically, would surely strike them as very much like a *colony*. A loaded word, one intentionally erased from the aspiring nation's name; as Bill Bryson notes in *Made in America*, at the time of the Revolution, "even the boldest patriot" referred to "the United Colonies" rather than "the United States," until Thomas Paine coined the latter term, and here we are.

Hamilton & Co. debated national expansion fervently as they planned for their new nation. Hamilton, for his part, didn't think a "free republic" could or should be "maintained in a large geographical area," but did hope that the United States would push westward to the strategic port of New Orleans. This, he told George Washington, "may be regarded . . . as essential to the unity of the Empire." Thomas Jefferson opposed expansion, using the slippery-slope argument to suggest that, if this became the trend, the United States "might receive England, Holland, Ireland, etc. into it."

The new nation's leaders drafted a colonial policy, the Northwest Ordinance, in 1787, a year before they ratified the Constitution. The ordinance was originally intended to address the Northwest Territory (what we now know as Ohio, Indiana, Michigan, Illinois, Wisconsin, and Minnesota) but came to serve as the precedent for further national expansion. New acquisitions would go through a three-stage process to become states. Step One: Congress appoints a governor, a secretary, and three-judge court. Step Two: Once a territory has "five thousand free male inhabitants of full age," it sets up a local legislature. Step Three: The territory writes up a local constitution and, *Congratulations, you're now a state!* Alternatively, if a territory reaches sixty thousand free inhabitants (slaves, alas, don't count), it can be admitted before drafting a constitution. Thirty-three of today's fifty states were previously territories.

The Constitution, too, considered the territories, although only briefly and in terms that, like everything else in that august document, are open to perpetual interpretation and argument. There are two relevant parts, both in Article IV, Section 3. The first says, "New States may be admitted by the Congress into this Union." The second, known as the Territorial Clause, decrees that "Congress shall have the Power to dispose of and make all needful Rules and Regulations respecting the Territory* and other Property belonging to the United States." In other words—and this is still true today—Congress has ultimate and full authority over the territories; states' rights, that fiercely protected hallmark of our democracy, far surpass territories' rights. Where, precisely, congressional authority begins and ends is a question that has kept the courts busy ever since.

The nation pushed ever westward—often, of course, at the expense of American Indians and other claimants to land, about

* Singular, because at that point there was only one.

whom much has been written elsewhere—and more than doubled with the Louisiana Purchase, in 1803. The sale was authorized by none other than longtime expansion-skeptic Thomas Jefferson, with encouragement from Alexander Hamilton in defiance of his Federalist Party compatriots. (Hamilton rival Aaron Burr, for his part, hoped the Louisiana territory would secede from the Union—and that he would be its leader.) Guided by the Northwest Ordinance, the new territories followed a gradual but straightforward process to statehood: Louisiana in 1812, Mississippi in 1817, Arkansas in 1836.

This was how the nation grew, at each step gaining more confidence and ambition, and feeling more emboldened to challenge the more established global powers. European nations had long dominated the Americas: France, Great Britain, Denmark, the Netherlands, Portugal, and, most of all, Spain. But Spain's holdings dwindled as independence movements swept through Mexico, Colombia, Venezuela, Argentina, Peru, and Chile in the 1810s and 1820s. The United States sensed an opportunity to assert its own power in the region, and in 1823, President James Monroe issued a command to Europe: *Back off.* The Monroe Doctrine was a geopolitical restraining order of sorts: *We'll stay out of your Continental affairs, and you'd better not mess around in our hemisphere, claiming new colonies or stirring things up.*

Expansion was a constant presidential campaign issue. James Polk was elected in 1844 after promising to annex Texas, which he did, antagonizing Mexico; the ensuing war netted the United States much of what we now know as the Southwest, plus all of California. To the north, Polk worked out the Oregon Treaty of 1846, adding what's now the Pacific Northwest.

What's often lost in the "Go west, young man" mythology of the nation is the fact that California and Oregon were not only desirable on their own terms but as stepping-stones for controlling the Pacific, just as Britain had long dominated the Atlantic. San Francisco was a superlative port; the rest of California was a nice bonus. In 1846, then-Senator William Seward decreed that "our population is destined to roll its resistless waves to the icy barriers of the north, and to encounter oriental civilization on the shores of the Pacific."

Expansion was never simply about having more people in more places—as Polk and Hamilton and Jefferson all understood, it was about claiming areas of strategic utility. It was about enhancing the nation's power in the world. Or, in some cases, it was about domestic strategy: in 1854, President Franklin Pierce, who had already given serious thought to acquiring Alaska, Hawaii, and Nicaragua, worked up plans for purchasing Cuba or "wresting it from Spain," for the purpose of adding another slave-owning state to the South.

At the root of this drive was a belief that, in the instantly famous words of the *United States Magazine and Democratic Review* in 1845, it was "our manifest destiny to overspread the continent allotted by Providence for the free development of our yearly multiplying millions." Expansion was a mission from God.

• • • • •

WITH THE VIEW and the Danes to keep me company, I was tempted to sit on Ronnie's porch all day. But I'd come here to see America. Precisely *what* I wanted to see, and how I planned to see it, I wasn't quite sure.

Enter Monica, with a loose white blouse, bronze skin, and her jet-black hair pulled into a tight bun. She was born and raised in Saint Thomas, lived there until she was about thirty, then fell in love with a Dane and moved to Denmark. She was going to take the three Danes on a tour of her old stomping grounds. Would I like to join them?

I nodded eagerly. The Danes looked disappointed.

Ten minutes later, the five of us were wedged into Monica's gray sedan and headed up a narrow, meandering roller-coaster road that veered through the jungle and across the island's plump hills, which top out at more than a thousand feet. As we slowed for one tight switchback, Monica said, "I used to come up here when I was learning to drive and my boyfriend was trying to quit smoking. This curve tested us both." When the trees thinned for a moment, we could see squiggly coastlines and small valleys, where a million shades of green were offset by scattered bursts of floral blooms, nature's fireworks in gold and pink and fire-truck-red. Humble but well-kept cinder-block houses perched on the inclines, some with flat roofs outlined with rebar reaching for the sky, an aspirational halo of hope for a second (or third) story sometime soon.

The trees tapered off and the road straightened out. We turned down a dirt road with a colorful hand-painted sign reading BORDEAUX FARMER'S MARKETPLACE. A wide path lined with wooden market stalls curved around a corner toward a pavilion the size of a small airplane hangar. The air was thick and humid after a brief sun shower, and the whirr of a weed-whacker signaled that just out sight someone was hard at work.

We followed Monica to the pavilion, where several men were chatting. Monica greeted them all warmly. "Good morning, good morning!" to the preppy white guy who was dropping off some solar panels, "Good morning, good morning!" to the black Rasta in dreadlocks (including his beard) and tall white rubber boots. It's standard practice in the USVI to greet everyone you see, friend or stranger, in restaurants, on buses, walking down the street. As one man would tell me, "You can call someone a *mutha*, say anything you want, but the worst insult is not saying 'Good morning' or 'Good afternoon . . . How you doing?'"

The marketplace stalls were painted with green, gold, and red stripes and symbols familiar to anyone who has wandered into the Bob Marley section of a poster shop: regal lions, black stars, slogans like HAIL D KING RASTAFARI LIVE. This, I realized, was what I'd seen on the retaining-wall murals the night before: Rastafari iconography, the real-deal kind.

The pavilion overlooked terraced hillsides, and Monica led us down a muddy path, exchanging pleasantries and gossip with everyone she passed. I got into the spirit, offering my own chipper greetings. The Danes gave me sideways glances.

On one of the terraces, a tall, burly man was clearing the field with a weed-whacker; he looked up and switched it off as Monica approached, giving her a familiar wave. His name was Elridge Thomas and he seemed to be in charge here. "We started as an agricultural group and evolved into a Rasta group," he said. They were preparing for their annual two-day festival, where farmers sold their goods—everything vegan and wholesome, a sort of Whole Foods of the islands—followed by concerts in the evenings.

The festival was a showcase of the specialty produce they grew on the farm, including some things I'd never heard of: eggfruit, breadfruit, and guavaberry, which Elridge said was *not* the same as a guava. He pointed out a type of mango called Guinness and multiple varieties of avocados ("pears" in the local parlance).

In my mind, I was slicing them open and taking messy bites. A sun shower began spritzing us, but I was in no hurry to take shelter and end the conversation—perhaps he'd offer us a sample if we stayed just a bit longer. I could see the Danes eying the pavilion.

"What kind of music do you play at the concerts?" I asked Elridge.

"Reggae, of course!" he said, and I caught the Danes snickering as I blushed.

I decided to change the subject. "Do you have many young people out here working the land?"

"Well . . ." Elridge began. His shoulders slumped a bit as he answered. *No.* They didn't have much interest from the younger generation. It's hard work, the kind that doesn't always pay off, even when you put in your best effort, he said. He pointed to an avocado tree that had been stubbornly refusing to yield fruit for more than twenty years. "She had all that time to prove herself," he said, "but we'll give her one more summer. We'll give her that.

"Local agriculture is in danger," he continued, lamenting Virgin Islanders' overreliance on imported goods and a general lack of support from the local and federal government. "The politicians just give money to people who already have it. They don't care about agriculture," he said, adding that it was only 1 percent of the USVI's overall budget.* Tourism gets all the attention, all the funding—all those ships in Charlotte Amalie, all those beachfront resorts. "But I keep telling them you have to invest in the people who *live* here, who will *stay* here."

Elridge sighed slightly, his muscular shoulders rolling. Then he fired up his weed-whacker and got back to work.

Up in the marketplace, another friend of Monica's was starting to set up shop, a tall woman named Menen, with a wavy

* The budget, I later learned, provides more money for the territory's public television station than for the Department of Agriculture.

mane of hair and a friendly but exhausted bearing. She smiled shyly as Monica made introductions. Menen made tinctures and other therapeutic items with traditional island herbs and inspiration from recipes she found online. Today, she was selling *moringa* vinegar, infused with the leaves of the local "tree of life," along with lemongrass hand cream and a sorrel wine, which she poured into little plastic cups for us to sample. It was fuchsia-colored, with a deep, sweet berry flavor (though sorrel is actually a flower, Menen said).

"Damn, that's good!" I sputtered, as Menen beamed and the Danes stared, clearly thinking, *What a lush.* No matter. *I* was enjoying myself.

• • • • •

THE IRONY of the lack of agriculture on Saint Thomas—aside from the fact that, as a quick glance at the landscape reveals, the whole place is immensely fertile, if hilly—is that one of the key moments in American overseas expansion started with a need to help struggling farmers.

In the early 1800s, back in the states, key crops like cotton and tobacco were in danger of catastrophic failure due to depleted soil: no nutrients, no sustenance, no growth. American farmland, Ralph Waldo Emerson said, "does not want a prayer, it wants manure." Across the Atlantic, the same problem was so pronounced that in the 1840s, according to historian Jimmy Skaggs, some European farmers "raided the Napoleonic battlefields . . . for bones to spread over their fields."

The United States had its eye on an equally unlikely source: remote, barren islands. It's here where the story of American expansion overseas and beyond the bounds of hemispheres truly begins, on these specks in the sea that we desperately wanted for their . . . *cue the trumpet fanfare* . . . bird poop. With its high nitrogen content, guano is an exceptional fertilizer,* and bird by bird, over the course of millennia, it built up until it was fifty meters deep on some islands. In 1856, the U.S. Congress passed the Guano Islands Act, which says:

> Whenever any citizen of the United States discovers a deposit of guano on any island, rock, or key, not within the lawful jurisdiction of any other Government . . . such island, rock, or key may, at the discretion of the President, be considered as appertaining to the United States.

In other words: *We know these unclaimed islands are covered in bird poop. So,* dibs, *that's all ours!* Within eight years, the USA had claimed fifty-nine islands and outcroppings in the Caribbean and the Pacific, as Skaggs details in his book *The Great Guano Rush: Entrepreneurs and American Overseas Expansion.*

Guano-mining operations didn't just mean a couple of ships filled with roughnecks wielding pickaxes, but large-scale operations that operated for decades, with quarries and railroads and small towns. On two-square-mile Navassa, about thirty-five miles west of Haiti, mining spanned forty years, and extracted nearly a million tons of guano. It was grueling work, days filled with swinging pickaxes, the air a haze, the equatorial sun on furnace-blast. There were almost one hundred fifty miners on Navassa at a time, most of them recently freed black men, with notoriously harsh white overseers. In September 1889, some of the workers rioted, killing five white overseers and making head-

* It's also useful for making an explosive called nitroguanidine.

lines across the USA. Three men were given the death sentence, which was commuted by President Benjamin Harrison, after much lobbying by Baltimore's African-American community and others who pointed out the inhumane conditions.

This is one of the more remarkable tales from the Guano Islands, but—as you can imagine from the work and the setting—far from the only intrigue on these distant specks. Navassa is just one of these now-abandoned islands with ghost towns and empty barracks and the ruins of railroads; some even have airstrips. If you're a James Bond movie villain looking to set up shop, here is your real estate.

Guano mining on Navassa ended in 1898, but the United States still holds on to it even though Haiti still claims it, citing the 1697 Treaty of Rijswijk and the fact that they're just thirty-five miles away.

So why not let Haiti have it? For that matter, what about Bajo Nuevo Bank and Serranilla Bank, two sets of islets and reefs some three hundred miles southwest of Navassa? They consist of little more than shipwrecks and strips of sand. Jamaica, Nicaragua, and Colombia all claim them; the Colombian Navy patrols the waters. Why does the United States care about these places at all?

Because when you claim one bit of land, you get its surrounding waters, twelve miles in every direction. You get the shipping lanes, the fishing rights, whatever minerals are under the sea. And you get the opportunity to just *be* in the area, to keep an eye on the neighbors, always a nice perk.

You find your scraps and hold on to them, no matter how small they may seem. Bit by bit, your dominion expands. As Hamilton said of New Orleans, and Jefferson and Pierce and Polk and Seward and many others also knew, these are the seeds of empire.

In 1864, it appeared that the United States was going to plant its flag on even larger, more consequential outposts. William Seward, now President Lincoln's Secretary of State in a nation at war, turned his attention from the Pacific to the Danish West Indies. Seward was an expansion advocate of long standing, but these islands were of particular interest, as the Union sought to combat Confederate ships that were operating in nearby waters. The islands were prime real estate, right where the Caribbean meets the Atlantic, and the harbor in Charlotte Amalie, formed from the caldera of a long-blown volcano, was the region's best spot for a naval base.

It took a few years to work out the details, and in 1867 the sale documents were drawn up. The price: $7.5 million. But Congress started having second thoughts. The war was over but the nation was still reeling and was having buyer's remorse after the purchase, earlier that year, of Alaska—widely known as Seward's Folly. In 1870, the USA reneged, much to Denmark's annoyance. King Christian was about as catty as a monarch could be, saying that "We . . . feel a satisfaction that circumstances have relieved Us from making a sacrifice [by selling the islands]."

The Danish West Indies stayed on the United States' wish list, and in 1896 the Republicans put annexation of the islands in their party platform. Expansion fervor was in full swing, and the Republicans' presidential candidate that year, William McKinley, won the election in part based on a promise to annex Hawaii, which he did in 1898. The United States tried to buy the Danish West Indies again in 1902, only to have the Danish Parliament reject the deal by one vote. In 1915, the United States gave it one more shot. The islands were more strategically desirable than ever, as a key transit point for ships going through the just-opened Panama Canal, which was also now American property. Plus, World War I had begun, and there were murmurs that Germany would take over Denmark and therefore the Danish West Indies. In Charlotte Amalie, the powerful Hamburg-American Line was rumored to be buying up more buildings. The company's owner also happened to be the German consul. *The New York Times* reported, "If the proposed sale should be rejected . . . an occupation of St. Thomas was thoroughly expected to be a consequence." This time, the deal went through. A new treaty was drafted, then signed by both nations on August 16, 1916. The cost had risen to $25 million (equal to about $460 million today, and the highest per-acre amount the United States has ever paid for land).

On March 31, 1917, in simultaneous ceremonies on Saint Thomas and Saint Croix, the Danish flag, the Dannebrog, was lowered and the Stars and Stripes went up. (Transfer Day is still a holiday there, but as Ronnie grumbled to me, "Some years, the government don't do nothin' to celebrate it.") The USA rechristened its new acquisition the Virgin Islands of the United States, after the broader island group, which Christopher Columbus had named during his Caribbean forays in 1492 and 1493.* In Charlotte Amalie, the United States Marines' first acts included rolling two fifteen-ton cannons up to the top of a hill overlooking the harbor and arresting the owner of the Hamburg-American Line and then marching him to the brig at Fort Christian, in the center of town.

Precisely six days later, the United States entered World War I.

* The official name of the neighboring British territory is simply the Virgin Islands.

• • • • •

FORT CHRISTIAN was all shuttered up, the tomato-red paint on its walls starting to peel, its crenellations seeming to sag. It hadn't been open to visitors for years, aside from the occasional school group (though local officials hoped to restore the fort and reopen it in time for the centennial of the territory's transfer to the USA).

"What's that?" I heard an American tourist ask his wife one morning. "Is it, like, important?"

She shrugged and they wandered off to join the crowds heading toward Main Street.

Charlotte Amalie is one of the planet's busiest cruise ports, welcoming more than five hundred ships each year. Right now, there were six in the harbor, including the *Oasis of the Seas*, the second-largest cruise ship in the world (missing the top spot by just two inches), a skyscraper tipped on its side and compelled to float, carrying around two thousand crew members and some six thousand passengers. The other ships brought many thousands more. The city's population of 18,500 had more than doubled since daybreak.

Most of the newcomers were headed to Main Street, narrow and lovely and lined with pastel-painted or brick buildings with small balconies and arched windows and sturdy, brightly colored shutters. It was a cacophony of conspicuous consumption. Dapper jewelry salesmen waved tourists into their stores. Jovial crowds compared bulging shopping bags with the logos of Cruzan rum and Tiffany & Co. and Mr. Tablecloth, a fine-linen boutique. The road was jammed with pedestrians and inching-along minibuses, known as safaris—essentially, modified pickup trucks with benches in the back, many with elaborate paint jobs featuring slogans like MR. WONDERFUL and POSITIVE IS HOW I LIVE.*

After a few minutes, I'd seen enough—I had no pressing need for a new Rolex or a pallet of rum—and made my way to Veterans Drive, the main drag on the waterfront, hoping to catch one of the safaris that follows a set route around Saint Thomas, serving as public transit. There were a handful of Virgin Islanders at the stop ("Good morning! How you doin'?"), and soon a safari approached. We stepped to the curb in unison, but it chugged past us, packed with cruisers. Every few minutes, more would-be riders appeared—a man carrying a folding table, a woman with a toddler son shyly holding her hand—and more safaris passed us by. I kept checking my watch: ten minutes, fifteen, twenty.

Aside from me, everyone waiting at the stop was black, and aside from a handful, every tourist on the safaris was white—wasn't this what Elridge was getting at? Tourism as leisure-class colonialism, taking away resources from locals?

By the half-hour mark, I was feeling a touch guilty by tourist-association. But the general mood was shoulder-shrugging resignation and a certain we're-all-in-this-together humor.

"Why they so busy?" one woman said to no one in particular.

The man with the folding table replied, "It's all them Caucasian tourists. The Yankee Taxi!"

* The safaris are all rather ad hoc, from the benches to the way you signal your stop, by pressing a doorbell wired to the roof. The whole setup makes a state-dweller recall both Developing World Transportation Disaster Tropes ("We're going to crash on one of those windy roads, I *know* it") and Inspiring Horatio Alger Stories ("What entrepreneurism! What DIY charm! That's the American way!").

Everyone chuckled. "You a comedian!" the woman with the toddler said.

"And you a good audience!" said the man. A moment later, he waved lightly at a passing safari driver. "Johnny's busy today. Good for him."

After an hour, I gave up and wandered to a marketplace at the end of Main Street, with twenty or thirty tents and vendors hawking beach towels and shell necklaces and smoothies. A Rasta selling Bob Marley T-shirts patiently told an American customer that, yes, he accepted dollars—*only* dollars, in fact; "You still in the USA"—which reminded me of Ronnie's tales of tourists shocked they could watch CBS here, buy a Snickers bar, communicate in English.

Just past the marketplace was Emancipation Garden, tranquillity with a front-row view of tourist frenzy. I sat on a bench near a middle-aged woman dressed for the office and eating her lunch from a plastic container. She looked bemused and slightly perturbed by the scene around her—behind her rimless glasses, her expression said, "Who *are* you people?"

• • • • •

IN THE MIDDLE of Emancipation Garden was a bust of King Christian. To one side was a replica of the Liberty Bell. Nearby was a bronze bust of a slave named Buddhoe blowing a conch shell, starting the rebellion that led to emancipation in 1848.

I was finally starting to understand the palimpsests of colonialism and globalization, now that I'd dug into my books—principally William Boyer's *America's Virgin Islands* and Isaac Dookhan's *A History of the Virgin Islands of the United States*—and talked to some locals and been corrected, at length, by

Anne the Dane. The statues weren't musty relics but potent cultural symbols whose legacies were embedded in the everyday life around me: the Danish architecture, the local residents descended from slaves, the overlay of American culture everywhere from the dollars trading hands to the hip-hop blasting from a safari painted with the words TRUST IN GOD.

It's a rollicking history. Christopher Columbus landed at Salt River in Saint Croix in 1493, whereupon the indigenous Caribs attacked, the first recorded instance of armed conflict between Europeans and Native Americans. European colonization started just over a hundred years later and, in turn, led to the enslavement and then total annihilation of the Caribs and their local counterparts, the Taínos, in just a few decades.

The first major contingent of European settlers on Saint Thomas were Dutch; they founded Charlotte Amalie, though they originally called it Tap Huis—Tap House. The Dutch, English, French, and Danish played a sort of musical-chairs colonialism, here and in the other Virgin Islands. Over on Saint Croix, the Dutch and English both arrived around 1625 and squabbled incessantly—in 1645, the Dutch governor killed the English governor(!), which sparked a battle in which the Dutch governor was himself mortally wounded. The Dutch fled, leaving the Brits in charge until 1650, when five Spanish ships sailed into Saint Croix at night. Then some French Knights of Malta in nearby Saint Kitts noticed the action ("*Zut alors, action!*"), so *they* invaded and drove out the Spaniards. The Danes took over Saint Thomas and Saint John in the 1670s (and Saint Croix in 1733) and platted Charlotte Amalie in 1681, naming the city after the Queen of Denmark, Charlotte Amalia, whose name was misspelled by a mapmaker. (The city's name is still pronounced "Charlotte *Amalia*.")

The Danes also brought the transatlantic slave trade here, in 1673. Sugar was the world's hottest commodity, shaping the global economy as cotton would in the 1800s and oil would in the 1900s, and the Caribbean was the hot spot for cultivation. Hundreds of sugar plantations dotted the Danish West Indies, and by 1800 they were home to more than thirty-five thousand slaves, more than 75 percent of the islands' overall population. The slaves built the local economy while enduring all the horrifying details of the "peculiar institution." By decree of the governor, runaway slaves were to be hung "unless the owner pardon him with the loss of one leg"; a slave who didn't step aside when meeting a white person was to be flogged; various other infractions would result in branding or having an ear or hand cut off. Even Anne made no attempts to gloss over the history.

For Americans, it's easy to think of colonialism in these history-book terms, misdeeds carried out long ago by other people in exotic places. Europeans arrive in pith helmets and jodhpurs, subjugate/annihilate indigenous people, build towns and economies through exploitation and/or slavery, sip coffee on verandas, write long letters to the Queen. These are the archetypes of empire and colonialism: the Belgian Congo, the Spanish Conquest of the Incas, the British Raj in India. Here in the Caribbean, British colonialism's ripple effects have famously been given form by writers like Nobel laureates Derek Walcott (a native of Saint Lucia) and V. S. Naipaul (Trinidad); it is a pulse beating through their every elegiac line, as it is in the music of Bob Marley, the world's best-known Rasta.

Rastafari was established in Jamaica in the 1930s as an anti-colonial movement and Afrocentric religion that worships Haile Selassie, the mid–twentieth century emperor of Ethiopia, the only African nation never to be colonized. It spread across the Caribbean, including the USVI, where there are Rastas in the territory's senate, Rastas at the grocery store, Rasta tour guides; they're a common part of the everyday culture here. But because they're so strongly associated with Jamaica, it's easy to categorize them as imports from another place, with no real relevance here, just as the Danish architecture and history of slavery are imports from another era, wholly separate from here-and-now. They're relics of the sins of others. (Surely it's no coincidence that the villain of our pop culture's most beloved saga, *Star Wars*, is the Empire—it is a term that conjures, to modern-day Americans, a Tyrannical Other.)

But where do we draw the line between colony and not-a-colony? If the Danish West Indies were a colony on March 16, 1917, what about the U.S. Virgin Islands on March 17, 1917? Did we make that politically charged label disappear simply by hanging up the UNDER NEW MANAGEMENT shingle?

• • • • •

I SPENT a few days poking around Charlotte Amalie, wandering around the waterfront and some of the backstreets and even Frenchtown, while constantly glancing over my shoulder, hearing both Ronnie and my distant wife in my mind, cautioning me to be careful. I trekked up a steep street, along with the tourist masses, for an obligatory lesson in the (robust, bloody) pirate history of Saint Thomas at Blackbeard's Castle, a stone tower that the guide said was actually the notorious buccaneer's *prison*. After I climbed to the top of the tower and back down—which took maybe five minutes, including the obligatory photos from the top—I asked the guide the way to the rest of the historic site.

"Well, okay, you saw the gift shop?" she asked. "And the pool and the rum bar?"

Yes, I said. Is there more?

She shook her head and wished me a pleasant day.

After a jerk-chicken lunch at a small café where the owner cranked up her Sinatra CD and serenaded me with "Pocketful of Miracles," I went back to the Crystal Palace, where I met Ronnie's cousin on the porch. She regaled me with stories about their parents and grandparents, including one who was "the dean of pit-bull fighting on the island" and once brought back a small alligator from his travels with the circus, which the kids played with until the parents had second thoughts. Ronnie listened quietly but with a pained expression on the other side of the porch, as he stared down at his domain. Finally, he interrupted and said, "You know, for *real* history, you need to go to the Historical Trust."

The next morning, my last on Saint Thomas, Ronnie called the executive director, a woman named Pamela, and said, "Mr. Mack is on his way."

I pushed my way through the Main Street crowds and a short walk later, I was standing in front of an old stone building with a sign reading ST. THOMAS HISTORICAL TRUST. Pamela buzzed me in and I signed the guest book; judging by the entries, only a handful of people came here every day, and I was the sole visitor now. Pamela was originally from the states. She had sandy, shoulder-length hair and a nervous jitter to her voice, hopeful to impress.

It was a small museum, just a few rooms, with the soothingly bland feel of a small-town doctor's office—but no worries, I thought, it's the history that counts. Pamela led me into a room with bottles and plates from a Danish ship, and picked up a football-sized chunk of coal from the days when this was a shipping way station, "the 7-Eleven of the Americas," Pamela said. This was followed by a room with an old-fashioned mahogany bed that had once belonged to a local doctor, and a small display of sepia photos, donated by Ronnie, showing daily life in Charlotte Amalie around the turn of the twentieth century.

And . . . that was about it. I kept waiting for more—another room, another floor. By now, I knew there was more to the story of the U.S. Virgin Islands than Danish industry and manor life. But those were the only story lines being told here, in the primary museum in the primary city of the territory, where tens of thousands of tourists arrive every day.

I was too shy to say it out loud but what was going through my mind was this: *Where is everything else?*

There was nothing about the indigenous Caribs and Taínos, nothing about the centuries of colonial battles, nothing about slaves or the multiple slave rebellions, like the one on Saint John in 1733, when the nearly eleven hundred slaves took over the island's fort and then the entire island for six months. Ran the place. Lived free. Successfully fought off Danish soldiers sent from Saint Thomas and two other takeover attempts by British troops called in by the frantic governor. (The gripping tale is ably told in *Night of the Silent Drums* by Lonzo Anderson.) And nothing, either, about the islands' still-vibrant African cultural roots, aside from some photos and a traditional broom made with dried palm fronds, forming broad bristles. Pamela demonstrated with a saleswoman's fervor: "Better than a vacuum!" *Yes, and what else you got?*

Heck, they didn't even have anything about that perpetual tourist-bait, pirates—not just Blackbeard came here but also Bluebeard, Captain William Kidd, and other swashbucklers, who literally left their mark here, cannons blasting, swords clashing.

I asked about the history of the past century. This was my

main interest, I told Pamela: the American era. She got very quiet and searched the room. Nothing. It was as though in 1917, the long arc of history screeched to a halt, skid marks on the timeline. Money's tight, Pamela explained, adding that she knew they had work to do. She was a recent hire, the only full-time employee. Some grant funding was starting to come in. I felt bad for her, and silently tried to come up with fund-raising schemes: *Sell Tap Huis T-shirts! Get a kiddie pool and reenact colonial battles with little toy ships!*

I walked away jarred, bewildered, and disappointed. That night, I ate dinner at one of the handful of restaurants open in the evening—most, along with nearly all the shops in central Charlotte Amalie, close down after the cruise ships leave in late afternoon—and moped over a beer and a burger. These past few days, I'd alternated between wide-eyed touristic wonder and a pronounced unease, from the safety concerns to the ever-present signs of the culture-skewing effects of tourists like me to . . . well, whatever was going on at the Saint Thomas Historical Trust. And I hoped that when I flew to Saint Croix the next day, I'd find something different. I finished my meal and sprinted back up the hill, past shuttered Main Street, to the Crystal Palace, where Ronnie was waiting on the porch.

"So," he asked, "did you learn anything today?"

• • • • •

THE EARLY DAYS of the American takeover, as it happens, don't make for an especially cheery, vacationer-education history lesson.

For the United States, the appeal of the USVI was its utility as a coaling station and vantage point for monitoring the Panama

Canal. The Navy officially ran the islands for the first decade after the transfer, and its general attitude toward Virgin Islanders was: *What gall of these savage people, to intrude on our islands.* Stories of Marines harassing black locals, including children, were commonplace, and public appeals for intervention by the Washington-appointed territorial governors were met with dismissals. In 1918, Governor James Oliver described one complainant as "a sort of half-witted negro . . . constantly causing agitation amongst the ignorant class." There were some positive developments, to be sure: the Navy improved the local hospitals, sanitation, and access to clean water. Death rates dropped by nearly half. But even beyond the racism and treatment of Virgin Islanders as second-class citizens, the transition proved detrimental in other ways, including the decline of agricultural cultivation by almost two-thirds. The economy plummeted.

Add it all up and it's clear that while the Navy may not have had pith helmets and bullwhips, this was still Colonialism 2.0. The bigger question is: When did the USVI stop being a colony?

Was it in 1927, when Virgin Islands residents were finally granted U.S. citizenship and governance transferred to a civilian—though still presidentially appointed—administration? Was it 1931, when President Herbert Hoover became the first American president to visit the islands since the transfer? Hoover's visit is still remembered here, with frustration and anger. He decreed the USVI "an effective poorhouse," adding that, "Viewed from every point except remote naval contingencies, it was unfortunate that we ever acquired these islands." The islands were struggling, it's true, but Hoover's derision ignored external factors: the world economy was reeling after the 1929 stock market crash, and a hurricane followed by a drought had tag-teamed to all but wipe out the islands' sugar plantations.

Hoover's assessment would shade the islands' collective mood and political outlook for decades. Archibald Alphonso Alexander, who was appointed governor in 1954, called Virgin Islanders "wards of the state," and his successor, Walter A. Gordon, characterized his constituents as lazy and standoffish.

Perhaps the shift away from "colony" happened in 1936, when Congress passed a Virgin Islands Organic Act, setting up a local legislature; or 1954, when they passed a stronger Revised Organic Act. Or maybe in 1969, when the territory was finally allowed to elect its own governor.

Decade by decade, the USVI gained more self-governance and became less and less like what we think of when we think of Quintessential Colonialism. But the question still nagged me: Does the USVI still fit the bill? Have we ever fully shed the label of Empire? What does a colony even *look* like in the twenty-first century?

• • • • •

SAINT THOMAS is known as the busy island, what counts for the big city around here. Saint John, more than two-thirds of which is the Virgin Islands National Park, is much smaller and more laid back. The vibe on Saint Croix, forty miles south, is somewhere in between. It has about the same population as Saint Thomas and twice the landmass in its wing-shaped form. The principal city, Christiansted, is on the northeastern part of the island and feels even more Old World than Charlotte Amalie; the Government House, a regal golden box lined with rows of white columns, seemed to have been teleported straight from Copenhagen. I texted Maren a barrage of photos.

The streets were lively with people and good cheer well into the evening. There's no cruise-ship port in Christiansted, and it operates as a normal town, with restaurants and stores open normal-town hours, the dinner options numerous. This particular evening turned out to be the monthly art crawl, with a dozen or so galleries open, and music and wine and the territory's highest concentration of tight black clothes and thick-framed glasses.

"Good evening, good evening!" I said to the art-crawlers, but none of them replied. Most of them seemed to be from the states, not tourists but people who'd moved down here to stake a claim in an island daydream. (Thanks largely to influxes of American mainlanders, who are mostly white, and "down-islanders" from other parts of the Caribbean, who are mostly black, USVI natives make up less than half of the territory's present-day population. While the newcomers are largely welcomed on an individual basis, locals told me, there's also a wariness about the demographic shifts to the islands, and questions of whose voices are heard—a parallel of sorts to the broader tourists-versus-locals anxieties. The native-born population feels the strongest kinship to each other, regardless of race, as their home is ever-changing.)

Away from the galleries, though, passersby greeted me warmly and I greeted them back and all was right with the world. Alongside the waterfront sat a bright yellow Danish fort, surrounded by a quiet park. A small group held a worship service and two young children played in the grass with their parents and an enthusiastic terrier. Sailboat halyards clinked and palm trees danced languidly in a light breeze.

I felt my posture relax.

• • • • •

THE CONSTANT greeting of everyone you encounter—art-crawlers aside, evidently—was quickly becoming one of my favorite things about the USVI. Even at the safari stop in Charlotte Amalie, and on safaris I later rode, the chorus of pleasantries directed my way never abated, despite the fact that everything about me, from my running shoes to my sunscreen-blotched cheeks, screamed, *Tourist!*

One night in Christiansted, I encountered a teenage Rasta sitting on the curb, flicking through photos on his phone. He greeted me warmly and I asked how his evening was going; he said it was real good. As an afterthought, he added, "Oh, hey, man, I got some nice kush if you need some." I politely declined.

"Okay, cool." With a thoughtful squint he added, "Well, yo, you looking for some powder? I can get you that, too."

"No, no. I'm all good."

"All right, man. Bless. You enjoy your evening. And be safe out there!"

At my hotel in Christiansted, I bade good morning to the cleaning woman, Pauline. She was a down-islander—an immigrant from elsewhere in the Caribbean—in a floral-print blouse, and, ice broken, we proceed on to small talk: the weather; her kids, who were in the U.S. military; and then the subject of lunch. "Go to Harvey's, ask for Richie, and tell him I said to take good care of you," she said.

Around noon, I reported to the twelve-table restaurant, its walls covered in framed newspaper clippings and photos of President Barack Obama and San Antonio Spurs star Tim Duncan, a Christiansted native. Richie presented me with a menu, which consisted of a notepad that he held in his hand. Pauline had recommended some local specialties: conch in a viscous butter sauce; *fungi*, a yellowy, cornmealy dome that was billed as a sort of vegetable-studded polenta; and *mauby* ("MAW-bee"), an iced drink made from a bark infusion, with flavors of anise and ginger.

I texted Maren a photo of my glass of *mauby*: *Instant refreshment—delicious!* It was her birthday and I felt guilty; here I was, romping around the tropics, while she weathered below-zero temperatures.

A lean man with a goatee and a blue polo shirt walked in, and I recalled that I'd seen him at breakfast at another restaurant that morning. We'd exchanged pleasantries then and began chatting more now. His name was Dexter, and he introduced me to his friend Sheldon, a stocky guy with a quick, eager smile and a white polo shirt with a red-and-yellow logo reading DA VYBE 107.9 FM. It was the local R&B radio station, where Sheldon worked and where they hosted a show together.

After two or three minutes of chitchat, Sheldon said matter-of-factly, "Hey, we should drive you around and show you the island." Just out of the blue. Like he said it to every stranger he met.

Dexter nodded. "Where we gonna go?"

I silently made predictions: an old plantation so they could tell me the heartbreaking legacy of slavery, or perhaps a shiny resort, the obvious tourist destination.

Dexter stroked his goatee. "We should get some ice cream!"

I laughed to myself. It doesn't get more middle-of-the-road Americana, more Norman Rockwell, than a trip to the local ice-cream parlor.

They finished their lunches and we got in Sheldon's blue Jeep Cherokee, brand-new and every inch shimmering in the bright sun. We drove up a hill and out of Christiansted, into an area called Orange Grove. The landscape was decidedly suburban: McDonald's, Subway, a big-box grocery store. We stopped at the radio station and at a print shop so I could meet a friend of

Sheldon's. As they shared their lives with me, I told them about Maren, freezing in Minnesota.

"It's her birthday? And you're here *without* her?" Sheldon said, more scold than question.

"Yeah," I replied sheepishly.

Sheldon's eyes lit up. "We gonna give her a big surprise. Text her and tell her to go to DaVybe.com and listen to the live stream."

I laughed and typed. Deep bass notes thumped softly from the car's stereo as Eminem issued a profane-yet-catchy rant. A few minutes later, Maren wrote back, *I'm listening. Whatever song this is, it's DEFINITELY not workplace-appropriate. What's going on?!*

Sheldon called the station and gave orders, grinning ear to ear. A moment later, the DJ came on the air.

"All right! All right, all right. We got a reeeal special request here." Pause for laughter. "This one's goin' out to Maren way up in Minnesooh-tah." He nailed the accent. "Happy birthday from her lovin' husband, Doug, sendin' all his love and tropical sunshine from the VI."

He put on a bouncy song called "Love and Affection." The entire car shook as we doubled over in laughter and triumphant whoops, and maybe even some moist eyes over the sweetness of it all.

"That was beautiful, Sheldon," Dexter said. I looked at Sheldon. He glowed with one of the broadest smiles I've seen in my life.

"Next time, you gonna bring her with you," he said.

We coasted to Armstrong's Ice Cream and gleefully stumbled inside. The owner came around the counter to shake our hands, and the woman in line ahead of us turned out to be Sheldon's former English teacher, who chatted with me about the writing life as she licked her cone. We got scoops of the best-selling flavor, gooseberry, with a subtle, not-too-sweet fruitiness and little pits that I kept swallowing rather than spitting out, desperate not to offend my hosts.

"It's good, right?" Sheldon asked as we got back in the car.

I nodded, my mouth full.

"It's all good," Sheldon said.

We drove back across the island, as Sheldon fielded periodic calls from the station and I marveled at the road signs. Saint Croix is divided into estates based on the former plantations, all two hundred of them, and many have exquisitely unexpected names: Great Princess, Mary's Fancy, Solitude, Adventure, Barren Spot, Rustop Twist, Prosperity, Hard Labour, Jealousy, Upper Love, Lower Love, Punch, Sprat Hole, Wheel of Fortune, and Body Slob.

Near the side of the highway, Sheldon pointed out a complex of apartment buildings, stout and handsome in that generic suburban way. They had recently been completed, replacing buildings destroyed in Hurricane Hugo.

Okay, I thought, *No big deal, so—*

"Hugo was in *1989.*" Sheldon said. "Some things still aren't rebuilt. Maybe they will, maybe they won't."

A few minutes later, we passed the local oil refinery, Hovensa, which opened in the 1960s and had long been one of the world's ten largest refineries, as well as the keystone of Saint Croix's economy. But it closed in 2012, putting more than twelve hundred Crucians out of work in an instant. I asked Sheldon about poverty and he visibly flinched: "Man, I don't know you'd call it *poverty.* We got poor people, yeah, but . . ." His voice trailed off. Times were tough, it was true, and I'd later look up the unemployment rate: in the USVI overall, it hovered above 12 percent.

But median income in the USVI was just a shade lower than that of the USA overall. On each island, I saw homeless people and shanties—but not shanty*towns* of the Hooverian, developing-world stereotype.

We drove on to the far side of Saint Croix, to see Point Udall, the easternmost point in the United States, a high, windswept cliff with a monument of tall, angular stones. The houses out here were farther apart and larger, and the overall effect reminded me of coastal Route 1 in California.

"Yeah, it's just like that," Sheldon agreed. "It's nice out here. In fact, lots of people don't realize all the nice things about the VI. They just think about, like, Fountain Valley, even though that was like three million years ago."

I'd wondered if any locals would bring up Fountain Valley, the mass shooting I'd read about in my pre-trip planning. It happened at the height of a flurry of high-end development in Saint Croix in the early 1970s, which brought in wealthy tourists and landowners and alienated locals whose own lot was far from improving. For the first time, island residents from other places outnumbered the native-born. A small independence movement arose, led by a local man named Mario Moorhead, known for his "Third World Marxist" books. Against this background, on September 6, 1972, five gunmen burst into the Fountain Valley clubhouse and killed eight people. It made headlines around the world, and a 1994 investigation in the *Virgin Islands Daily News*, uncovering new details of the case, won a Pulitzer Prize for Public Service. Five young black men, three of them Vietnam War veterans, were arrested.

"They were a bunch of crazy Rastas," Sheldon said. "It was bad, but not something big that should've scared people away, or that they should still talk about like it was yesterday."

There is crime here, as Ronnie warned. In fact, the previous year, there had been more than thirty murders on Saint Croix alone, a rate higher than that of any major American city. But another Crucian, echoing Sheldon, told me not to get too concerned. He'd gone back and looked at the list. He knew all the names. Tragic as they all were, all but one were "folks involved in the wrong sort of activities"; tourists and most residents were perfectly safe.

On the way back into town, Sheldon decided to give me a taste of the island's high life. We pulled up to the gate of a resort called Buccaneer, and Sheldon talked his way inside. He took an accidental wrong turn onto a golf-cart path and kept going, which fortuitously led us to a postcard vista at the top of hill, the town of Christiansted laid out to our left, a trio of perplexed golfers to our right. "If anyone asks," Sheldon said, "Dexter was driving." He pointed toward Christiansted. "And, look. Look at that view."

• • • • •

"IT'S NOT MAYBERRY, but it's not Detroit, either," a man named John Beagles told me that night, as he and his wife, Karen, and I tucked into bowls of pad thai and ramen at an Asian fusion bistro in Christiantsted. John was a native Crucian, with large glasses that accentuated a perpetually ruminative gaze. Karen had blond hair and an amused smirk, and was from the mainland; she came down years ago to be a dive master, and never moved back.

As we ate, a steady stream of passing friends stopped at our table to say hello; no more than a few minutes passed before the "Good evening!" call-and-response resumed.

I asked John and Karen to tell me stories about life here. Well, they said, there's the sense of community.

"Yeah," I said, silently adding, *And how.*

"It can also be . . . a bit tiring," John said. Everybody knows each other's business, whether you want them to or not, and they know it right away, through "the Coconut Telegraph."* The territory also seemed to attract more than its share of odd outsiders, John added, sizing me up with a look that said I might fit this description. Given its less-than-full federal oversight, he went on, "It's the end of the line. There's a bar down at Coral Bay where you get all the fugitives from the states. Go in there and just whisper, 'FBI,' and just like that it'll clear out, just you and the bartender." There were the more benign eccentrics, like the disheveled woman who used to go into their friend's store and shoplift all the time, and turned out to be a prominent heiress missing from New York. There was a mysterious woman known as the Contessa who wore coordinated polyester outfits, picked up hitchhikers in her limo, and lived in a stone castle at the top of a hill.

John and Karen shared a shrug of *so-it-goes* amusement before turning to greet more friends who had just entered the restaurant, an elegantly dressed couple.

John and Karen introduced me to their friends, and for a minute the four riffed on some of the minor annoyances of life on Saint Croix. Groceries were expensive—a gallon of milk cost $7. Ordering online could be difficult because many retailers charge international rates, not understanding that this is the

* I hadn't told John and Karen about my driving tour with Sheldon and Dexter, but John emailed a few days later to say that he'd heard them talking about me on their radio show, and that Sheldon had also confessed to driving on the Buccaneer golf cart path.

USA; sometimes the islands were listed in a drop-down menu as "Virgin Islands, U.S. and British." Often, though, you could use a workaround: select Virginia from the drop-down menu, then enter the proper zip code.

And territory residents pay into Medicare and Medicaid taxes, yet the programs' payouts are disproportionately low. John and Karen knew a young woman who was hard of hearing. If she'd been in the states, they said, she would have been eligible for subsidies for interpreters and hearing aids. Because they live in a territory, nothing. And the Affordable Care Act essentially forgot about the territories. It required the local insurers to comply with all the new regulations, like doing away with existing-conditions clauses, but failed to mandate that residents purchase insurance, or give them subsidies to do so. Healthy people were neither compelled nor inclined to buy into the system and give it the necessary strength in numbers, and premiums soared. In 2014, the Department of Health and Human Services came up with a solution: it exempted insurers in the territories from many of the requirements they had to follow in the states, starting with—and this is the big one—"guaranteed availability."

Eventually we finished our meal, and then moved on to another nearby restaurant, where Karen wanted me to try the rum cake, and John wanted to make the rounds and see who else was out. He got back to the table just as Karen was telling me about a voodoo-like practice called obeah, whose adherents sometimes place offerings at various local crossroads: a metal bowl filled with lettuce, money, and a dead chicken.

"Did you see the one at the end of our road the other day?" Karen asked offhandedly.

She and John chuckled and then looked at me with matching half smiles, which I read as both, *This-is-home-I-love it*, and, *Seriously-this-place-is-nuts*.

And here was the point that they, and all the hospitality-minded, stranger-welcoming locals I'd met—Monica, the Rastas at Bordeaux Farmer's Market, Sheldon, Dexter—had been trying to impress upon me: They're making it work. Yes, there are some problems, some oddities, some kinks in the system. It can be paradise; it can be utterly maddening; it's both, and also, for many residents, just a pleasingly average, American working- and middle-class existence. Farmers, cleaning ladies, radio DJs. Malls, softball leagues (or pickup cricket), happy hour with your friends. It's just that, well, sometimes there's a voodoo shrine on the way to the mall. Sometimes there are little pits in your ice cream. That's just how it goes.

• • • • •

ALL OF THIS was making it ever harder for me to answer the question of colony, which grew even more muddled when I asked people how they felt about the territory's political status. Nearly everyone bemoaned their inability to vote for president, the lack of full-fledged congressional representation, the general attitudes and misconceptions of the stateside tourists, and the myriad ways in which the federal and local governments try to outdo themselves in their bumbling.

But to my great surprise, no one I talked to was particularly worked up about the political status. In fact, I had to drag opinions out of them; they weren't offered readily. John and Karen waffled when I asked, over dinner, and the sudden awkwardness was such that I immediately changed the subject. When I emailed later, John replied, *The change would be a concern,* noting, for example, the tax incentives. All territories have tax codes unlike those in the states—in the USVI, Guam, and the Northern Marianas, there's a "mirror" system set up, in which many basic rules of the IRS apply, but the money goes straight into the territorial coffers—but the USVI, in particular, is "A Made-in-America Offshore Tax Haven," as *Newsweek* put it: "With the blessing of the U.S. Treasury and Congress, the islands offer a 90 percent reduction in U.S. corporate and personal income taxes."

We would have to weigh those as a cost to vote for president, John wrote. He and everyone else I spoke to said most Virgin Islanders favored the status quo. It wasn't just about taxes but a fear of the unknown, a sense of we've-got-it-good-enough, and a fundamental distrust of the American government to really, truly put them on equal footing, economically, politically, or otherwise.

The issue was the focus of a Status Commission that was planned to convene in early 1990, but it was canceled after the destruction caused by Hurricane Hugo. Local dignitaries took to the newspapers' editorial pages to voice their opinions, with nothing even close to a consensus. Some argued to keep the status quo, others wanted independence. Or statehood. Or commonwealth status, like Puerto Rico. The whole range of possibilities.

Three years later, the USVI held a referendum on the political status, with options for staying a territory, becoming a state, or becoming independent. More than 80 percent of voters favored maintaining territorial status—but only 30 percent of eligible voters cast a ballot at all, and 50 percent turnout was required for the results to be binding, so they were invalidated. There has not been another referendum.

The attempts to set up a territorial constitution—which would take the place of the Revised Organic Act of 1954 and would be a necessary precursor to a statehood push—have met similar fates. Constitutional conventions met in 1964, 1971, 1977, and 1980, but all failed to agree on terms. In 2010, the Fifth Constitutional Convention sent a draft constitution to Governor John de Jongh, who promptly rejected it. Foremost among de Jongh's objections was a section granting special privileges to "native Virgin Islanders" (born here) or "ancestral native Virgin Islanders" (people whose ancestors lived in the islands prior to 1932, when American citizenship was officially extended to the territory). For example, ancestral native Virgin Islanders would be exempt from property taxes, and only native Virgin Islanders would be allowed to run for governor. The proposed provisions highlighted the feeling, among many island natives, that they deserve a greater voice in what happens to their homeland; de Jongh, however, called them "inconsistent with basic tenets of equal protection and fairness as established by the United States Constitution." A lawsuit forced him to forward the draft to Congress and the Obama administration, both of which rejected it for much the same reasons. In 2012, USVI delegates reconvened to start over, but again could not reach an agreement.

• • • • •

ON MY last day in Saint Croix, I walked to the Budget car rental office in Christiansted to finally try this whole driving-on-the-left thing. My mind was a newsreel of predicted crashes: being flattened by a semi, soaring over a cliff edge and onto kayaking tourists below, plowing into an obeah shrine. I signed up for every conceivable insurance policy and some inconceivable ones—the clerk kept inventing, I kept buying. I sat in the car psyching myself up for a few minutes, until the clerk came outside to ask if I was okay. With a nervous nod, I started the car, cranked up Da Vybe, and puttered east.

First stop: Estate Whim, a former sugar plantation, where I hoped to get a deeper history lesson than I'd found at the Saint Thomas Historical Trust Museum. Da Vybe was playing a bouncy kids' song about the months of the year, creating an incongruously cheery feel as I pulled into a long, shaded driveway and parked in an empty lot. On the porch of the estate's great house I was greeted by a docent, Mr. Meyers, a tall, soft-spoken black man in a coral polo shirt and dreadlocks. He took me on a long tour of the house, offering a dissertation on the materials and design of each piece of furniture: a mahogany bed, a side table hiding a chamber pot.

We came to a lounge chair, with a low-angle back and long, straight arms that almost looked like skis. "Do you know what this is?" Mr. Meyers asked.

I shook my head.

He sat down and swung his legs onto the arms. "It's designed to help the master take off his shoes. He feels so stiff after a long day watching the fields. He just wants to relax." Mr. Meyers sold the scene well; I empathized with this poor, fatigued master.

Then we went out to the porch and Mr. Meyers started pointing at the other parts of the estate—the slave quarters, the kitchen building, the field—and said that everything else was self-guided. "And over there are some gravestones of slaves," Mr. Myers said, pointing to a weed-choked lawn. "Those are my ancestors. So you can look at that, too." Their aches got no elaboration. "And right here is the gift shop," Mr. Meyers added. With that, he went off to greet a freshly arrived busload of Danes.

I wandered the grounds for a while, reading the plaques—half of which were faded to illegibility—and eventually ended up by the old sugar mill, where the Danes were gathered with their own guide, who was giving a long lecture in Danish, captivating to them, useless to me.

As I drove off, I recalled Anne's comments about the ubiquity of her compatriots in the USVI, and something clicked. They come to the territory in droves, specifically for the history, for the portal to their nineteenth century glory days. The American tourists come for the beaches and the shopping. The museums and historic sites, intentionally or not, reflect this imbalance and tailor their content to their ticket-buying audience: the Danes. History is written not just by the victors but by those who are most eager to underwrite it.

All of this skews the story that's told. And this is compounded, I later learned, by the fact that most primary documents about the transfer and the early American era are held at the U.S. National Archives in Washington, D.C., and the majority of materials from the Danish era are *in Danish* and held in Copenhagen, at the Danish National Archives (which in 2012 began scanning two hundred fifty linear miles of documents, with plans to put them online in 2017, in time for the hundredth anniversary of the transfer).

It's difficult for Virgin Islanders to research their own history, because it has literally been taken away from them, as Jeannette Allis Bastian discusses in her book *Owning Memory: How a Caribbean Community Lost Its Archives and Found Its History.* One noteworthy example is the story of Buddhoe, the slave I'd seen memorialized in Emancipation Garden in Charlotte Amalie. He's a local legend, a folk hero, who famously led the 1847 rebellion that led to emancipation of all Danish West Indies slaves, after gathering thousands of his comrades in Saint Croix and taking over the fort in Frederiksted, where I was headed now. Anne the Dane had told me that a friend of hers had uncovered evidence at the Danish National Archives that Buddhoe *wasn't* the rebellion leader—that, in fact, he wasn't even a real person, purely a myth. What Anne didn't mention, but I later learned, was the considerable public outcry after her friend offered this new narrative. It wasn't just the challenge to the Virgin Islands' collective memory and identity that angered locals, but its source: an outsider, using colonial-era documents held half a world away. And, not incidentally, the findings directly contradicted those of another scholar who'd pored over the same materials in 1984 and concluded that the core of the Buddhoe legend *was* true.

In Frederiksted, I made my way to a waterfront park, where there was another Buddhoe statue, blowing his conch shell. A dozen or so tourists, wearing lanyards from the cruise ship docked at the town's pier, loitered in the park, comparing purchases from the cluster of vendors who'd set up shop nearby. On the street, a parked car blasted a reggae tune with a mournful plaint.

I sat in the park, listening and thinking, until the song ended and I recalled that I had an altogether more frivolous task to undertake while I was on this side of Saint Croix: I had a tip about a nearby bar. It had come from one of Sheldon's friends, a guy named Mike, whose drinking-establishment recommendation I knew I could trust because he was from New Jersey and wore a gold Tasmanian Devil necklace.

• • • • •

Which was how I ended up at the Montpellier Domino Club, the rum bar in the jungle with the beer-drinking pigs out back, and the crew of regulars—Leon, Ray, Linda—holding court. I sat there long enough, soaking up the camaraderie, that Norma, the owner, comped me a drink. She mixed me a concoction she called Cheesecake, with vanilla Cruzan rum and pineapple and cranberry juice, and then told me to introduce myself so that everybody would know my name.

So now it was official: this was the rain-forest version of *Cheers*. Even when I'd pictured monkeys in malls when I first imagined the territories, I hadn't actually *expected* this sort of thing, nor I had imagined that, in fact, it would feel so natural.

Just then, a dreadlocked Rasta tour guide walked up with a seventyish Danish tourist couple.

"Pigs running, Norma?"

"No, they're all worn out for today."

The three decided to stay, joining our conversation and completing our tableau. Of all the possible embodiments of the American melting pot, I had never considered that one might be a Rasta and a pair of Danish tourists sharing brightly colored cocktails mixed by a Trinidadian in a West Indies jungle bar.

But here it was, and it was glorious.

I texted Maren: *This is the good life.*

She wrote back: *Next time, I'm coming with you.*

Chapter 2

FOREIGN IN A DOMESTIC SENSE

American Samoa

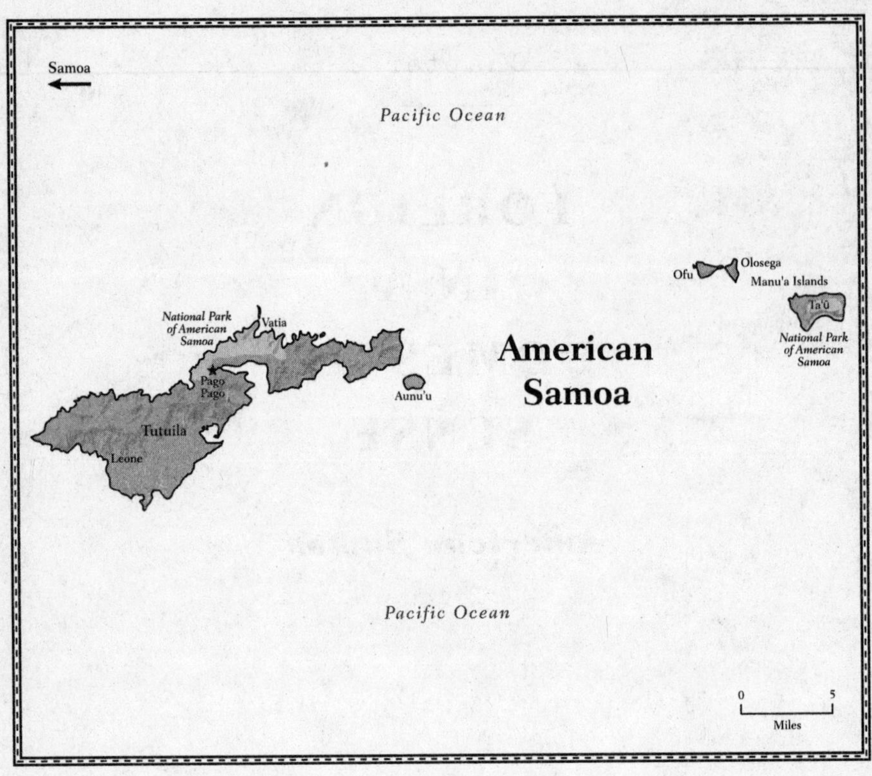
Samoa
Pacific Ocean
National Park of American Samoa
Vatia
Pago Pago
Tutuila
Leone
Aunu'u
American Samoa
Ofu
Olosega
Manu'a Islands
Ta'ū
National Park of American Samoa
Pacific Ocean
0
5
Miles

I ARRIVED HOME FROM THE USVI WITH A TAN AND a million questions.

My trek across the territories had begun largely as a catalog of Americana at its most far-flung and mixed-up. The history and culture were fascinating, to be sure, but I'd also stumbled across political and legal issues that had left me with all sorts of questions: How, when, and why had the empire gotten weird? Why were there so many differences compared to the states, particularly with regard to the myriad laws that shape everyday life? And why were the territories still territories, rather than states?

It was becoming clear that if I really, truly wanted to understand these places, I'd have to roll up my sleeves and dig into the esoteric details. I searched again for books that examined the territories in a broad, all-encompassing sort of way, and found precisely one: *Defining Status: A Comprehensive Analysis of United States Territorial Policy* by Arnold Leibowitz, more than seven hundred pages long and published in 1989. There were also a few academic works focusing on legal matters, including *Does the Constitution Follow the Flag?*; *Colonial Constitutionalism*; and, most helpful, *Foreign in a Domestic Sense.* I bought them, opened them, and panicked: even to an interested reader, they were dense and daunting.

I needed some help. I called up Columbia Law Professor Christina Duffy Ponsa, one of the editors of *Foreign in a Domestic Sense*.* Months earlier, she had also presented at a conference hosted by the Harvard Law School to examine the history and legal issues regarding the territories. It was a one-day event and the first such conference since Ponsa organized one at Yale in 1998. In the opening remarks, the dean of the Harvard Law School noted that in all her years of study and teaching, she had never once discussed the territories.

When I told Professor Ponsa what I was looking for, she laughed and said, "Simple!" She spent more than an hour walking me through the basics and standing by as a massive thunderstorm in Minneapolis kept knocking out reception on my end.

Ponsa's answers all pointed back to the turn of the twentieth century, the USA's so-called Imperial Moment. "That's what the historical actors at the time see as the question: *Can we do empire?*" she said. "In the wake of the Civil War, the federal government has become more powerful and the United States is now flexing its muscle on the international stage and European powers have been annexing colonies, so the question arises, *Do we do this, too?*"

The nation's answer: "Let's go for it!" In 1898, the United States annexed Hawaii and then claimed Puerto Rico, Guam, and the Philippines in the Spanish-American War. In 1900, it added American Samoa to its holdings. In a flash, the scope of the American empire had grown from the North America con-

* At the time *Foreign in a Domestic Sense* was published, in 2001, her name was Christina Duffy Burnett.

tinent and assorted guano-covered islands to distant, *populated* corners of the map.

Ponsa spoke animatedly and rapidly, and I could imagine her in a lecture hall, gesturing and pausing every now and then to make sure everyone was keeping up.

"Right," I said.

"Okay," she continued, racing onward. "And as people look at these places"—these newly acquired islands, so far away and with cultures so seemingly *different* from the USA's—"they can't quite imagine them being states. So the debate heats up: Can we take places that we don't intend to make states? It's primarily a constitutional debate: Does the Constitution permit the U.S. to do this? And the question makes its way to the Supreme Court."

The resulting set of cases are known, collectively, as the Insular Cases (because they affect the insular areas, the parts of the USA that aren't states); there were approximately two dozen, the primary of which were decided between 1901 and 1922.* The key case, the one that underlies all the others, was *Downes v. Bidwell*, in 1901, which began with a tax on oranges shipped from Puerto Rico to New York. The Constitution forbids taxation on interstate commerce, so the issue was whether this was true of commerce with Puerto Rico, and, more to the point, whether Puerto Rico and the other newly acquired territories were part of the United States in strict constitutional terms. The court said no: the territories *belonged to* the USA but were not wholly *part* of it. Therefore, Congress could decide what laws and parts of the Constitution did and did not apply to territories, treating them like states or like foreign countries, depending on the mood.

* Some scholars, including Ponsa, argue that a handful of other territory-related cases should also be considered among the Insular Cases.

What *Downes v. Bidwell* established was this key principle: American soil does not necessarily mean all American laws apply. Or, as the academics put it, the Constitution does not follow the flag.

Adding the territories to the nation as true equals, on the traditional path to statehood, the court's majority decision said, could be "a false step [that] might be fatal to the development of . . . the American empire." The United States would likely continue to annex "distant possessions," and, "If those possessions are inhabited by alien races, differing from us in religion, customs, laws, methods of taxation, and modes of thought, the administration of government and justice, according to Anglo-Saxon principles, may for a time be impossible."

Puerto Rico was therefore "foreign in a domestic sense because the island had not been incorporated into the United States." This is where we get the distinction between *incorporated* and *unincorporated* territories, which added a major and previously nonexistent step on the path to full statehood, and—

Hold on, I said, asking Ponsa to back up to the language of the ruling. It really called these places "alien races" not capable of living up to Anglo-Saxon ideals? Well, *that* was pretty racist.

"Oh, it's a racist idea," she said, "but it's also an idea about cultural difference," adding that after President Polk took over a portion of Mexico, the treaty of the annexation had a guarantee of citizenship in it—and there's no question that Mexicans were not perceived as Anglo-Saxon. But by 1900 the USA had come up with more legal alternatives. Moreover, Ponsa said, "Part of the thinking wasn't just that these people are different and therefore inferior, but it also was, 'This is a wholly developed foreign culture, and it really isn't clear how well their cultural, legal, social, political traditions can mesh with ours.'" (The *Downes v.*

Bidwell ruling made a distinction between "the annexation of distant and outlying possessions" and earlier expansion within "contiguous territory inhabited only by people of the same race or by scattered bodies of native Indians"—the Indians and *their* rights, it's clear, were also of little concern to the court.)

It was an issue of assimilation, one that called to mind not just present-day immigration debates but also the question of how, exactly, we define what it means to be American, and who gets to set that definition. As Professor Ponsa kept going, full speed ahead, my mind fixed on this question.

I'd spent the hour before our call planning the next leg of my trip, to American Samoa, and the topic of cultural evolution, of colliding traditions, recurred throughout my guidebooks and historical research. The common theme was that even by the pluralistic standards of the USA, American Samoa was *different*, more foreign than familiar.

• • • • •

Of all the territories, American Samoa was the one I could most clearly imagine—I'd seen it, or approximations of it, in tiki bars, in *South Pacific*, in *Moby-Dick*'s Queequeg, in Gaugin's paintings of Tahiti. The Packaged Polynesia of jungles and bougainvillea and volcanoes, hulaing women in grass skirts and coconut bras, spear-wielding men, stone-totem gods—Eden with a dash of danger. I knew, on an intellectual level, that this was not reality but commodified exoticism. I've read *Orientalism* and *The Image*. I get it. But my Tourist Lizard Brain was hard to tune out. *Let me have my South Seas Fantasy*, it said. *Gimme.* It was all the more alluring since Maren was, indeed, coming along. After that beach photo she'd seen months earlier, and Sheldon's radio shout-out, she wasn't going to just get by on text messages and postcards. She wanted a piece of the fantasy, too.

We booked a room at a hotel called Sadie's by the Sea, named for the lady-of-the-night protagonist of Somerset Maugham's 1921 short story "Miss Thompson," which was turned into the movie *Rain*, starring Joan Crawford, and also inspired its share of stateside theme restaurants with rain sound effects.* And in late June, we flew to LAX, then Honolulu, then five hours south by southwest, across the equator and just a few miles shy of the International Date Line, to Tutuila, the main island in American Samoa (in the independent nation of Samoa, forty miles west, it was already the next day).

We arrived at night in a haze of jet lag and collapsed in bed. In the morning, refreshed and bright-eyed, we poked our heads outside to see if any of our fantasy was true. The hotel sat near the mouth of the broad Pago Pago Harbor, which thrust so far inland that we couldn't see, from here, where it ended up. White tuna-fishing boats lolled in the cobalt waters. Jungle-shrouded snaggletooth hills ran up and down the coastline, forming the spine of the twenty-mile-long island; straight across the harbor was Rainmaker Mountain, scratching the clouds that swirled on a whispering trade wind, the only sign that it was the beginning of winter here in the only bit of the USA south of the equator. We walked up a path past a sliver of a beach and a swimming pool in the shape of a fruit bat, to the reception desk, where we were welcomed by a young woman in a blue muumuu and with a white hibiscus flower tucked behind her ear. She gave us directions into town, a short walk away, and then turned to two burly

* The Joan Crawford film is, somehow, better remembered than the 1953 version, *Miss Sadie Thompson*, a 3-D musical starring Rita Hayworth.

men who had just entered, wearing sarong-like wrap skirts called *lavalavas* and swirling geometric tattoos on their bulging biceps. The men greeted us in unaccented English, then addressed the receptionist in a flowing melody of glottal stops that I took to be Samoan. The road into town, Route 1, was narrow, and traffic proceeded slowly. Tutuila's speed limit is twenty-five miles per hour and there are no stoplights in the territory. The sidewalk was edged with shoulder-height bushes with bright bursts of flowers.

Maren and I exchanged looks: *So far, so good.*

• • • • •

In the beginning, there was the god Tagaloa, who lived in the expanse of infinite space. There was nothing else until Tagaloa grew tired and created a rock to rest on. He called the rock Manu'atele, but we know it as the Manu'a Islands, out in the eastern part of American Samoa. Tagaloa split the rock into pieces. They became sky and earth and water and everything that exists. From the original rock, he made the rest of the islands of Polynesia, and also the first people: a man named Fatu—Heart—and a woman named Ele'ele—Earth. He put them on Manu'atele, and then he placed two more people on each of the other islands: Fi and Ti on Fiji, To and Ga on Tonga, Tutu and Ila on Tutuila. This is how we all got here.

Or, according to the archaeologists' version, American Samoa was settled about thirty-five hundred years ago, by the Lapita people from Fiji. They've found pottery that connects the cultures. The Lapita were masters of the sea, just like their ancestors and *their* ancestors, going back to people who left Malaysia and Indonesia around 7,000 BC. Entire families spent weeks on outrigger canoes, not knowing where they were heading, but hoping they'd reach somewhere nice, and they settled here.

"Either history is pretty impressive, right?"

This was the earnest-faced question from a young docent named Ioane—"Samoan for William, but you can call me Will." Maren and I had stopped at the National Oceanic and Atmospheric (NOAA) Center on our way into Pago Pago—the territory's capital—and Will led us around a one-room exhibit space about the territory's marine conservation areas, of which there are ten. The history and traditional stories were all Will's addition, told with an eager smile. This, he said, would help us understand *why* people cared so much about keeping their surroundings as pristine as possible. When we'd arrived, the center's main room, a high-ceilinged hexagon, had been filled with a conservation day camp, forty or so kids hunched over small tables, eyeing a PowerPoint projection reading *VERTEBRATES*, with a still from *Finding Nemo* as the background.

Will continued, adding that the Lapita used wave patterns and stars and clouds to find their way; there are still a handful of people, he said, who can navigate this way.

Our Bearer of Traditional Tales wore a yellow polo shirt and tan cargo shorts and a fauxhawk. "How long do you think you'd last out there in a canoe?" he asked me with a smirk.

I laughed. Maren laughed harder. Me? An effete Tocqueville-quoter from a landlocked city? Mere seconds.

"How about you?" I asked. Dude was *big*—when we shook hands, my fingers were saplings among redwoods—but he had an athletic lightness on his feet. Plus, despite his preppy appearance, he was probably well schooled in all traditional ways and—

"Maybe a few hours," he said, flashing me a brief sideways look followed by an eye-bug of exaggerated fear. He seemed to be saying: *I know what you're thinking. I know your expectations here.*

He pointed to the next display. "Have you been to Vaitogi?"

We shook our heads. Just got here last night.

Outside the village, he said, was a cove known as Turtle and Shark, drawing its name from the story of a grandmother and granddaughter who were cast out of their family and leapt off a cliff in despair, but transformed into a turtle and a shark when they hit the water.

Stories like this, Will said, were intrinsic to *fa'asamoa*, the Samoan Way. *Fa'asamoa* encapsulates food, music, architecture, rituals and traditions, the organization of families and communities. Every village has its own defining stories.

"If you go over to Vaitogi and look at the water, you might be able to see them." Will's fauxhawk bobbed again. I wasn't sure how to read the suggestion: Was it earnest, full of cultural pride? Or was it, "*Yeah, go spend an afternoon staring at waves—good luck with that, tourist*?

Will moved on to a photo of a giant clam. "Old people think it's a delicacy, so I guess I'm supposed to, too," he said.

"And?" Maren prompted.

"I don't really like it very much." Will grimaced reflexively and then looked guilty for the grimace.

• • • • •

PAGO PAGO is even more enjoyably Seussian when said correctly—*Pongo Pongo*—and, in conversation, it's typically halved: "Let's go into Pago," Maren said as we left the NOAA Center. (Also, Samoa is properly pronounced "SAH-moa," not "Sam-

OH-a.") It's a small town, population 3,656;* the entire territory has about 55,000, the vast majority of whom live on Tutuila. The architecture is plain, the atmosphere calm and working-class and notably safer than Charlotte Amalie; "You can walk around anywhere," a local man told us shortly after we arrived. "Your only concern is stray dogs." There are no colonial forts here, and also no thatch-roofed huts, just a lot of one- and two-story cinder-block buildings. It's not South Seas Wonderland, but it does have its own low-key charm, which comes in part from its lack of tourist flash. There are no duty-free shops on Tutuila, no chain hotels, no resorts. (Tourists are so rare that hotels peg their rates to the U.S. government's current per-diem limits, knowing that bureaucrats here on business are their core clientele.)

At one end of downtown was the territorial legislature—called the Fono—which looked like an exact cross between a modern government building (stately, lots of windows) and a *fale*, a traditional Samoan structure with a domed roof perched atop wooden posts. Across the way was a row of small shops and markets and, in a parking lot, a slickly branded cell-phone kiosk with a short line of patrons. At the public market, vendors had set out baskets woven from palm fronds and filled with papayas and breadfruit and bananas whose amber color was so vibrant they seemed internally lit. An elderly woman in a long green dress was selling coconuts, and when we handed over our $2 each, she pulled out a machete and sliced a tiny piece off the top of each shaggy brown orb and inserted pink straws. We loitered

* Technically, Pago Pago is actually one village among several strung together along the harbor, all of them seemingly a contiguous town to the untrained eye. If you called them, collectively, the Greater Pago Pago Metropolitan Area, you could add in a couple thousand more people. But still: small.

for a few minutes, watching buses—which looked like close-sided versions of the USVI's safaris—come and go from a parking lot set between the market and a new-looking McDonald's. Across the water, we could see the island's economic lifeblood: tuna canneries, large and hulking and industrial, *The Jungle* at the edge of the jungle.

A pair of teenage boys watched us with amusement. They were wearing Golden State Warriors jerseys and matching flat-brimmed baseball caps, paired with *lavalavas*. They looked sharp—they were pulling off the combo. I couldn't help but notice a silvery glint underneath the hats—not diamond studs on their ears but large silver disks inside their ears. They were quarters, bus fare. Most *lavalavas* have no pockets, so you make do.

I took stock of my surroundings: the market, the people, the Fono, which was flying the territorial flag, featuring a bald eagle with two traditional objects in its talons: a *fue* whisk and a *uatogi* war club. If Charlotte Amalie was a swirl of cultures, this was a perfect split between Mainland American and Samoan. And in the push-pull of cultural interaction, it was hard to see which way the balance was tipping.

"Are there a lot of traditions the old people keep up but young people don't?" I'd asked Will.

Maren had shot me a look that I immediately translated as: *Dude, no need to make him explain the universal truth that culture evolves. We all know this and now you're just obnoxiously forcing him to say, "Yes, of course," and to enumerate all the ways—*

"Well . . ." Will said, his expression suddenly ruminative after all that joking around. "It's pretty complicated."

• • • • •

The first European to arrive on Tutuila was the French explorer Jean-François de Galaup de la Pérouse, who landed here in 1787. In the next century, he was followed by a string of merchants, whalers, missionaries, and colonizers. Germans staked a major claim first. Then came the British and the Americans, around 1869, when the Union Pacific Railroad opened, connecting the United States coasts and improving prospects for trade with the British colonies of Australia and New Zealand. That tremendous slash of a harbor in Pago Pago was a perfect coaling station for Pacific-crossing ships. As with the USVI and California and Oregon, commerce was the key.

At the same time, Samoa's village chiefs, called *matais*, were feuding. A civil war simmered throughout the 1870s and 1880s, with Germany, Britain, and the USA opportunistically nudging the fighting and power struggles toward their own interests. By the early 1880s, as Foster Rhea Dulles recounted in his 1932 book *America in the Pacific*, "the diplomatic wires between Washington, London, and Berlin began to hum." It was strictly a political matter, nothing that riled up the American public, until there were reports that the Germans had destroyed American property and defaced an American flag, which "awoke a storm of indignation throughout the country."

In the nineteenth century, Republicans generally supported overseas expansion and Democrats typically opposed it. President Grover Cleveland, a Democrat, refused calls to annex Hawaii, on the grounds that this would violate the Monroe Doctrine, since it was outside the Americas. He also didn't think annexation of American Samoa was constitutionally justified, but here there was another factor on his mind: the possibility that Germany might take the islands if the Americans did not.

Pressure built from Congress and the public, aided by the fact that, as Christina Ponsa had said, Reconstruction had ended and the nation was again looking to prove its place in the world.

"Interest in Samoa was a straw which showed which way the wind was blowing" in terms of foreign policy, Dulles wrote, "and it is not without significance that . . . these events coincided with the successful movement for building up a new navy."

In August 1888, American warships stationed at Tutuila smuggled rifles to supporters of a *matai* named Mata'afa, who "felt the time was right to test his army against the forces of Tamasese, who were backed by German marines."

On March 11, 1889, it all came to a head in Apia, on the island of Upolu, in what's now the independent nation of Samoa. Seven warships were anchored in the harbor—three American, three German, one British—and, onshore, stood Mata'afa and six thousand troops. Everything was set up for a ferocious, bloody battle, soldiers just waiting for the command. And then, before a shot was fired, a hurricane hit. The ships were tossed about in the looming waves. The German ship *Eber* was the first to go down, after it struck a reef; another German vessel, *Olga*, lost control and hit the British ship *Calliope* and the Americans' *Nipsic*. Of all the ships, only *Calliope* rode out the storm; all the others sank or ran aground, killing 150 sailors. Local Samoans, their own villages flattened, risked their lives to swim out and help, forming a human chain to rescue the men from the sinking ships.

Their battle ruined by the storm, the British, Americans, and Germans decided to simply share the administrative duties of Samoa. The Americans requested and received full control of Pago Pago Harbor. For ten years this was the setup: Samoa remained officially sovereign but was a quasi-colony with three overseers. But in 1899, the USA, Britain, and Germany decided they'd had enough with the sharing, and split Samoa in two: the Americans got Tutuila (because they already had that claim to Pago Pago) and the islands to the east, and Germany claimed the western islands, including Savai'i and Upolu, both more than twice the landmass of Tutuila. Britain got none of the Samoan islands but, in exchange, received German claims elsewhere in the Pacific and in West Africa, whose residents were presumably mystified about how they'd gotten dragged into all of this.

The deal had the blessing of the highest-ranking *matais* on Tutuila and its small neighbor, Aunu'u, who drafted the paperwork to turn the islands over to the United States officially and with full-throated approval: "SALUTATIONS!!" the Deed of Cession begins. "We rejoice with our whole hearts on account of the tidings we have received . . ." The United States had annexed the Kingdom of Hawaii in 1898, and the *matais* were aware that American annexation was inevitable here, too. There was pressure, even duress, but the fact remains—and American Samoans are deeply proud of this fact—that these islands were granted to, not claimed by, the USA.

On February 19, 1900, President William McKinley signed an executive order decreeing that "the Island of Tutuila, of the Samoan Group, and all other islands of the group east of longitude 171 degrees west of Greenwich, are hereby placed under the control of the Department of the Navy for a naval station." Two months later, on April 17, 1900, in a ceremony in Pago Pago, the American flag was raised, while Samoan students from a missionary-run school sang "America" in English. And then: a big party, with games and sports and a feast of roasted pigs. (The three Manu'a Islands were ceded to the United States in 1904, and the territory's final parcel, Swain's Island, in 1925.)*

The *matais* who opposed becoming American decamped to Western Samoa, forty miles west, which was claimed by New Zealand in 1914, during World War I, and gained independence in 1962. The nation, which now has a population just under two hundred thousand, dropped "Western" from its name in 1997, although most people in American Samoa still refer to their neighbor this way, a not-so-subtle way of saying, *You aren't the only real Samoans—we are, too.*

• • • • •

WITH HAWAII and American Samoa now part of the USA, the interest in all things Polynesian began to build back in the states. As Sven A. Kirsten details in his excellent 2014 book *Tiki Pop*, the decades-long trend began with nineteenth century books by the likes of Herman Melville and Robert Louis Stevenson, but took off after the turn of the century, progressing to music—"Uncle Joe has sold his banjo / Plays his ukulele soft and low" went one 1917 song—and then to movies such as *Hurricane* and *Mutiny on the Bounty*, and spreading tiki bars, tiki motels, and even tiki bowling alleys. In the 1960s, near the end

* Swain's is an odd outlier of a place, listed separately on many present-day U.S. government documents. This includes college financial-aid materials, even though Swain's has no permanent population. It was abandoned not long ago, due to lack of potable water and general remoteness, although it still has a seat in American Samoa's legislature—which is held by one Alexander Jenning, Swain's Island having been a privately held coconut plantation owned by the Jenning family since the mid-1800s.

of this pop-culture moment, shows featuring actual South Seas performers were a mainstay of glitzy hotels in Las Vegas and Miami, Kirsten notes, showcasing "the Samoan fire dance, the Maori haka, the Hawaiian hula, the Tahitian drum dance"—aggregated and tailored for tourists, to be sure, but with at least some basis in actual tradition and performed "with an honest and joyful sense of ambassadorship."

At the Showboat Casino & Hotel in Las Vegas in the late 1960s, the marquee revue was Evalani & Her South Seas Islanders. Its star, Evalani Pearson, eventually moved back home to American Samoa and opened a restaurant called Evalani's Cabaret Lounge, which Maren and I had heard was one of the few places to get a glimpse of the Packaged Polynesia we'd been picturing back in Minneapolis.

It was raining when Maren and I arrived at Evalani's one night. We'd been walking around for hours and were thoroughly soaked. As my eyes adjusted to the dim lighting inside, I felt like I'd stepped into a time warp, but not the tiki-bar throwback I'd expected—it had the air of a Rat-Pack-style lounge, with semicircular red vinyl booths, sconces with red and green bulbs, and photos of radiant Evalani, with lively eyes and a tight satin dress and a white flower tucked into her long black hair. Evalani had helped bring Polynesia to Las Vegas, and, evidently, she brought some of Vegas back to Polynesia.

Maren and I slid into seats at the bar as a server poured herself a start-of-the-shift glass of milk, then greeted us.

"My name is Em," she said. "Tonight's special is one-dollar tacos." She handed us menus, which had a long list of fajitas, enchiladas, and burritos. It was like some kind of marvelous cultural riddle: What do you get when you filter Polynesia through Las Vegas and back again? *Tex-Mex.*

Em, who I guessed to be in her mid-twenties, explained that her aunt, the chef, had lived in California for many years, and had come to love Mexican food. She wasn't the only one—at the grocery store, we'd seen a sprawling section of tortillas and salsas. The biggest Samoan population on the mainland is in Southern California. Em grew up there and in American Samoa, "a fifty-fifty split." Each time she came back to the bar, she stayed a bit longer and our conversation got a bit deeper.

Em delivered our tacos, wrapped in waxed paper: hard shell, ground beef, shredded cheese, iceberg lettuce, an agreeable greasiness. Classic American bar food. Em lingered as we started to eat, and I asked her if she thought there was generally a strong cultural connection between American Samoa and the states. She nodded vigorously. "Many Samoans spend time living in the states or have relatives there, so they know what's going on and feel connected. But at the same time, there are unique traditions and culture here. So you get the best of both worlds."

She left and then came back and asked, "Do you guys like to go out?"

"Well, we were thinking about doing karaoke over by the cannery," I said. In truth, we'd just come from an ill-fated attempt at doing just that. I'd thought it would be oh-so-droll to belt out "Sittin' on the Dock of the Bay" with an eclectic assortment of cannery workers, not just Samoan but also Chinese and Filipino. But Maren insisted that she had a bad feeling about the bars, with their lack of windows and general rough, foreboding air; outside one, a particularly mangy dog stared us down. Maren had been palpably relieved when it turned out none of the bars were open.

I was about to relate this story to Em, with much smirking commentary about how my wife was *so* skittish and *I* knew this island was totally safe, when Em's eyes grew large and she took a step back.

"Don't go over there! We call that 'the dark side.'"

Maren was triumphant in that I-love-you-but-I'm-right spousal way: "That's what I was trying to tell him!"

Em made air quotes. "*Karaoke rooms* . . . you know?"

"Wait . . ." I said. "You mean . . ." I didn't have to finish the thought. Maren and Em were looking at me like I'd just tried to shove my last bites of taco into my ear. *Way to figure things out, dumbass.* Days later, another local described one building near the canneries as "the trifecta: they've got an illegal mah-jongg parlor on the second floor, karaoke on the ground floor, girls in the basement."

A small pile of crumpled, greasy waxed paper slowly grew on the bar in front of us, bathed in a pool of red light. A pair of young Samoan women sat at a nearby booth, the only other customers, and Em excused herself to take their order. When she came back to the bar, we continued talking about American versus Samoan cultures, and I asked her if she felt like she was more one culture or the other.

She gave a small laugh, like it was a ridiculous question. It was the same muffled chuckle I'd hear in the coming days as I posed the query to many other American Samoans—conservation workers, football coaches, lawyers.

Their answer was the same as Em's: "I'm American and I'm Samoan, and I like being both."

• • • • •

THE QUESTION of culture was widely debated during the Imperial Moment, tied up as it was with the hot topic of expansion. The newly acquired lands were curiosities, with a steady stream of stories in national magazines like *Harper's* and the *Atlantic*, and numerous widely read travelogues, including *Neely's Color Photos of America's New Possessions*; *Pictorial History of America's New Possessions*; *The History and Conquest of the Philippines and Our Other Island Possessions*; *Our Island Empire*; and *Our New Possessions*. The most popular was the two-volume *Our Islands and Their People*, published around 1902, whose first edition sold four hundred thousand copies. (These travelogues, along with other depictions of the territories in stateside popular media around 1900, are the subject of historian Lanny Thompson's fascinating book *Imperial Archipelago*.)

Overseas expansion was one of the central issues of the 1900 presidential campaign, a rematch of Republican William McKinley and Democrat William Jennings Bryan, who had faced off four years earlier, in part over the possibility of annexing Hawaii. McKinley won in 1896, and in 1900 the Democrats put the issue of expansion near the top of their official platform:

> We declare again that all governments instituted among men derive their just powers from the consent of the governed; that any government not based upon the consent of the governed is a tyranny; and that to impose upon any people a government of force is to substitute the methods of imperialism for those of a republic.
>
> We hold that the Constitution follows the flag . . . We assert that no nation can long endure half republic and half empire, and we warn the American people that imperial-

ism abroad will lead quickly and inevitably to despotism at home.

It was the era of Jim Crow and the Chinese Exclusion Act, and deep-seated racism and xenophobia also informed both sides of the expansion debate. Opposition was in some cases grounded in a belief that the "half-civilized" people of these lands, while more worthy of pity than outright contempt, were simply unfit for inclusion in the nation. The Democrats' platform also said, "The Filipinos cannot be citizens without endangering our civilization." For others, though, there was a deeper moral underpinning. One prominent Democratic leader, Richard Croker, offered a succinct, timeless definition of anti-imperialism: "It means opposition to the fashion of shooting down everybody who doesn't speak English."

Rudyard Kipling's "White Man's Burden," which he wrote in 1899 and subtitled "The United States and the Philippine Islands," summed up the most xenophobic strains of the pro-expansion crowd. Here's the first stanza:

Take up the White Man's burden, Send forth the best ye breed
Go bind your sons to exile, to serve your captives' need;
To wait in heavy harness, On fluttered folk and wild—
Your new-caught, sullen peoples, Half-devil and half-child.

"White Man's Burden" was a viral hit of its day: "In winged words it circled the earth in a day, and by repetition it became hackneyed in a week," one commentator said.

William McKinley won the 1900 presidential election. The United States had chosen the path of empire. The question now was what to do with these new territories: How would they fit with the existing American system?

Enter the Insular Cases. They quickly made things complicated for the territories. In *Downes v. Bidwell*, the Supreme Court said, essentially, that not all parts of the Constitution applied to the territories, but didn't specify which parts did and which did not—that was up to Congress to decide. In the 1922 Insular Case *Balzac v. Porto Rico*, the Supreme Court ruled that only "fundamental" constitutional rights were in effect in the territories. But what, exactly, is "fundamental"? Broadly speaking, as things currently stand, the courts have upheld the Bill of Rights in the territories, but there are some exceptions: the Sixth Amendment right to a criminal trial by jury, for example, has not been held applicable in local courts in Puerto Rico.

The most striking legal outlier, however, is found in American Samoa, where residents are left out of one of the most significant markers of being an American: citizenship. If you're born here, you're an American *national* but not a citizen of this or any other country.

Being a national means you have different, more limited visa eligibility when traveling abroad. If you move to the states, you can't serve on juries, and you may have a hard time applying for jobs because you're not a citizen but also don't have a green card or work visa, and employers don't know what to do. You also can't vote in elections—presidential or otherwise—if you move to the states, which means that, although thousands of American Samoans live in Southern California, they don't have much of a political voice.

To gain all these rights, you have to become naturalized, like any immigrant, even though you were born in the USA just as surely as any Springsteen-song protagonist. You have to pay nearly $700 and take a civics test (which, incidentally, asks applicants to list their U.S. representative, and if you live in the territories, there are two correct answers: you can name your nonvoting delegate or you can say, "I don't have one").

"To become a citizen, I had to go with my mother to the U.S. embassy in New Zealand," an American Samoan named Charles Ala'ilima told me.* "So I understood from a young age that this was absurd and unacceptable."

Charles is an attorney and now lives in Seattle. He was co-counsel for a group of American Samoans who were, as we spoke, suing the federal government for birthright citizenship; the case, *Tuaua v. United States*, was making its way through the courts. He was working with the nation's sole nongovernmental organization dedicated to advocacy for the territories as a whole, the We the People Project, founded in 2013, a one-man operation run by a young lawyer from Guam named Neil Weare.

I spoke to Charles via Skype shortly before I left for Pago Pago; he popped onto my screen wearing a flannel shirt and slightly wild hair, a sort of grunge-rock intellectual.

"It boils down to the Fourteenth Amendment," he told me. "Is this American soil? Because if it is—and it *clearly* is—then the Fourteenth Amendment applies, and citizenship is a birthright."

Here it is, the first sentence of the Fourteenth Amendment: *All persons born or naturalized in the United States, and subject to the jurisdiction thereof, are citizens of the United States.*

Seems straightforward, but this is the Constitution, the true American religious text: there's *always* room for interpretation

* When Ala'ilima was born, in 1955, this was the American embassy closest to Tutuila. The United States established diplomatic relations with (Western) Samoa in 1971, and there is now an American embassy in Apia.

and alternate meanings, every calligraphied stroke parsed for the hidden but singular truth-above-all. The federal government, for one, says that the Fourteenth Amendment doesn't apply in American Samoa, that this isn't the United States in the sense that the Fourteenth Amendment means the United States, since it's neither *incorporated* nor *organized*. (American Samoa has a local government but no Organic Act.) The USA, in other words, is making this argument: being a citizen is not an innate right of being an American, even one born on American soil.

Before the Spanish-American War in 1898, American treaties of annexation promised citizenship to the new territories' residents, excluding American Indians, who had to wait until Congress passed the Indian Citizenship Act of 1924. But when the United States claimed Puerto Rico, the Philippines, and Guam after the war, American citizenship was not part of the package for anyone.

Here, again, the issue came to the Supreme Court, in the 1904 Insular Case *Gonzales v. Williams*. Isabel González (whose name immigration officials misspelled) was a Puerto Rican woman who intended to move to New York in 1902. When she arrived at Ellis Island, she was detained as an "alien immigrant" who was "likely to become a public charge," on the grounds that she was unmarried and pregnant. González argued that, since the United States had annexed Puerto Rico, she was an American citizen, not an alien. The Supreme Court didn't quite know how to rule—clearly, she was American, if nothing else, but was she a *citizen*? The court decided no. She was a *noncitizen national*, a designation that had not previously been used in the United States but mirrored the practice of European empires when labeling their colonial subjects. After *Gonzales v. Williams*, that's how all residents of the territories were categorized, until, one by one, each territory set up an Organic Act, became *organized*, and its residents gained citizenship. But in American Samoa, that change has never happened: it's unorganized, and residents are not, by birth, American citizens.

Charles Ala'ilima explained all of this with an understandably exasperated tone. He added, in a follow-up email, that "to become a citizen one normally has to leave the territory and reside in the U.S. However, recently, someone was flown to the territory to have [military] service members born in American Samoa take their oath of allegiance before him. It seemed oddly redundant to have a U.S. national who was born owing his allegiance only to the United States having to take an oath of allegiance to the United States."

The issue isn't just a matter of federal government obstruction or neglect. The most vociferous opposition to birthright citizenship comes from an unexpected source: other American Samoans. This includes the governor, the territory's member of Congress, and many of the all-powerful *matais*. (Ala'ilima also told me that "our local judges, lawyers, and public office holders, in taking their oath of office, swear to uphold the U.S. Constitution provisions that apply to American Samoa rather than the U.S. Constitution in its entirety.") It was Professor Ponsa—who had filed an amicus curiae brief in Charles Ala'ilima's case, providing expert information without taking sides—who first explained this to me, and I sputtered with incredulity when she said it. *They . . . they don't want to be citizens?*

Their argument is that there's a delicate cultural balance in American Samoa, one that citizenship would disrupt. They embrace the Insular Cases precisely because the laws offer a certain protection of their status as foreign in a domestic sense—it's a means to insulate *themselves* from the culture-leveling forces of

Americanization, or at least to have some power to curate which of these elements takes hold.

• • • • •

THERE ARE some aspects of mainland USA culture that American Samoans welcome with open arms. Exhibit A: football. Turns out they're good at it. *Really* good.

Christian missionaries brought rugby here—American Samoans are still good at that sport, too, although it's more popular in (Western) Samoa, where the cultural gaze is toward its former overseer, New Zealand*—and in the mid-century, as modernization brought American television, local rugby players saw the NFL and thought, *I can do that.* At the start of the 2015–2016 season, there were twenty-eight NFL players of American Samoan ancestry and more than *two hundred* in Division I college programs.

I spoke to the football coach at Samoana High School, Silasila Samelou, in his office—a small, austere room with a desk and a computer—above the open-air gym after he'd finished morning workouts one day. He holds practices multiple times a day, in part to accommodate players' work schedules. Silasila's young granddaughter played nearby, and then came to sit on his lap as we spoke, and he patiently switched between answering her questions and mine. His school alone has produced *six* NFL players, he told me with a wide smile.

* (Western) Samoa recently switched to the west side of the International Date Line so that it would be on the same business day as New Zealand and Australia, instead of being twenty-one hours behind these important trade partners. At the end of the day on Thursday, December 29, 2011, (Western) Samoa jumped ahead to Saturday, December 31.

The territory's seemingly unlikely football legacy has been covered in feature stories by *60 Minutes*, *ESPN the Magazine*, the *Washington Post*, and many others, the rare time the media has paid any attention to American Samoa. Honestly, it's an easy story to write, with predictable narrative beats about "bootstrapping their way to football glory." You talk about how the seafarer history and Warrior Culture created brawny, sure-footed young men who are fierce on the field but also disciplined and soft-spoken, thanks in part to their devout Christianity and the respect for authority ingrained in the *matai* system. You note certain shoddy facilities (threadbare fields, shipping-container locker rooms), lament the lack of economic opportunity on the island (it's either the tuna cannery or the NFL—these are your options!). You wryly observe how football prowess stands in contrast to the territory's ineptitude at soccer—they have their own national team, which was for years FIFA's lowest-ranked side in the world (and was the subject of the delightful documentary *Next Goal Wins*, released in 2014).* And you frame it all with a condescending tone that says, *Isn't it cool how these Native Islanders are playing at being American?*

But, of course, they *are* American. This was becoming clearer and clearer to me, from aisles of salsa in the grocery store, to the teenagers in basketball jerseys or on their way to football practice with pads in hand, to the dozens of men and women we'd seen carrying U.S. Army duffel bags on our plane from Hawaii. American Samoa has the highest enlistment rate and casualty rate of

* You might also note that the second-ever non-Japanese sumo wrestler to attain the sport's highest rank, *yokozuna*, was the American Samoa–born Musashimaru Kōyō. "I guess I got my start in sumo thanks to the American football and Greco-Roman wrestling I was doing at school in Hawaii," he told the *Japan Times*.

any state or territory. There are two McDonald's on the island and packaged foods are so ubiquitous that the territory has one of the highest diabetes rates in the world: 47 percent of the adult population (but only one dialysis clinic). And while Samoan is the default language, pretty much everyone under the age of, say, sixty, will switch over to English without a second thought, and sound exactly like your archetypal West Coast mainlander, in accent, idioms, slang, sarcasm, and every other conversational marker—talking to them, you feel like you're in the states.

You can't define culture merely by tallying data points, of course. Japan has baseball and jazz clubs and Wild West theme parks and impeccably tailored blue jeans, but it's clearly not part of the United States. You also need the broader societal mesh that holds all these elements together: a collective agreement that these things, specifically and together, form a particular identity and represent particular ideals. And you'll find that in American Samoa—the sense of being American is deeply ingrained here, at both the personal and community levels. There's no independence movement to speak of; even the staunchest opponents of citizenship want to maintain the territorial relationship with the United States. In official statements from the governor and even online discussions I read—the comments on any *Samoa News* website story about citizenship go on for miles—there was a strong tendency for anti-citizenship arguments to be followed, without irony, by "God Bless America." There is a pride in being American . . . and in being Samoan.

So what would the Supreme Court, circa 1901, make of American Samoa? Would they see the *lavalava* or the NFL jersey? Or what about today's self-appointed Guardians of the Culture, the commentators and politicians who talk about immigrants' need to assimilate and speak rhapsodically of the "Real America"?

That stump-speech fantasyland is, roughly speaking, a place of small, working-class towns with a deep reverence for church, football, military service, and *tradition*, all of which sounds a lot like American Samoa. Is it the "Real America"?

For that matter, given that there's clearly lots of Americanization and globalization in American Samoa, and given the importance of Samoan tradition and history to the fabric of the culture, there was another important question to ask: Is this still the "Real Samoa"?

The biggest question: Can American Samoa be both "real" America and "real" Samoa at once?

• • • • •

A friend of mine had put me in touch with a local man named John Wasko, who'd offered to show us around the Tutuila. One day, he drove up in a black Jeep and emerged looking for all the world like Joe Biden's brother, with a saunter, aviator shades, and baggy jeans. He'd just turned seventy the previous week, described himself as "old but not a geezer," and designed websites for a living. John was from the states and had come to American Samoa for a work assignment thirty years ago. He married a Samoan woman named Luaao, and they'd raised their two kids in the village of Nu'uuli.

John drove west along Route 1, which runs the length of the island. Ocean waves lapped at broad reefs on one side of the road; the other side was a steep hill with palm trees and banana trees and leaves you could use as a bedsheet.

We passed a small mall anchored by a Carl's Jr., a first-run movie theater, many tailor shops (most run by Filipino immigrants, John said) and convenience stores (where the person behind the counter was typically Chinese), and countless churches. American Samoa has churches like Dublin has bars, ubiquitous and culture-defining. Capstone Church. House of Faith. First Samoan Pentecostal. Calvary Assembly of God. Lion of Judah. Lighthouse Assembly of God. Anchorage of the Soul Jesus Embassy. Harvest Vision Church. Sharing space with a convenience store was the South Pacific Presbyterian Theological Seminary and Medical Mission School. The first Christian missionary on the island was an Englishman named John Williams, who founded a hulking Gothic-in-the-tropics church in the village of Leone in 1832 and remains a revered figure. People notice if you *don't* pray before eating, even at McDonald's, John told us, and abortion is illegal in the territory. In the most devout villages, there's a prayer time called *Sa* every night. Christianity is now as much a part of *fa'asamoa* as any legend Will told us.

We pulled into John's village, Nu'uuli, as he explained that, most of all, *fa'asamoa* is tied to the village itself, of which there are about fifty on Tutuila. There are virtually no fences around houses, and nearly all land is owned communally, by villages or extended families (called *'aiga*s)—of the territory's seventy-six square miles, just one and a half are privately held. In the middle of the village was an open area with a large *fale*. A *fale* is a community center, a guesthouse for visitors, whatever you need it to be—even, we saw one day in Leone, an animal field-surgery center, where veterinarians in blue scrubs were spaying and neutering dogs sprawled on folding tables. Many homes had their own *fales*, which were sometimes freestanding and sometimes directly attached to a small cinder-block house, outside of which stood two or three cross-topped white concrete boxes: the graves of loved ones. Your village isn't merely a set of geographic coordinates, John said, but the fundamental basis of who you are, even in the afterlife.

After the American takeover, in April 1900, the territory was—like the USVI—initially under naval rule. The first naval governor, B. F. Tilley, recognized the importance of the land to *fa'asamoa*, and believed that Samoans "must be protected from the harmful elements" of the outside influences that had entered the islands, particularly their habit of taking Samoan land by deceit or violence. One of Tilley's very first acts, less than two weeks after the Deeds of Cession were signed, was the Native Lands Ordinance, which forbade the sale of land to non-Samoans. That's why there are no Westins or Club Meds here—they couldn't buy the land even if an *'aiga* wanted to sell it. Technically, American Samoa was never colonized, but the need for an ordinance shows that there was a tangible threat from outsiders, a de facto colonialism.

We stopped at a convenience store for a snack of doughnuts filled with toasted coconut, chewy and greasy and deeply satisfying, and went to a lagoon-front park to eat, spilling crumbs on a picnic table while a dozen or so teenage boys played football in thigh-deep water, with much splashing and giddy yelling. John continued his American Samoa 101 spiel.

Each village is run by *matais*, who gather in the central *fale* for their formal meeting, called the *fono*. (This is the basis for the name of the territorial legislature.) Village *fonos* are highly ritualized and use the objects I'd seen on the territorial quarter and in the clutch of the bald eagle on the flag, including the *'ava* bowl, used for the sacred *'ava*-drinking ceremony (the beverage is derived from kava leaves and has mildly sedative properties), and the *fue* whisk and *to'oto'o* staff, used by the talking chief, an orator/spokesperson for the high chief. The *matais* are the trustees of the land, the political leaders, the disseminators of information, the power brokers. The territorial legislature is bicameral, with the house elected by standard-issue direct democracy, while the senate consists of *matais* who have been elected by their peers, the other the village *matais*—regular citizens can neither serve in the senate nor participate in the selection of senators. The *matais* are even the law enforcement; it's their oversight, and the close-knit nature of the communities, that makes this such a safe place.

"I guess the police could come to my village," John said, but there's no need. American Samoa's police don't even carry guns. "The *matais* will take care of everything. Like, if you're drunk in public, you might be fined a couple of pigs."

"And if you do something worse?" I asked.

"Well, the *matais* will send their boys to talk to you, rough you up a bit, you know what I mean?" He chuckled softly. He took a bite of doughnut. "If it's really bad, you'll be kicked out of the village." In other words: stripped of the biggest part of your identity.

• • • • •

AMERICAN SAMOANS who oppose birthright citizenship argue, essentially, that it would bring the Constitution into greater power here and, as a consequence, certain long-standing cultural practices might be deemed unconstitutional. In other words, citizenship would be a slippery slope of court cases, leading to an existential threat to *fa'asamoa*. There are three things they single out:

- The Native Land Ordinance (which would seem to be discriminatory and conflict with the Equal Protection Clause of the Constitution).

- The *matai*-only senate ("No titles of nobility shall be granted by the United States," says Article 1 of Constitution).
- *Sa*, the roads-closed prayer time observed in some villages (arguably an establishment of religion and contrary to the mandated separation of church and state).

"There's a reason why the argument [against citizenship] is tenuous, and yet American Samoan opponents of citizenship do have concerns that need to be taken seriously," Professor Ponsa told me.

The anti-citizenship case was shaky, she said, because none of those constitutional concerns had anything to do with citizenship per se. They were separate issues, and should be treated as such—Ala'ilima's case shouldn't be judged based on the hypothetical possibility of inspiring future cases on indirectly related issues. Besides which, elsewhere in the United States, there was already legal precedent allowing practices very similar to those in question in American Samoa. For example, you can find similar land-ownership laws in Alaska, Hawaii, Guam, and the Northern Mariana Islands. This is also Ala'ilima's argument: the case is about citizenship, period, and doesn't expressly affect anything else. It would give American Samoans full access to employment and improve their ability to stand up for their rights and their traditional ways. It would be the government finally redressing its oppression of indigenous peoples—and it would give them a voice and a spotlight to make their concerns known.

In addition, Neil Weare of the We the People Project told me, at the time of the American takeover in 1900, American Samoans expected that they *would* become citizens, and petitioned Congress to grant them citizenship several times over the next fifty years. A group of American congressmen and senators traveled to American Samoa in 1930 to prepare a report on the territory, and found not just broad support for citizenship but a general *demand* for it. One of the visiting senators was Hiram Bingham III (best known for an earlier career as an explorer, when he brought Machu Picchu to the world's attention), who in 1946 recounted, for the *New York Times,* his commission's recommendation that citizenship be granted to American Samoans, which led to two separate bills to do so. The U.S. Senate unanimously passed each but both then failed in the House of Representatives after lobbying from the Navy. "So the Samoans are still 'subjects,' but not 'citizens' of the United States," Bingham said. "It is a blot on our record for fair dealing and democracy." He called for no "further delay in doing justice." But around this time, many of American Samoa's leaders started to shift their views toward the positions that hold today.

There's some merit to the idea that birthright citizenship would nudge the Samoan-American balance, Professor Ponsa said. "When you're that much closer to the U.S., it could encourage challenges and encourage courts to see things as unconstitutional."

For those who oppose citizenship, being American involves the freedom to move around the states, to serve in the military, to play football and eat McDonald's, to have a free press—and to reject what you see as government imposition on your right to do your own damn thing. (Stubbornness may be the most American of traits.) *Look*, say citizenship foes, *we understand the rights we're giving up. But those rights actually aren't so important to us, given that they'd come, inevitably, as a forced package deal with greater federal scrutiny of our island and our culture—and with ever-greater American cultural and political takeover. It will lead, inevitably, to further erosion if not willful eradication of our traditional ways. Just look at Hawaii.*

• • • • •

IN 1893, American business interests violently overthrew Queen Lili'uokalani, the ruler of the Kingdom of Hawaii, imprisoning her in her bedroom at 'Iolani Palace, and taking over the government. The Americans hoped that their nation would annex Hawaii, and in 1898 they got their wish. Said President McKinley: "We need Hawaii just as much and a good deal more than we did California. It is manifest destiny." With this came land-grabs of the sort American Samoans fear, tearing apart communities and fulfilling a prediction made in 1837 by Native Hawaiian historian Davida Malo: "If a big wave comes in, large and unfamiliar fishes will come from the dark ocean, and when they see the small fishes of the shallows they will eat them up." (Notably, Hawaiians *were* open to cultural evolution and many aspects of modernization. 'Iolani Palace had electricity before the White House.)

Statehood wasn't in the initial plans—Hawaii was merely a territory, a far-off one, full of seemingly inscrutable Polynesians. "It would indeed be profitable . . . to keep the United States forever a compact, continent Republic," wrote Willis Fletcher Johnson in his 1903 book *A Century of Expansion*, which might as well be subtitled "And Here's to a Century More!" Johnson lauded American leaders for not promising Hawaii statehood at the outset:

> That wise policy should be forever maintained. If so, the Hawaiian annexation will not prove unfruitful of at least one important and beneficent constitutional principle—the abil-

> ity and right of this nation to acquire and to hold colonies, never intended for statehood, at any distance in any part of the world. That is a power which all other important nations possess and exercise at will.

Of course, in 1959, Hawaii did get statehood. The republic was no longer compact and continental, but this had no ill effects on the union. Indeed, there was much interest and celebration back on the continent—Elvis sang "Hawaii, USA!," *Boys Life* celebrated with a cover story, and James Michener published his best-selling novel about the fiftieth state. Hawaii boomed as a tourist destination, fueled by the all-things-Polynesian craze.

And then, perhaps inevitably, came the fate that has befallen many tropical lands across the globe: "Developers, seeing dollars, began destroying exactly what Americans were seeking," Sven A. Kirsten writes in *Tiki Pop.* "Beaches were bulldozed for high-rise resorts; cars raced feet from the sand on multilane highways." In 1965, *Look* magazine ran a cover story on "Problems in Paradise," with a swimsuit-clad model lying awkwardly in shallow water, not quite drowning, but not happy, either.

Today, just 6 percent of Hawaii's population is of Native Hawaiian ancestry (another 15 percent identify as part-Hawaiian). Their rites and rituals, though still practiced by some, are also the stuff of tourist shows. And in 1993 Congress passed a resolution "to offer an apology to Native Hawaiians on behalf of the United States for the overthrow of the Kingdom of Hawaii." If all of that is not a warning sign, American Samoa's citizenship opponents argue, then what is?

If you dig deeper into the history books and cast your eyes fifteen hundred miles north of Tutuila, you'll find another noteworthy case study in American governmental ineptitude and the vast unfairness of rights-granting. Palmyra Atoll, an uninhabited scattering of islets with less than five square miles of land, was annexed and incorporated into the United States along with Hawaii. But when Maui & Co. received a promotion to statehood, Palmyra was left in the purgatory of territoryhood, making it the sole insular possession that is *incorporated*. This means that, though Palmyra is a wildlife refuge with no legislature or courts and an official population of zero—aside from the occasional scientists who come to study its million-plus seabirds, the researchers flying in via an airstrip laid during World War II, when the atoll was a naval air station—it's the only territory where the Constitution fully applies and is, in legal if not practical terms, a candidate for statehood.* By the letter of the law, it is Palmyra, not one of the inhabited territories, that is in the best position to nudge our flag's star count to fifty-one.

How does that make sense? Why would you want closer ties with a nation so maddening?

• • • • •

DURING AMERICAN Samoa's first few decades as a territory, the federal government's attitude was essentially one of neglect, aside from military utility; the naval base at Pago Pago was a key refueling port during World War II.

In 1961, *Reader's Digest* published an article titled "Samoa: America's Shame in the South Seas." Writer Clarence Hall

* Births are understandably rare there, but not without precedent: in January 1947, a baby boy was born to parents who were stationed at the atoll's American Radio Propagation Field Station. Even if his parents hadn't been American, because of the atoll's political status he would have been a citizen by birth.

observed that although the United States had "been doling out billions to underdeveloped nations, we have let our only South Pacific possession sink to the level of a slum." There's some debate about whether Hall was paternalistically seeing *traditional* as *impoverished*, but the end result remained the same: Congress and President John F. Kennedy, embarrassed, authorized major funding for projects in the territory, including new schools, new roads, and a new airport terminal. A new television tower was built at the top of Mount Alava, bringing American pop culture—including football—into local homes, and an innovative educational television program into classrooms. To provide technicians easy access to the tower, a cable car was constructed, spanning the mouth of Pago Pago Harbor, and becoming a tourist attraction in its own right. American Samoa even got a taste of the space race—the command modules for Apollo 10, 12, 13, 14, and 17 all splashed down near Tutuila, and the astronauts were helicoptered to Pago Pago before heading back to the mainland United States. At the Jean P. Haydon Museum in Pago Pago, among the historic artifacts, is a display showing a few tiny lunar rocks.*

But space missions don't end up near American Samoa anymore, and the educational television program ended in 1978. Two years later, during ceremonies marking Flag Day—the big local holiday, commemorating the April 17, 1900, handover of

* Incidentally, the USVI also played a supporting role in NASA history, by way of an undersea habitat program that the agency helped sponsor. Tektite I (1969) and Tektite II (1970), both based in Saint John's Great Lameshur Bay, were intended to measure the effects of extended stays underwater by humans. In Tektite II, four "aquanauts" stayed in the undersea capsule for fifty-eight days as NASA analyzed the psychological effects of working in such close, confined quarters.

the islands to the United States—an Air Force plane doing a flyby of Pago Pago Harbor clipped the cable-car line, sending the plane and the cable crashing to earth, killing eight people. A memorial marker now stands near the lower end of the decades-closed cable-car line, where Maren and I poked around the old yellow cars, which were rusting and being consumed by the jungle, a symbol of a lost era.

John lamented the current state of the island's educational system and noted that the only higher-ed option on Tutuila is a community college. "They have good intentions," he said, "but if you really care about education, you go off the island." His kids had attended college in the states. One of John's many projects was trying to start a university on Tutuila, focusing on environmental studies and nursing. He figured he needed about six hundred thousand dollars to get it going and hoped to capitalize on the fact that, he said, Internet speeds on Tutuila were faster than on the mainland United States—a rare bright spot in the local infrastructure.

The federal government's general policy, John said, was "benign neglect." Distant, not particularly trustworthy. Outside a building that looked like an Army barracks was a sign reading LYNDON B. JOHNSON TROPICAL MEDICAL CENTER; the territory's primary medical facility, where John's wife, Luaao, worked as a nurse. "It's named for the last president to visit American Samoa," John said with a sigh. "He came here in 1967." (Vice President Dan Quayle came here in 1989 and gave a speech known for this infamously odd line: "You all look like happy campers to me. Happy campers you are, happy campers you have been, and, as far as I am concerned, happy campers you will always be." That about sums up the federal government's view of American Samoa.)

Disaster relief is slow—in 2009, an earthquake triggered a tsunami, killing thirty-four people in American Samoa. Five years later, there were still leveled buildings by Pago Pago Harbor. I peered into one to find a rusting boat, picked up by the wave and dropped there. The same week as the tsunami, the territory lost two thousand jobs when one of the tuna canneries closed. Now there was one cannery, Starkist, with another in the works; tuna comprised 80 percent of the territory's economy. The local government was the territory's largest employer overall, and its finances were in free-fall—John told us that some employees couldn't even get home loans because banks didn't trust that they had a reliable paycheck coming in. The local unemployment rate was around 20 percent.

And federal oversight was often lacking. At our hotel, we met a woman who investigated labor complaints for the U.S. Department of Labor. There was a huge backlog, since she was the first person from the department to come down here for years. Her original assignment was for a few weeks, but it had just been extended by four months.

When the government did pay attention, there were still issues. One evening in Tutuila, I met with Charles Ala'ilima's sister, Marie Alailima (the two spell their last names slightly differently), who is also a lawyer, who told me that many federal agencies were culturally tone-deaf. In 2014, the Western Pacific Regional Fishery Management Council sought public input on a proposal to change the area in which long-line fishing vessels could harvest their catch. They had been restricted to operating at least fifty miles offshore, but the council proposed to reduce this restricted area to twelve miles. Many *matais*, Marie said, believed this went against U.S. promises to protect the marine waters and resources for native Samoans, and would also introduce harmful competition to village fishermen who operated smaller vessels known as *alias*. The council held a public hearing at Sadie's by the Sea, announcing the event in the federal register and local media. But they didn't take their message where it needed to go: to the villages, including those on the Manu'a Islands, for whom travel to Tutuila would be cost-prohibitive. More than fifty *matais* issued a joint statement asking the council to hold further public hearings in the local communities—including those on the other islands—and in the Samoan language, to better inform the local population of the proposal. "You cannot just come and assume that your system is their system," Marie said, but the council ignored the *matais'* request and, as Marie put it, "denied American Samoans meaningful due process."

It's the locally based organizations that are most effective, John [Wasko] told us, particularly when it comes to conservation. He took us to the small Pago Pago office of the Community Fisheries Management Program to meet a young biologist named Tepora Toliniu Lavatai. She was casual in a gray hoodie and jeans, and her passion for her work was infectious, even when she lost me with the scientific details—a page of my notebook says, "Belt Transects???" The program included meticulous monitoring of the reefs, she said, but a big part of her work was simply maintaining relationships. "We try to visit each village once a month. It's nothing formal; it's like stopping by your aunt's house: 'Hi, Auntie, how's it going?' And you have to go to the church if you want to really reach people."

• • • • •

WE WORRY *about the land*, everyone told me, even those who supported citizenship. *This land is who we are. We don't want a*

Westin, we don't want Club Med—that would ruin it. Protecting the land means protecting the culture. Even the National Park of American Samoa, established in 1988, is actually owned by the local *'aigas*; the park has a yearly lease. Unique among all national parks, it has a homestay program, allowing visitors to spend the night with the local families and see their everyday lives: tending their stands of taro, holding traditional ceremonies, checking their email.

We took a few different hikes with John, one up the hillside above the mouth of the harbor, to see the giant guns installed during World War II, and another to see the southernmost point of the island, which, though it's not advertised or marked as such, is also the southernmost point in the United States (aside from uninhabited Rose Atoll, an outlying area of American Samoa). The second hike took us through *'aiga* land, and John got permission to pass from the local family sitting in their *fale*, chatting with them in Samoan, telling them what village he was from, and going through the list of any potential mutual acquaintances, the local way of making connections and smoothing interactions. He nodded at me and Maren and said with a chuckle, *"Palagi"*—outsiders, white people. "Welcome," one of the women said with a warm laugh.

There was one particular hike that John wanted to take with us as a seventieth birthday gift to himself: the Mount Alava Adventure Trail.

"Sounds great," we said, though we had some second thoughts when he showed us the route on a map—it traced the ridgelines above the harbor, winding along jungle paths up to the summit where the cable car once led. Still, we were game. And so, one morning, we stopped at a convenience store to stock up on oranges and bottles of water ("This is one place where Fiji is the *cheap* brand, because we're so close," John said), our pile of purchases eliciting a perplexed smile from the young Chinese clerk. Then we took a bus up a hill so steep I swear I heard a roller coaster ratcheting below us. We lurched over a pass and the road briefly leveled out near a *fale* and a small interpretive sign.

"This is us," John announced.

I've visited my share of national parks, and I know generally what to expect: RV parking and gift shops and graded trails leading straight to the key scenic overlooks. The allure of the frontiersman meets the reality of the mall-shopper, in that grand American tradition. (Let's not forget that when Henry David Thoreau holed up at Walden Pond, a defining act of American Escape to the Wilderness, he was actually only a mile from the town of Concord, his mom did his laundry, and he was a frequent dinner guest at neighbor Ralph Waldo Emerson's house, where he "scandalize[d] the women of the house with his talk of the sexual habits of various animals.")

But this was not most national parks. I couldn't even figure out where the trailhead was. All I saw was a tangle of trees on either side of the road.

"Over there," John said, pointing to a mud-covered incline embedded with thick concrete slabs every two feet or so, like a boot-camp obstacle course. A rope dangled down the middle, stippled green with moss and mold. Next to it was a reassuringly familiar sign, a white-print backpacker icon against a brown background—standard-issue national park. John raced ahead.

"Definitely not a geezer," Maren said, as we struggled to keep up. She added brightly, "If we die out here, at least we'll be together."

The trail, such as it was, twisted and turned with the muddy topography, shimmied around massive roots, high-stepped up more of those quasi-ladders, following the ragtag choreography of Mother Nature. And after half an hour, it disappeared.

John plunged into the bush, out of sight. We heard him stumble, followed by a yelp that unfurled into a scream of existential fear. "WaaAAAAAAAUGH!"

Maren and I exchanged bug-eyed looks. I knew that scream. That was a Hollywood scream, a beloved-sidekick-dying-in-a-sudden-and-dramatic-fashion scream. We'd gone hiking with a seventy-year-old—why did he think this was a good idea? Why did *we?*

"Shit, shit, shit," I said, looking at my ever-practical wife for deeper insight.

"Shit," she said.

The bushes rustled and I heard a grunt and then a shout of glee: "Found the trail!" We spotted John peeking down at us from atop a steep, muddy slope, his face framed by a downed tree trunk, his expression elated and mischievous.

The hike that followed turned out to be nearly six hours up and down a seemingly endless series of peaks, traversing muddy and sometimes wholly overgrown paths, including more than fifty ladders. By the time we were halfway through, my legs were caked with mud, every muscle burned, and I felt a giddiness I hadn't felt since I was a kid, a sense of unalloyed, carefree *fun*. Maren and I took turns giving each other the thumbs-up. We had the trails to ourselves—there were zero other hikers—and there was a certain summer-camp vibe, especially when John started telling us creepy stories, like the time he hired a Fijian witch doctor (for "ten bucks, a pack of Kools, and a bag of kava") to put a curse on a neighbor who'd been annoying him.

"Another time," he said, "I was hiking up a mountain in Manu'a by myself." It was supposed to be a day hike but he realized he wasn't going to make it down before dark, so he lay down to sleep in a clearing. He woke up with the sunrise, "and sitting right there next to me were an orange and a bottle of water. They just appeared, you know what I mean? No one knew I was up there. Must have been an *aitu*"—a trickster spirit. He cackled, and Maren and I humored him with a smile.

Back in the lower elevation, the trees had been banyans and leafy hardwoods; now it was moss-draped cloud forest, with an appropriately eerie mist and the occasional flicker of a chilly breeze. The trail got wider, and ahead I could see a sawed-off branch jutting partway into the path. As we got closer, I noticed that it had a mold-covered baseball cap perched on the end. It was so grimy, it must've been here for years and—

Oh, shit.

It said MACK on it. The trucking company logo, but still: MACK. My not-that-common last name. Way up here. My heart raced and I hoped John wouldn't notice. He cackled. "See? It's from an *aitu*!"

I looked at it for a few moments, honestly thinking it might be a fatigue-induced hallucination.

"Don't touch it!" John said, still laughing, though I could tell he really meant it. "You don't want to chance anything. Leave it here."

Not to worry, I assured him, already striding away.

An hour or so later, we came to a small clearing with two benches hewn from thick logs. My legs ached and the benches were transforming into pillow-top mattresses before my eyes. And then I stopped in my tracks. It was not just a clearing but a vista.

Directly below us, the lush hills eased down to the isolated village of Vatia, its *fales* and churches snug against a cozy bay where waves crashed along the reef and glided calmly to shore.

My feet were stuck, my brain transfixed. And it wasn't just the combination of ocean plus jungle plus mountains plus village, rare and enrapturing as that is, but something about the specific arrangement of it all. The far side of the bay was formed by a narrow peninsula, a serrated edge of hills that undulated before dropping sheer into the ocean. There was a short gap of open water before the rock rose again, four hundred feet straight up and then tapering away. With its curves and scaly eminences, it looked for all the world like a massive dragon's tail arching into the Pacific.*

When I'd talked to Marie Alailima, she ended our conversation with a few tourist tips, first and foremost, "Go to Vatia. It's just breathtaking."

Literally, it turned out.

I looked at John. He was sweating but grinning. His shirt read: YOU ONLY LIVE ONCE.

• • • • •

WE RODE the bus back into town, and as we walked to John's car, we heard a loud clanging noise. We looked up the road to see a man in a blue *lavalava* hitting a metal bar against an air compression tank while a trio of kids nearby plugged their ears, and more men in blue *lavalavas* stood along the side of the road. Their job, John said, was to prevent anyone from driving or even walking in the village during *Sa*—they were the literal keepers of the peace.

It's something you read about in the guidebooks: *Respect Sa,*

* In fact, I would later learn that this is one of the local names for it: Dragon's Tail. The official Samoan name, though, is even better, translating to Cockscomb Point.

don't walk through the villages. Over dinner at a Chinese restaurant, I mentioned this to John and he laughed. "The idea is that you're supposed to be praying. And I suppose there might be two grandmas who do that. But mostly it means just turn down the TV a little bit. And these guys out on the road aren't always out here, so it's not entirely consistent.

"I bet you also read that you're not supposed to keep your feet out when you sit down in a *fale*," John added as he tucked into his seafood soup, a massive crab leg projecting out of the bowl.

"Yeah, we did see that," Maren said. In a national park brochure and *Lonely Planet* and several other places.

"Well . . ." John said. "Have you seen a lot of people sitting down in *fales*? Or have you seen tables and chairs?"

We thought for a moment. "Tables and chairs," Maren said.

"Exactly."

"And you're not supposed to eat food while walking through a village, right? But there's a guy with a bag of chips in one hand and a Pepsi in the other. And a lot of these guys coming back after decades in the military are so used to life in the states or on base. They build houses surrounded by fences."

Is this erosion or simply evolution of a culture? In every conversation, at every sight, I'd gone back and forth in my mind. Up on the trail, I'd thought, *Save it all! Put this whole place under a dome and keep it as it is!* At Evalani's, it was, *Cultures change! We all adapt! Better living through tacos and tiki drinks!*

Countless outside observers—among them anthropologist Margaret Mead, whose book *Coming of Age in Samoa* grew out of her fieldwork in the Manu'a Islands—have marveled at the adaptability and elasticity of Samoan culture. When the missionaries arrived, Samoans picked and chose which Christian dictates to follow—*fa'asamoa* was flexible and could be compartmentalized, so it followed that the same must be true of the newcomers' worldviews. Per missionary command, out went the leaf skirts and bare tops, in came the long, modest dresses that are common today (along with *lavalavas* and shorts, jeans, and T-shirts). Keeping the Sabbath remains important, and *Sa*. But other Samoan traditions persevered, like the *'ava* ceremonies and dancing. There's also the *fa'afafine* ("way of the woman"), Samoa's "third gender," born male but identifying as female, here not just accepted but celebrated as an important part of the culture, even if it seems an unlikely fit for an evangelical Christian environment.

I asked Charles Ala'ilima about the cultural picking-and-choosing and he said, with a laugh, "Well, they do say that the true sign of intelligence is to hold two mutually exclusive concepts in your mind . . ."

He added, though, that this was one of the key points of his argument for birthright citizenship. *Fa'asamoa* had proven remarkably flexible and resilient—accommodating Christianity, Americanization, changing diets, workdays spent in offices and canneries. If it could survive all this time, surely citizenship wouldn't be the end of it.

• • • • •

BACK AT the restaurant in Pago Pago, John introduced us to the owner, a beaming Chinese woman in a black-and-white-striped dress. She had married a Portuguese fishing-boat captain she'd met here, John said, and she had the freshest seafood in town. John had recently begun taking Chinese language lessons so he could communicate with this growing immigrant community.

"It's the twenty-year plan," he said. You emigrate here from

China, because the territory runs its own immigration with no federal oversight, and it's easier to get in. You save up money, have a family. Your kids are born U.S. nationals, which allows them to travel to the states—and eventually they do just that, going off to college and settling on the mainland, with their parents right behind. But none of them have the full rights of citizenship.

Here was a twist to the citizenship issue, something that hadn't occurred to me before: its impact on non-Samoans.

Citizenship opponents typically framed the issue in terms of Americanization versus indigenous traditions, but American Samoa isn't exclusively American or Samoan. The territories are no more culturally static than the states. They may be reminders of a different era in American history—the Imperial Moment, the Age of Empire—but they're always evolving, situated as they are on the front lines of globalization, closer to other countries than to the United States and abuzz with competing cultural influences.

It's a key point, one that the overarching debates about territorial policy often ignore. The Insular Cases intentionally shut out people of "alien races"; now, Charles Ala'ilima said, some American Samoans were using the rulings to discriminate against immigrants from China and the Philippines. Even if the Insular Cases did help protect some Samoan traditions, their legal consequences affected everyone in the territory—a blanket *geographic* approach to a *cultural* concern, the widely cast net going far beyond Samoans fending off Hawaii-style development interests.

In fact, Charles Ala'ilma asserted, some *matais* have set up "an exploitive system," bringing in foreign laborers to work in stores and other businesses they run, knowing that immigration and labor department oversights are lax. He called it "an abusive local alien sponsorship program which promotes something very much like indentured servitude upon foreigners working in the territory." One day in Pago Pago, I bought a newspaper and found a front-page headline reading "Over 2,400 illegal aliens register for amnesty campaign." The largest human trafficking case in United States history was in American Samoa, at a garment factory that operated from 1998 to 2001. The owner, a South Korean businessman named Kil Soo Lee, was sentenced to forty years in prison in 2005, after being convicted of luring about three hundred women from China and Vietnam to work in his factory (after charging them up to $8,000 for the privilege) and holding them against their will in atrocious conditions, documented in a *Seattle Post-Intelligencer* report titled "Made in Misery." In 2010, during investigations of another human trafficking case, local and federal officials raided American Samoa's own Office of Immigration, which was suspected of aiding traffickers in illegally bringing hundreds of people from China, the Philippines, and South Korea to the territory, according to the search warrant. American Samoa didn't even have a law against human trafficking until March 2014. "With citizenship, you'd get the [federal] immigration authorities down here," Charles Ala'ilima told me.

Beyond the issue of immigration, it's worth examining the underlying motives of some *matais'* opposition to citizenship for the simple fact that the current power structure, which they argue is embedded in *fa'asamoa*, places them squarely at the top. They may be genuinely concerned about broader issues of *fa'asamoa*, but any cracks in that foundation would likely affect their own status. And why would they advocate for that?

The Insular Cases have always been about maintaining power and cultural imbalance; it just turns out that this functions in more ways than one.

• • • • •

WE STILL wanted a taste of sunny-isle stereotypes. No flame-twirlers or hula-dancing; just a little hut on the beach to ourselves and maybe an umbrella drink or two. A pod of semi-domesticated whales would be ideal, but not mandatory. Of course, there was no way such a thing actually existed.

Sure it does, John said. "Let's call Tisa. She's a friend."

One afternoon, he dropped us off at Tisa's Barefoot Bar, built on a deck above a powdery beach, with railings and beams hewn from driftwood, orange life rings and glass floats hanging from rafters, and a scattering of hand-painted signs. It was all salvaged by Tisa and her boyfriend, who goes by the name Candyman, from their private cove, and formed a knowingly Don the Beach-comber aesthetic. In addition to the sporadically open bar and restaurant, Tisa had two small A-frame *fales* she rented out, each with a thatch roof and a tiny veranda jutting over the high-tide mark.

There were no other guests; it was just me, Maren, Tisa (guessing fiftyish, short hair, radiant), Candyman (about the same age, tall, Aussie, utterly laid-back), and their dog, Palusami (watch your step). Over dinner, Tisa boasted of how healthy her reef is and how, in August, the trade winds subside and the water is like glass, and whales come into her cove to calf. She gets out her ukulele and sings them traditional Samoan songs.

"I stand here, and just *siiiing* and sing to them," she said, strumming an air ukulele.

"Do they respond?" I asked. She stared at me like I'd asked if the whales get wet.

"Of course! I can tell they like it. They sort of look at me."

Candyman mixed us cocktails with layers of color and juice and inadvisable amounts of rum and then brought out dinner. He'd just caught the parrotfish himself. "Grilled it, squeezed a little bit of lemon on it, should be nice and light." Next to it was boiled green banana with a coconut sauce and a green salad. After days of meats in thick brown sauce and salads consisting of wilted cabbage, I had almost forgotten what this looked like, greens that were actually green.

"I like it nice and quiet like this," Tisa said as we ate. She gets crowds when cruise ships call in Pago Pago, about a dozen times a year. There's good turnout for her weekly feast of traditional Samoan barbecue, called *umu*, cooked in a mound of heated basalt rocks covered with banana leaves, served with hefty helpings of *palusami*, her dog's namesake dish, consisting of taro leaves cooked in coconut milk, rich and sweet enough to make even the most devoted vegetable-shunner ask for seconds. And she rents out her two *fales* a few nights a week. But that's enough. Tisa has no interest in tourist crowds disrupting her comfortable life. Besides, they might come here expecting a plush resort. There's no room service, no air-conditioning, and the bed is surrounded by a much-needed mosquito net. The shared bathroom is bare-bones and up a sandy path that, for Tisa's sake, I should note is covered with slowly pinballing hermit crabs that could probably snap off your toe if they wanted to.

But there's also this: That night, covered in the sticky residue of the ocean after an hour of splashing in the waves with Maren, I walked to the shared outdoor shower to clean up. The water was hot and the stall's side was open to the cove, the waves crashing some fifteen feet below me. And when I rinsed the soap off my face and looked up through a broad frame of tree branches, there was the Milky Way, brighter than I'd ever seen it before, not just a sprinkle of points on a hazy scrim but a flowing wash of white against pure black, with depth and layers and glittering eddies. I walked back to the *fale* and sat on the porch with Maren, looking out at the starlit water in wordless contentment, before we fell asleep to the lullaby of the rising tide whispering in and out, in and out, in and out below our hut.

• • • • •

Our days in American Samoa were numbered. Soon I would continue on to Guam and Maren would fly back to Minneapolis, back to her job, her vacation days depleted. For now, though, we wanted to make the most of what time remained. In the morning, we dawdled on Tisa's deck, enjoying a breakfast of pillowy pancakes topped with banana sautéed in its own juice, with a side of fresh papaya, so soft and rich that it seemed like something you'd buy by the scoop in a gourmet shop in Rome or Paris. Candyman brought out mugs of thick, robust Samoan hot chocolate.

Eventually, we dragged ourselves off the deck and hopped a passing bus to the eastern end of Tutuila, then took a ten-minute boat ride to Aunu'u, a mile-wide dot of an island. Tisa and John had described it in terms that city-dwellers often use to describe the country—*more rural, more traditional*—which was a jarring thing to hear from people who lived in a place that was itself, to our mainlander minds, pretty rural and "traditional." John also warned us that the local stray dogs were particularly vicious.

Kids swam under the boat as we arrived and the Mormon missionary on board deftly jumped out onto the dock ahead of us. A cell-phone tower stood near the dock, and the village (population five hundred or so) looked much like any other we'd seen:

one-story houses in various states of repair (from the recently remodeled to the just-about-falling-down) and arranged around an open lawn; assorted *fales*; a few churches, which were the largest and best-kept buildings around.

Heeding John's warning about dogs, we armed ourselves with long sticks. The island's village is concentrated near the dock, but not far away we began to understand what John and Tisa were getting at. The houses became sparser and we passed a hut constructed of leaves and tarps, a Mormon church—characteristically tidy and sparkling white—and a school, before the road ran out, leaving water and jungle. Along the beach, two people were fishing in the shallows and a young girl of perhaps six years old was poking at something in a tide pool. As we passed her, a dog came bounding over the low-lying shrubs at the beach's edge, barking at us. Maren held out her stick with a fencer's poise while I simply flailed at the air. The girl calmly pulled her hand out of the water to reveal a six-inch knife. She flashed it at the dog and yelled, and it stopped in its tracks before trotting away. The girl nonchalantly turned her attention back to the tide pool. The air was still, the only sound the crashing waves.

For the first time on my territory journey, I felt like I was a galaxy away from the states, somewhere wholly unfamiliar to my own American experience.

There's so little on Aunu'u that one of our guidebook's highlighted attractions was a swamp known for its reddish hue. In search of this local landmark, we headed back through the village, where we inadvertently picked up an entourage of four kids, ranging in age from four to eight.

"You know Christina?" they asked.

"No, sorry," Maren replied.

"You know Masina?"

"No.

"You know Shakira?"

"The singer?" I said, startled.

"No, my friend."

"Sorry, don't know her." I couldn't resist asking, "Do you know Prince? He lives in my village, Minneapolis."

"No," the kids chorused.

They merrily followed us for ten minutes or so, trying out their English and continuing to list names, seeking common ground with us. They were good company.

We got the impression, from the kids' gesturing and chatter among themselves in Samoan, that they hoped we'd give them money if they led us to the swamp—although they couldn't agree on where, exactly, it was. So we gave them the only cash we had, a five-dollar bill, to split four ways on an island with no stores or, really, anywhere to spend it. A series of thoughts flashed through my mind: (1) a cosmic guilt for embodying, in this small way, the Corrupting, Patronizing Forces of Outsiders; (2) an indignant self-scolding: *Geez, haven't they earned it? Can't we spare it? Couldn't it maybe possibly help them a teeny-tiny bit?*; and (3) a realization that it was best not to read too much into this; we were neither saviors nor corrupters, just tourists passing through, forgotten by tomorrow.

The boat puttered back to Tutuila, where I realized that, somewhere on Aunu'u, I'd lost my hat—evidently the trickster *aitu* of Mount Alava had followed us. We waited for a bus that didn't come, and then we started walking. It was a couple of miles back to Tisa's, we figured. After a few minutes, though, a truck pulled up next us, a giant white Chevy with a Seattle Seahawks flag and tinted windows—archetypal "Real America."

"Do you want a ride?" asked the driver, a man in his sixties.

His name was Tony, he said, as I climbed into the front seat and Maren got in back. He had a thick mustache and a white polo shirt, and sipped from a Coors can; he had another in the cup holder and offered it to me.

"Um . . ." I hesitated, not really wanting to encourage drinking and driving on winding roads.

"Doug, take the beer!" Maren hissed from the backseat. "Be polite!"

I took the beer.

"I am retired from the government, so it's okay," Tony said, nodding toward his Coors. He, too, started listing the people he knew; his brother, he said, used to be the governor.

Tony turned into his family compound. "I want to show you where I live." We stopped outside a white house with red trim, then walked around the side and found a small cove. "Here is my beach. And my *fale*." Part of the roof was a section of an old Charlie the Tuna sign.

"Here is my boat," Tony said, pointing to a small powerboat. "And here is my *umu*. I will have a barbecue with my friends tomorrow.

"It's nice?" he asked, gesturing around—to his spread, his view, the ocean, and then to the island beyond. His expression was pure contentment. It said: *This is why we live here. This is what we cherish. This is* fa'asamoa *writ small.*

"It's really nice," I said, nodding.

• • • • •

Back on Tisa's deck, our host proffered a series of monologues as she alternated between making a palm-frond basket and looking at her iPad, periodically scrolling through photos or finding a document. She wore her hair in tight curls and a teal *lavalava* and a white T-shirt that advertised her "Barefoot Bar."

Tisa supported citizenship, she said, although she was worried about the possibility of outsider land-grabs, which seemed to be the main concern of everyone I talked to about citizenship (*matai* power and *Sa*, not so much; they directly affected a much smaller portion of the population). Her nephew served in the military and had problems getting a job on the mainland, even after he served, because he wasn't a U.S. citizen.

"That makes me so mad!" Tisa said. "I went to California and I had the same issues when I was looking for a job." Eventually she started working as a real estate agent.

"That's why I know how to sell," she said. "Right now I'm working on our tattoo festival." She pulled up a document on her iPad, promotional copy for the annual event, which draws hundreds of people, with live streaming online.

"My first festival was in 1993," she said. "It was before its time."

Tattooing here goes back thousands of years; the Pacific is where the very word originated. (It's *tatau* in Samoan.) The most traditional tattoo, called a *pe'a*, runs from the waist to the knees, and is created by a master tattooist called a *tufuga ta tatau*, using ink created with the soot from a burned candlenut, a blade made with tortoiseshell, and a bone comb. The predominant feature of a *pe'a* is a sequence of horizontal lines of various thicknesses, with diagonal lines and color blocks and intricate, angular patterns—an aesthetic theme, but always personalized. Today, the most popular tattoos—which you see on nearly all adult men, and some women—swirl from the breast to the shoulder and halfway to the elbow, and feature abstracted motifs of sharks and turtles and outrigger canoes interlocked with shapes and lines, all telling a story representing your *'aiga*.

When the Christian missionaries came, tattooing was one of their prohibitions. It stuck for generations.

"I think it was that first festival that planted the seed" and started to bring tattooing back, Tisa said. "But people looked at me like I was some kind of heathen." She didn't have another festival until 2005.

By then, tattoos had inked their ever-growing spot in the American psyche, with teenagers and soccer moms and retirees going under the needle; even Miss America contestants have tattoos. There are TV shows devoted to tattoos, shops on seemingly every corner of most large cities. Along with Maori and Hawaiian motifs, Samoan designs have been part of the trend, spurred on by celebrities, including Dwayne "the Rock" Johnson and other professional wrestling stars of Samoan descent, as well as NFL players. (The Rock is part of the extended Anoa'i family, which includes at least seventeen professional wrestlers, among them his father and grandfather.) Meanwhile, Peace Corps volunteers in Samoa started getting armband tattoos as souvenirs before heading back to the states, where they helped popularize this stripped-down version of the traditional designs.

Tisa said she didn't mind outsiders getting tattoos with Samoan motifs. "It's helping spread the culture and bring it back here," she said. "It's the only traditional art the kids get really excited about. Not so much the dancing and other crafts, but the tattoos go viral and the kids are always showing them off and tweeting it."

Today, Samoan tattoo artists are in high demand. Like Tisa's brother: "He used to come to me for money but now he's doing really well and traveling all over. Right now he's at the Smithsonian showing his designs," she said. "The revival has been a blessing to the island." It was reclaiming their roots, but also sharing them with the world, at thousands of dollars a pop for the larger designs.

American Samoa has become more Americanized, Big Mac by Big Mac, but the flow of culture isn't one-way. The USA has also become incrementally more *Samoan*, even if we haven't realized it, through tattoos and Polynesia's myriad pop-culture influences and, more important, person by person, in the form of everyday Samoans who make their mark on the mainland, from everyday citizens—or at least nationals—to NFL stars to the forest-fire fighter we met one day, biding his time back home while awaiting his next assignment in a mainland national park, with the rest of his crew of hotshots, all Samoan.

Like so many other "alien races," the people of the territories have changed the fabric of the USA—and what a magnificent thing that is.

"I'm probably the only one not making any money from tattooing, and I'm fine with that. I'm just sitting here with my cocoa and papaya," Tisa said, beaming. "For so many years, we've been poor. You either had a government job or worked in the cannery." This was still the reality for many American Samoans, of course, but for some, "The whole clan, they're teaching everybody, even the babies, how to be a traditional artist and use your skill and make the most of yourself. That's the American Dream."

Chapter 3

OFFSHORING THE AMERICAN EXPERIENCE

Guam

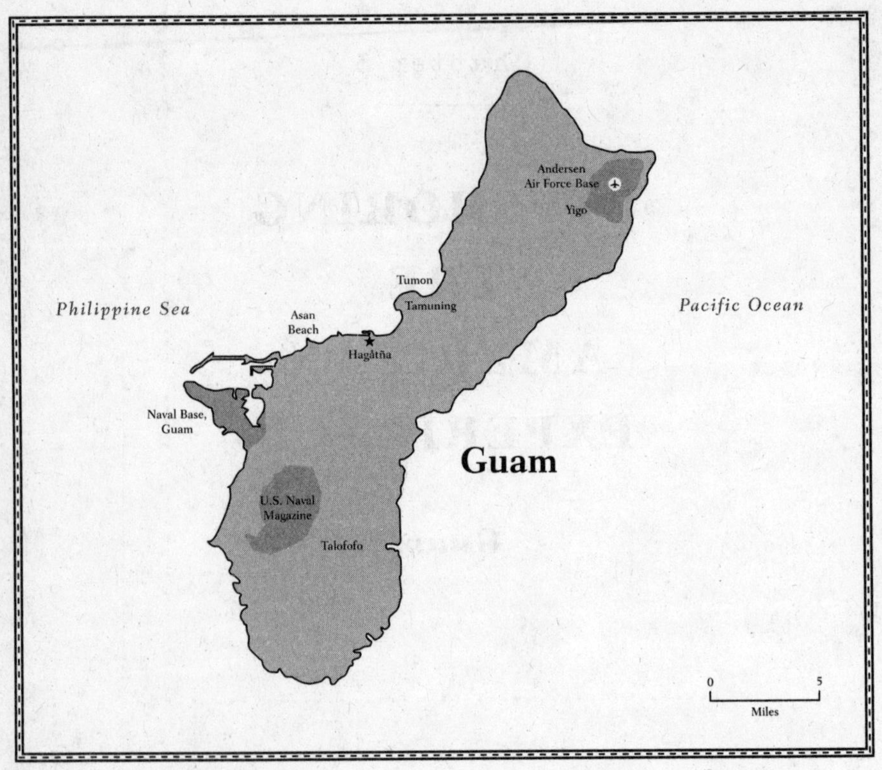
Andersen
Air Force Base
Yigo
Tumon
Tamuning
Philippine Sea
Pacific Ocean
Asan
Beach
Hagåtña
Naval Base,
Guam
Guam
U.S. Naval
Magazine
Talofofo
0
5
Miles

"HAPPY FOURTH OF JULY, EVERYBODY! ARE YOU ALL HAVING A GOOD TIIIIIME?" A goateed radio DJ bellowed from a stage set up in the middle of a pulsing crowd of thousands of revelers in the heart of Guam's Tumon tourist district. High-rise hotels and hulking malls formed a canyon around me and illuminated the cloud of meaty smoke rising from the food stands set up in the middle of Pale San Vitores Road. It was the second annual Guam BBQ Block Party and the local visitors' bureau had gone all-out to make it a truly archetypal American extravaganza, with shredding rock bands and a barbecue contest headlined by celebrity pitmasters flown in from Vladivostok and Seoul.

To get to Guam from American Samoa requires backtracking to Hawaii and then flying seven and a half hours west. In terms of distance and direction, this is like starting in Jacksonville, Florida, traveling northeast of Hudson Bay, in the outer reaches of Canada, and then back across the continent to Anchorage, Alaska. Guam is north of the equator, in the western Pacific; it's part of Micronesia, not Polynesia—same ocean but different regions and different cultures. And compared to the pastoral quiet of Tutuila, Tumon was a different world, a shock to the system, a farce, a twisted fantasy of brands and brashness and bustle. Here was the Westin, the Hyatt; here was the nearly block-sized duty-free complex with Bulgari and Dior and Hermès and Rolex boutiques; here was a water park, an amusement park, and the Guam Slingshot, a sort of reverse bungee-jump contraption that shoots you high into the sky.

My GOD, I thought. *This is so crass and commercialized, so overbuilt and—*

Aaaaah. And then it kicked in. The sweet, synthetic all-American high of Brand Overload. I hadn't realized I missed it. It may not have stirred my soul in the same way as the natural wonders of American Samoa, but it felt . . . so good.

Maybe I needed to blow my rent money on some new shoes at the two-story Gucci store. Maybe I needed to see some artfully lit fish at UnderWater World. And hello, Häagen-Dazs. I *definitely* needed a triple-scoop to go with all the smoked meat I was about to consume.

A cluster of young, muscle-bound Americans laughed and shoveled barbecue into their mouths, military personnel from the island's Navy and Air Force bases. Nearly everyone else in the crowd was a tourist from Korea, China, Russia, or Japan. Half the glowing signs around me seemed to be in at least one of these languages; near my hotel, I'd seen an Outback Steakhouse—the Australian-themed chain—with a large sign reading AMERICA'S FAVORITE STEAKHOUSE in Japanese. Nearly a million Japanese citizens visit Guam every year; it's an easy three-hour-and-forty-five-minute flight from Tokyo, with daily service on multiple airlines. (It's also a four-hour flight from Taipei, and if you're so inclined, you can travel on an EVA Air jet called Hello Kitty Happy Music.)

I bought a plate of brisket and ribs and kept scanning my surroundings—Louis Vuitton! Hard Rock Café!—when suddenly there was a warp in the Luxury Tourist Zone template. Next to the Prada store was a shabbier three-story building. Here was a sex-toy shop. A massage parlor that sure looked like it offered more than sore-muscle relief. And Hollywood Shooting, which was advertised with a backlit sign of Japanese tourists dressed up as cowboys and holding pistols and rifles. It was jarring to see high and low culture cozying up like this, but also refreshing. They weren't so different, really, in their appeal to base desires. Just different recipes for swagger. Choose Door A to drop a few grand on clothes and accessories that will make you feel powerful and sexy. Or strut through Door B, grab an M16, shoot shit, and get laid.

On the stage set up in the alley between these two versions of America, the DJ brought out a local dignitary. The mayor? The governor? I don't know. I couldn't take notes. I was too busy eating some of the best barbecue I've had in my life, the brisket fall-apart tender and served with a heady coconut-flecked sauce. But some guy in rimless glasses strode to the mic and announced the barbecue-contest winners with a sportscaster bellow: "*And in first place . . . AAaaaassssuu*!"

Asu was a local restaurant, run by indigenous Chamorros, who comprise the majority of the population of 165,000 here in the second-largest territory, a thirty-mile-long island shaped sort of like Florida, if the top half of the Sunshine State started to droop to the east. (Also, because Guam is the name of the island, not just the territory, the convention is to say that you're "*on* Guam" not "*in* Guam.") The runners-up were also from Guam.

The crowd cheered wildly. No one seemed to care that Team Vladivostok and Team Seoul got shut out, not even the Koreans and Russians, two rising tourism markets the visitors' bureau was clearly trying to impress—Guam attracted some 208,000 Koreans in 2013 and 6,000 Russians (comparatively low, but they're big spenders, dropping an average of $1,600 every day). But they hadn't come here for a taste of Russia or South Korea. They'd come here to mainline the American Experience.

If you're so inclined, in the course of a single afternoon, you can rent a canary-yellow Chevy Mustang or a Harley-Davidson, dress up like a cowboy and fire a machine gun at Wild West Frontier Village, eat a burger at the Route 66 Pub & Club, buy a bulk-sized bag of your favorite flavor of beef jerky from the dedicated section at the souvenir shop, and pose with the Statue of Liberty, with a baseball field in the background, before ending the day with a Las Vegas–style magic show replete with white tigers and dancing showgirls with feathery headdresses.

"Guam, USA," it says on postcards, on T-shirts, on boxes of dolphin-shaped chocolates, on the seven varieties of souvenir ashtrays I counted at a sprawling gift shop. There are two other common postcard slogans: "Hafa adai" (the Chamorro term for "Hello") and "Where America's Day Begins." The latter is a sly way of turning its distance from the mainland USA into a selling point—Guam's so far away that it's literally a different day, on the other side of the International Dateline, thirteen hours ahead of New York. It offers easy access for Asian tourists who want a taste of the states in an affordable weekend trip. Nowhere have I been surrounded by so many people yearning, desperately, to *feel* American. As I squeezed through the crowd, I could usually tell, even before hearing languages, who lived here and who didn't: the more red, white, and blue, the less likely to be from the United States.

• • • • •

"IT'S LIKE the samurai in America—we like the samurai, they like the cowboy," one Chamorro man explained to me. Fair enough. Stereotypes sell. In contrast with the Packaged Polynesia and its hula girls, though, the cowboy isn't just a stereotype but an archetype wholeheartedly embraced by the people it ostensibly embodies. The cowboy is the quintessential American icon.

"Tales of Wild West men and women, from Kit Carson to Wild Bill Hickok, to Calamity Jane, to Annie Oakley, are woven into the dreams of our youth and the standards we aim to live by in our adult lives," then-President Ronald Reagan—himself a onetime Hollywood cowboy—said in 1983. "Ideals of courageous and self-reliant heroes, both men and women, are the stuff of Western lore."

Alexis de Tocqueville thought that mythology of this sort was the stuff of the musty Old World, of monarchies, and that the United States, as a newer, purer sort of place, was above such frippery. "Among a democratic people poetry will not be fed with legends or the memorials of old traditions," he wrote in *Democracy in America*. But it turns out that we do nationalistic hagiography as well as anyone. It came as a package deal with Manifest Destiny and American Exceptionalism and the fervor for expansion and a growing role in the world. If the United States was going to become a global power, it had to follow its predecessors in methodology—control ports to control the seas—as well as in *mythology*, forming a collective identity and a face to the world. To rise quickly requires not only a belief in legends but a confidence that you yourself are legendary.

In the post–Imperial Moment era, perhaps no single figure looms larger in the nation's mythology than Teddy Roosevelt—Rough Rider, national park booster, and progressive leader, a

Founding Father of the American Century. Here was a man who, like no one else, paired rugged individualism with coalition-building Washington refinement. Count me among his fans. "There were all kinds of things I was afraid of at first," he writes in his autobiography, "ranging from grizzly bears to 'mean' horses and gun-fighters; but by acting as if I was not afraid I gradually ceased to be afraid." I read that—as someone known to bolt in fright when he disturbs a garter snake in his backyard, as someone who has only been camping for two nights, at his wife's insistence—and I think, *Badass.* I start dreaming of saddling up a horse and heading out to the open range with a rifle and a bedroll, come what may. The real key to my admiration, though, is the fact that Teddy wasn't all empty-headed bluster; he was also someone who, after his wife and his mother died on the same day in 1884, moved to the South Dakota badlands and contemplated the landscape and the poems of Edgar Allan Poe. We are, famously, a nation of guileless cockiness, leaving the rumination to those espresso-drinking Old Worlders, but in Mr. Speak Softly and Carry a Big Stick we get dashes of all of the above.

After brooding and playing cowboy for a couple of years—there's a remarkable photo of him wearing a leather jacket and pants edged with a prairie of fringe—Teddy moved back East, serving as New York City's police commissioner and then, in 1897, being appointed by President William McKinley as the Assistant Secretary of the Navy. He was a key voice in McKinley's chorus of expansionism-enablers, with a particular itch to go after Spain's colonies, a goal he endorsed "on the grounds both of humanity and [national] self-interest."

The cowboy-statesman was relishing his—and his nation's—next moves, preparing for Manifest Destiny's biggest leaps away from the North American continent.

• • • • •

EACH DAY in Tumon, I delighted in taking an inventory of the amped-up America on display: the tommy-gun-shaped vodka bottles at the gift shop, the American-style diner where I sat next to a young Korean couple who studied the six-inch mound of whipped cream on their waffle as though it were an endangered-species specimen. At Hollywood Shooting, surrounded by *Tombstone* and *Die Hard* movie posters, the sixty-something Japanese man behind the counter tried to talk me into the Rambo Package (M16, machine gun, shotgun, $150); what he lacked in English vocabulary he got across with pantomiming, gesturing to show just how big and powerful these weapons were. A chic Japanese couple—she in a green sundress, he in a white linen shirt and a fedora—took selfies with a wooden drugstore Indian in the corner as they awaited their turn to shoot.

When my appetite for Americana was finally sated, I went to a Japanese restaurant, and was delighted to see the temple-like interior and the table of Japanese retirees next to me. The server came over to take their order, and though she shared their ancestry, she was American through and through, startling the tourists when she told them she only spoke English.

I looked up an old college friend named Mars, who had grown up on Guam and now lived there, working as a lawyer. It's the ideal place to pursue a legal career, he said, because territorial law so rarely matches up cleanly with stateside precedent, so "everything's a new, crazy challenge," and even some nationally applicable laws disproportionately affect Guam. (He mentioned as an example the 1920 Jones Act, which regulates shipping between American ports and, long story short, significantly increases the cost of many goods and commodities, including gas, on Guam, as well as Hawaii and Puerto Rico.) I was hoping he'd help me get out of the tourist bubble, which he did, sort of—he took me to a place called Jamaican Grill, a Chamorro-Jamaican barbecue spot, where we feasted on jerk ribs and chicken *kelaguen*, the latter a bit like chicken salad, the meat finely chopped and marinated in lemon juice and soy sauce and with a hot-pepper kick. We washed it down with bottles of Guam1 Beer, which turns out to be made in Wisconsin.

Guam has long been a whirl of cultures, mixing in all kinds of ways, by choice, by circumstance, by force. It was a Spanish colony long before the United States arrived on the scene.

"The Chamorro tradition is a design for life, which was constructed with and under the influence of Spaniards, Filipinos, Mexicans, and Americans," Guam's then-Congressman Dr. Robert Underwood noted at the Centennial Conference in 1998. "But it is a unique tradition, which many will find a familiar thread in, but in which no one can claim ownership except Chamorros."

Mars and I met up again the next evening, for more feasting at the Chamorro Village, a marketplace with a scattering of permanent buildings clustered around a pavilion, along with tents set up in the open spaces just for the night. We bought some barbecue from Asu—the street-party winner, and deserving of the title—and stood on a staircase landing overlooking the market, perching our black Styrofoam clamshells on the ledge and enjoying the view as crowds milled about and daylight faded and a barbecue haze hung in the air. In the pavilion, families danced the Electric Slide.

When the Chamorro Village opened in 1990, "there was more of a focus on local crafts and culture," Mars said. "Now it's a lot of mass-produced stuff for tourists. Plenty of locals still come here, but it's not really a snapshot of the traditional ways." But, he added, "there's also a debate among Chamorros about what's authentic culture. Is it pre-war? Pre-USA? Pre-Spanish?"

He pointed to one of the compartments of food in my Styrofoam container. By now there wasn't much left. "That red rice is the traditional side dish for Chamorro barbecue. It's from Spain," the distinctive color derived from the achiote plant. Another compartment held coleslaw—America! And then there was the star of the Styrofoam: the pork ribs. Barbecue on Guam goes back thousands of years—Chamorros first cooked turtles and fruit bats, expanding the menu when the Spanish brought pork and chicken and beef. But present-day Chamorro barbecue also has its roots in more recent history, the ribs and other packaged meats coming from the American military influence, and the marinade that gives the barbecue its distinct flavor and fall-apart texture has a base of vinegar, introduced by the Americans, and soy sauce, from the considerable Japanese population that has made its way here.

These particular ribs had a perfect pink-brown hue, imbued with wood smoke, finished with a subtle dry rub, and with a buttery, porky sublimity. I've eaten my share of barbecue around the USA—including a pilgrimage to Kansas City for that express purpose—and this was as good as it gets; if there were any justice, Guam would be lauded as one of the nation's great culinary regions, with foodies flocking here by the planeful.

It was clear that this seemingly all-American dish had a more complicated story to tell.

• • • • •

UNLIKE THE USVI and American Samoa, where the early European influences were many, Guam's story is a bit more straightforward, starting with Ferdinand Magellan's stop here in 1521. As the Spanish galleons neared the shore, they were surrounded by Chamorros in outriggers called *proas*. The Chamorros climbed on board the ships and, Robert F. Rogers details in *Destiny's Landfall: A History of Guam* (1995), "carr[ied] away anything loose," not out of hostility but per the local custom "whereby new arrivals on an island present gifts to their hosts, who can take whatever they wish from the newcomers." The Spanish, though, saw only theft and aggression, and responded with crossbows, killing several Chamorros and burning down more than forty huts. They named Guam and its surrounding islands Islas de Ladrones, the Islands of the Thieves. A bloody theme was set.

In 1565, Spain officially decreed the Ladrones—which we now call the Mariana Islands—a Spanish colony, not that they'd cleared that with the Chamorros. Today, the Chamorro language—seldom used in everyday life—bears a striking resemblance to Spanish in vocabulary, though not in grammar. (Drawing on my college Spanish, I kept thinking, *I know this phrase . . . wait, no, I don't.*) The last three governors were Eddie Calvo, Felix Camacho, and Carl Gutierrez; and the Catholic Church is still front and center, with regular community fiestas in honor of local patron saints. (One day, driving around Tumon, I saw a large banner advertising the Fiesta of Saint Rita, featuring a cockfight—another Spanish legacy.) Jesuit missionaries first arrived on Guam in the 1660s; as Rogers notes, this was "not just a minor evangelical effort but a commitment by church and state to a modest but strategically significant expansion of the Spanish empire into the Pacific Ocean."

The fact that the Spanish and the British Empires had grown in large part because of their domination of the sea was much-discussed among early American leaders, but got even more attention in 1890, when the president of the Naval War College, Captain Alfred Thayer Mahan, published a book called *The Influence of Sea Power upon History, 1660–1783*. If the United States was serious in its own ambition, this was the template to follow: the path to empire led across the ocean. It was arguably the decade's defining policy treatise, one that formed the views of American leaders including McKinley and Roosevelt, its influence growing as the emboldened nation annexed Hawaii and continued looking for places to expand overseas.

The same year as Thayer's book, the United States surpassed Great Britain to become the world's largest industrial economy. The national press was strengthening in reach, most famously through the newspapers of rivals William Randolph Hearst (the *New York Journal*) and Joseph Pulitzer (the *New York World*). The USA had a strut in its step and the megaphones to announce it.

One way to mimic the empire-building of others: take it from them. The Spanish Empire was faltering and their holdings seemed easy pickings, particularly Cuba. The United States had long coveted the island. John Quincy Adams, among other early leaders, presumed that Cuba would eventually become part of the United States, and the Americans unsuccessfully tried to buy it after the Mexican-American War in the late 1840s. American business interests were deeply invested in the Cuban economy, to the tune of some $100 million by the 1890s, at which point the U.S. government was eager to try again to claim the island or at least a larger stake in it. Cubans had fought a long war of independence, from 1868 to 1878, and a shorter one from 1879 to 1880, both of which had failed. But in 1895 revolution was brewing again, and the United States saw an opportunity to insert itself into the conflict.

In the American conception, the Spanish were "primitive Iberian savagery"; taking them on wasn't just a matter of expansion but of liberating oppressed peoples. Pulitzer and Hearst led the way in decrying the Spanish, and their sensational headlines and blustering articles—crafted to stir up outrage and sell more newspapers than the other guy—famously gave rise to the term "yellow journalism." "You furnish the pictures and I'll furnish the war," Hearst reputedly told one of his reporters, a tale historians believe is apocryphal but accurately conveys his (and Pulitzer's) general sentiment.

Importantly, it wasn't just Hearst and Pulitzer denouncing Spain, but also more high-minded publications like *Harper's* and the *Atlantic*. The latter ran a story titled "The Decadence of Spain," with tales of corruption and general high-living excess on the part of the monarchy and the Catholic Church: "To a greater or less degree, all Spanish colonies were fields in which clericalism rioted at will." Other *Atlantic* stories included jabs that the Spanish embodied both "Christian obscurantism and . . . Oriental incuriousness" and were innately "self-centered" and "warlike."

To be sure, the Spanish had a lot to answer for. On Guam, some of the earliest missionaries had offered the Chamorros a choice: convert to Christianity or be killed. The ultimatum led to a slow-burning war that lasted for twenty-six years, from 1672 to 1698; just over a hundred Spanish were killed in the fighting, and more than a thousand Chamorros. Add to that "deprivation, diseases, disease-induced infertility, societal demoralization," Rogers says, and "the Spanish colonial system as a whole, including the church as well as the military, was responsible for the decimation of the very people it sought to save." Similar events unfolded in Spain's other colonies, including Cuba, Puerto Rico, and the Philippines, all of which the United States was eyeing as the clamor for war—and, implicitly and explicitly, overseas expansion—grew in the late 1890s.

The United States aided the Cuban rebels, including sending the battleship USS *Maine* into Havana Harbor in January 1898. On February 15, 1898, the *Maine* blew up. The cause is still unknown and widely debated to this day. Was it an accident? Intentionally set off by Americans as a pretext for war? Hearst and Pulitzer splashed it on their front pages. "DESTRUCTION OF THE WAR SHIP MAINE WAS THE WORK OF AN ENEMY," declared the *Journal*, offering a $50,000 reward "for the detection of the perpetrator of the Maine outrage!" Teddy Roosevelt, the Assistant Secretary of the Navy, proclaimed it "an act of dirty treachery." Soon, the national rallying cry was, "Remember the Maine, to hell with Spain!" A few months of posturing ensued before the Spanish declared war on April 23, after the U.S. Navy set up a blockade of Cuba.

News was slow to reach Guam. Very slow. The mail had come from Manila on April 9 with nothing of note, and more than two months passed without any more information about goings-on in the world, until June 20, 1898, when four unfamiliar ships appeared on the horizon. They were American military vessels under the command of Captain Henry Glass, a Union veteran who, with his hard stare and thick mustache, could have passed for Roosevelt's brother. He was eager to get to the Philippines, which he regarded as the real action in the war, but had orders to "capture the port of Guam . . . in one or two days" on the way.

As the ships rounded Orote Peninsula on the island's west side, the cruiser USS *Charleston* fired several shells at Fort Santa Cruz, yielding no return fire, because the fort had long been abandoned. So Glass steamed on toward the harbor, where everyone had heard the blasts but assumed that these ships, whoever they were, had been firing a ceremonial salute. Ever hospitable, the locals reciprocated the greeting with "little antique brass cannons" and local health and customs officials dutifully rowed out to greet the *Charleston*, at which point Captain Glass harrumphed words that are lost to history but were presumably to the effect of, *Did you not hear? There's a* war *on*.

The following day, after a flurry of letters between Glass and Governor Juan Marina, the latter surrendered Guam to the Americans, and Glass steamed on to the Philippines. The rest of the war went quickly, with a decisive American victory, led by Teddy Roosevelt and his Rough Riders, at the Battle of San Juan Hill, on July 1. A peace protocol between the United States and Spain was signed on August 12. Fighting across the various theaters, in the Pacific and the Caribbean, had lasted less than four months. American Secretary of State John Hay called it "a splendid little war."

On December 10, 1898, the two nations signed the Treaty of Paris, with Spain selling the Philippines to the United States for $20 million, ceding Puerto Rico and Guam outright, and giving up control of Cuba (which the United States would officially control until granting the nation independence in 1902). The American poet Carl Sandburg, who had fought in Puerto Rico, attended a banquet in Paris, at which Americans toasted their homeland:

> The first one [said], "Here's to the United States, bounded on the north by Canada, on the south by Mexico, on the east by the Atlantic Ocean, on the west by the Pacific." The second speaker: "In view of what President McKinley has termed manifest destiny and in consideration of the vast new respon-

sibilities that loom before our country, I offer the toast: To the United States, bounded on the north by the North Pole, on the south by the South Pole, on the east by the rising sun, on the west by the setting sun." The third speaker: "With all due humility in view of the staggering tasks our country faces in the future, I would offer the toast: To the United States, bounded on the north by the Aurora Borealis, on the south by the Precession of the Equinoxes, on the east by Primeval Chaos, on the west by the Day of Judgment."

Sandburg's kicker: "It was a small war edging toward immense consequences."

• • • • •

BY THE TIME of the Spanish-American War, many markers of Chamorro culture of the pre-Magellan variety had been erased or altered beyond recognition. To see a traditional village (or an approximation of it, anyway) these days, you have to settle for a ticketed tourist attraction at the edge of Tumon. The day I went, a young man in a loincloth showed me around thatch-roof houses—here's where the chief lived, here's the school—and demonstrated how to open a coconut, before pointing me toward a display of local animals. The enclosure for the brown tree snake, I noted, was empty, which I pointed out with mild alarm, glancing around the overhanging branches, remembering the story I'd read months earlier about the plan to combat the snakes with Tylenol-laced dead mice. "Yeah, ours died," my guide said with a shrug. "We haven't found a new one yet. Everyone thinks they're, like, everywhere, but it's actually pretty rare that you see them." He added, "Okay, that's the end of the tour," and informed me that my ticket would get me a deal on drinks at the bar next door.

But after a few days spent gaping at the attractions and malls around Tumon, eating copious amounts of barbecue, and generally enjoying the cross-cultural people-watching ("Check out those *Russians* haggling over that *Guam, USA*, coffee mug with that *Japanese* shopkeeper!"), I started to feel restless, the high of Tourism Overload slowly wearing off.

I left Tumon and drove south. The buildings were lower and a bit shabbier, the highways lined with familiar chain stores and strip malls with coffee shops and storefront churches and dive bars. The terrain rolled gently with subdivisions and scrubby, wide-open fields and swaths of jungle. Every now and then I came across an old Spanish bridge or church, but the general impression was postwar Americana, modest yet aspirational, *The Brady Brunch* with a hint of *The Jetsons.* Small white ranch houses with some minor modernist grace note, like a rounded corner. A Citibank with a blue roof like a geodesic dome. Even the monument in Plaza de España marking Pope John Paul II's visit in 1981 felt like it dated to thirty years earlier, sinuous and white and rocket-like, like something off of Eero Saarinen's drafting table.

There was one recurring design motif, a stubby mushroom-looking shape that appeared in bus shelters, on political signs and corporate logos, even on the façade of the world's largest Kmart, which stands near the airport and where I went to buy a new hat to replace the one claimed by the *aitu* of American Samoa.* It was the same shape I'd seen on Maren's Guam

* The World's Largest Kmart looks exactly like you'd expect. I spent fifty-two minutes there, entering by walking through a triumphal arch of snacks emblazoned with the proclamation CELEBRATE FREEDOM WITH FRITO-LAY.

quarter: *Lattes* (or *latte stones*), pronounced "lottie" or "laddie." The traditional versions were made of basalt or limestone: a pillar (*haligi*) and a stubby capstone (*tasa*), the whole thing four to seven feet tall. From about 1,000 BC until Spanish colonization, they were literally the foundation of Chamorro culture, with key village structures built atop six or eight *lattes*. They were found only in Micronesia and have become the symbol of Guam.

Just south of Hagåtña, the commercial center, was the Latte of Freedom, which stands eighty feet tall. It is Guam's version of that American standby, the roadside attraction, albeit one with a deeper cultural significance than, say, New Jersey's Lucy the Elephant or Minnesota's World's Largest Ball of Twine Rolled by One Man. I snapped a handful of photos, carefully framing them to make it seem even larger and kitschier than it was—admitting to myself that maybe I wasn't done with being a clichéd tourist *quite* yet—before buying a ticket to enter. Inside the spacious *tasa*-cum-observation deck, a plaque explained that the structure opened in 2010, as a symbol of "the endurance of the belief that freedom is the indestructible and unquenchable desire of all people. The Latte of Freedom like the Statue of Liberty in the East . . . [stands] boldly as America's Western gatepost from Asia and the Pacific Rim."

For the United States, Guam, like all the other places the nation claimed or bought in its expansion efforts, was initially an advertisement to the world: *Look what we can do. We're an empire now, too!* But the Latte of Freedom, even as it celebrated Chamorro culture, also presented an updated view of the territories: they are living showcases of the American Experience.

• • • • •

In my visits to the USVI and American Samoa, I'd been intrigued by the long-ago battles and the ongoing political posturing, but largely compartmentalized these tales as one-off anecdotes, without fully understanding how they fit into the recurring themes of American territorial history. But when I started to read about Guam after the American takeover, there were so many parallels to what I'd heard before that the broader trends were suddenly obvious.

The pros: improvements to basic infrastructure, schools, and public health. The Navy built an ice plant and brought electricity and telephones. The earliest U.S. Census of Guam, in 1901, counted 9,630 Chamorros; by 1920, this population had increased 70 percent. The cons: a hefty amount of racism, efforts to change or forbid fundamental elements of the local culture, and efforts to prevent the territory from gaining political power. Guam's 1905 *Annual Report of the Governor* said:

> The location of Guam [makes] it of great and recognized strategic value to the U.S., as a point to be occupied and held for naval purposes alone. It has neither present nor prospective economic value and should not, then, excite the interest of other than scientific or military men.

Until the Guam Organic Act of 1950, Guamanians (the catchall term for people who live there, regardless of ethnicity) were nationals, not citizens, because the naval government was "of the opinion that the enactment of [citizenship] would be prejudicial to the best interests of both the United States and the native population of Guam." (In 1947, a congressional committee report stated that "the people of both Guam and American Samoa are entitled to full American citizenship and should be made citizens at the earliest possible date by Congress." The report later added, in direct answer to the strong lobbying from Guam, "In our opinion citizenship is long overdue and should be granted forthwith. Indeed, an apology is due the Guamanians for the long delay. . . .")

The Navy forbade the speaking of Chamorro in public places and—because the early governors were strict Protestants—dismantled the power of the Catholic Church, including sending every Spanish priest to Manila. The overall situation was bad enough that in 1901, thirty-two Chamorros petitioned Washington to end naval rule and establish a civilian government because, "It is not an exaggeration to say that fewer permanent guarantees of liberty and property rights exist now than under Spanish domain." At various points, governors outlawed smoking, drinking, and even whistling. Naval Governor William Gilmer, who took office in 1918, tried to ban interracial marriage, which was met with such protest that it led to his removal from office in 1920.*

The thing about secondhand colonies is that taking them over by force requires a two-step chain of logic. First: *The current colonizers are evil and oppressing the natives.* And second: *But the natives are a fundamentally inferior race, incapable of ruling themselves. This place should remain a colony, just with a new ruler: us.* It was a double whammy of racism, based specifically on the same belief in white Anglo-Saxon Protestant exceptionalism that guided the Insular Cases. "The American flag has not been planted in foreign soil to acquire more territory but for humanity's sake," William McKinley said on the campaign trail in 1900.

• • • • •

* Gilmer was a special one. His other orders included one to outlaw "dancing the fandango" after ten p.m.

In 1917, Guam was thrust into another war, and again its role was that of an offbeat footnote: this was where the first American shots of World War I were fired. The German naval ship SMS *Cormoran* had been interned at Apra Harbor since coming in to refuel in August 1914, just a few weeks after the war started in Europe, at a time when the United States was still officially neutral but diplomatic relations with Germany were already strained. The ship and its crew remained in port without incident until the United States declared war on Germany on April 6, 1917 (on Guam, it was already April 7), and the small U.S. naval force on Guam fired two shots across the bow of the *Cormoran* as they attempted to seize it. The captain agreed to surrender the men but not the vessel, and in short order the Germans set off explosives to sink the *Cormoran*. Seven crew members drowned as they swam to shore; the other three hundred fifty or so survived and were taken prisoners of war.

After World War I, life continued apace on Guam, with continuing Americanization, but the neighborhood was changing. Guam is the southernmost of the fifteen islands in the Mariana archipelago, the rest of which had been controlled by Germany prior to the war, but were ceded after the conflict to Japan—a new empire on the rise.

By the 1930s, Japan's aspirations and expansion efforts were starting to make the rest of the world nervous. Their version of manifest destiny was the "Greater East Asia Co-Prosperity Sphere," spreading across East Asia and the islands of Micronesia. Japan transformed Guam's Mariana Islands neighbors Saipan, Rota, and Tinian into bustling agricultural hubs and military bases, and invaded mineral-rich Manchuria, prompting a League of Nations reprimand in 1933. In response, the

Japanese delegates walked out in a statement-making huff. As tensions grew through the rest of the decade, Japan knew that the small Pacific islands, spread across thousands of miles of ocean, formed a strategic chain. To win a war would require claiming nearly every link. This time, Guam would not be a mere footnote.

On Guam there were resources, there were harbors for naval fleets, there were the strips of land for runways. In an update of Alfred Mahan's empire-building guidance, Japanese Lieutenant General Yoshitsugu Saito observed, "There is no hope of victory in places where we do not have control of the air."

Guam was a critical gap in Japan's chain and a nexus for American naval communications and airplane refueling. On December 8, 1941, hours after the attacks on Pearl Harbor, Japanese bombers based on nearby Saipan began air raids on Guam. The next day, a fleet of Japanese Navy vessels arrived with nearly 6,000 troops, easily overwhelming the U.S. forces, which consisted of some 125 Marines and a Chamorro Insular Guard of 84. Naval Governor George McMillin surrendered the island. Guam and the Aleutian islands of Attu and Kiska were the only parts of the United States to fall to Axis control during World War II.

• • • • •

As I drove around the southern end of the island, I spotted a sign reading TALOFOFO FALLS PARK/YOKOI'S CAVE, which I'd heard was a particularly notable tourist trap. I couldn't resist.

I took a hard right onto a bumpy road that led into the jungle, and then to a broad parking lot in front of a long shed-like building with a faux-castle façade. It was a broiler of a day, and the instant I emerged from the air-conditioned bubble of the car, my skin cells resigned themselves to melanoma.

I bought a ticket and entered the grounds, greeted by a handful of amusement-park attractions, including bumper cars and spinning teacups, none of them in use, advertised with hand-painted cartoon characters that may or may not have violated certain Disney trademarks. There were only two or three other people around, plus a couple of wild pigs poking around in the bushes.

I walked on to a shaded area with a fenced-in garden. Through the vegetation, I caught a fleeting, veiled glimpse of some sculptures, and it looked like an area of tranquillity and repose. The sign on the gate read:

ATTENTION
Only 19 yrs. and Older
May Enter the Love Land

Hold on, I thought. *Is this* . . .

My question trailed off as I saw the first sculpture, a man about to drop his trousers. The next was a woman pulling down her top. I followed the path and one at a time, from behind each tree or bush, the statues revealed themselves—in every possible way. There were twenty or thirty statues in all, doing things to themselves, with others, and in threesomes, often performing sexual contortions that defied all laws of physics and real-life possibilities of anatomy. Some of the statues had bulldog heads. I've never seen a more compelling ad for abstinence.

But as they added up, they became less droll and more wearying in their efforts to enthrall and titillate. The next stop was the Ghost House, and after a couple of minutes with its motion-activated lurching mannequins, fake blood, and creepy sound effects, I'd had enough. This time, I didn't even have any snarky comments to make, and I thought, finally, *All right, I've reached my limit for quirk and kitsch*—for real this time.

I could feel my energy draining away in the midday heat as I boarded a gondola and rode over a waterfall and down into a small valley, where hand-painted signs pointed to a museum that told the story of Guam. There were a few rooms of dioramas, a half step more lifelike than the Ghost House, depicting Chamorro settlement and Spanish conquest and World War II. One showed a Japanese soldier, gaunt and shirtless and alone in the jungle, one Sergeant Shoichi Yokoi.

Japan's occupation of Guam lasted until August 1944, when American troops came back in full force and reclaimed the island. As the fighting wound down, thousands of Japanese soldiers fled into the jungle, among them Yokoi. A piece of paper taped to the glass told his story:

> Shoichi Yokoi went into hiding with two other men, Shichi Mikio and Nakawa Sato, [who both] died around 1964 from starvation. Alone for eight years, Yokoi was discovered by two hunters . . . on January 24, 1972. Yokoi survived 28 years . . . eating rats, frogs, snails, shrimp, coconuts, and tropical fruit from the area.

Without even realizing what I was doing, I raised a hand to the paper and underlined the words "28 years."

Outside the museum, a narrow path threaded through the jungle, and led to a clearing with a Buddhist shrine and a tall stand of bamboo that splintered the midday sun, the patchwork light like a stained-glass window. Here, at the edge of the river, was Yokoi's hideout, dug into the earth. Actually, this was a replica—the original was destroyed by a storm some years ago—but this fact does nothing to diminish the quiet power of the sight. A breeze twisted through the bamboo and, despite the heat, a scattering of goose bumps rose on my arm.

Here was the square opening, a couple of feet across, and the two-and-a-half-meter shaft leading to Yokoi's cave. Picture him living down there, in a hole one meter high by three meters long, with a set of bamboo shelves at one end and a makeshift toilet at the other. Home. Picture him shimmying up his bamboo ladder every day, in search of food, water, light, pausing at the top before reentering a world he believed wanted him dead, a world he had to enter to survive. Every day. For twenty-eight years.

Yokoi was one of many Japanese holdouts after the war, as I later learned. For decades, even into the 1980s, people from Japan trekked around the jungles of Guam and other Pacific islands in search of remaining soldiers, leaving newspapers and flyers wrapped in plastic, in hopes that the soldiers would understand that the war was over. Some who saw these messages, or heard the news on their radios, assumed it was all a propaganda campaign; others, like Yokoi, believed it but were simply too afraid of what would happen to them if they surrendered. Yokoi was the last holdout soldier found on Guam, although others were found in the Philippines and Indonesia in 1974.

Given that the cave's surroundings have been transformed into one of the world's most superlatively odd amusement parks—built to entertain the pilgrims who come to pay their respects to this story of perseverance—there was a bit of cognitive whiplash as I stood by the cave and reminded myself, *This is real*. The last traces of smart-aleck snickering from Love Land now crumpled into heartache.

I wasn't sure what to make of it, to bawl or to beam.

On the one hand: *The human capacity for fear of the Other is astonishing.*

But on the other hand: *Look at what he pulled off in spite of that. Let's hear it for the human capacity for survival under duress.*

• • • • •

While Japan was claiming its Pacific Islands, gearing up for war, the United States was doing the same. The Americans built runways and outposts on Wake Island, Midway Atoll, and Palmyra Atoll, in some cases in the guise of tourism. Wake Island, for example, was a stopover point for trans-Pacific commercial flights, primarily by Pan Am, which also built a forty-eight-room hotel along with one of the world's first hydroponic gardens, to provide the hotel with fresh produce.

The Americans also made plans for three smaller Guano Islands, Howland, Baker, and Jarvis, all of which had long since been mined out and left to the birds. To officially reassert its claim to these islands, the United States needed to populate them, and the Navy decided, in an official memorandum, that "native Hawaiians be used for this purpose."

Government officials went to the Kamehameha School for Boys in Honolulu and asked, *How would you like an adventure? We'll pay you three dollars a day.* The stipulations were that they "know how to fish in the native manner, swim excellently and handle a boat, that they be disciplined, friendly, and unattached, that they could stand the rigors of a South Seas existence."

"They just said you're going to an island. They didn't say why, what, or where," recalled one of the men, Kenneth Bell, in the documentary *Under a Jarvis Moon*, produced by Honolulu's Bishop Museum in 2010, under the direction of Noelle Kahanu, granddaughter of one of the Jarvis Island colonizers, George Kahanu, Sr. The islands were a five-day trip from Honolulu, aboard the Coast Guard cutter *Itasca*. The men went in groups of five, rotating every couple of months. The youngest colonists were seventeen years old. Between 1935 and 1942, the United States sent more than one hundred thirty young men, most of them students or recent alums of the Kamehameha School and native Hawaiians, to be Hui Panalä'au—the colonists.

Paul Phillips, who was on Jarvis from July 1941 through February 1942, recounted arriving: "The islands did not look like posters of tropical islands, with lush vegetation and waterfalls. They were flat, barren. . . . There's scrub brush and birds, that's all."

At first, a couple of military personnel stayed on the islands, too, but they quickly burned out, unaccustomed to the hard work of island life. The Hawaiians did much better; some, like George Kahanu, signed on for a second round, for which there were no military representatives—it was just these young men, the birds, and the sea. When the settlements had been in place for a full year, the United States formally decreed to the world that it had sovereignty over these islands.

The men stayed in platform tents and later built shacks. They radioed weather reports to other Pacific outposts, collected plant life for the Bishop Museum in Honolulu, tended small stands of agricultural crops, studied birds, and fished—*lots* of fishing. They kept detailed logs, per their government mandate. Said one colonist: "I did the same thing yesterday and today. And tomorrow I'll do the same thing." But from photos, the general impression you get is of young men enthralled with island life, strapping and carefree, goofing around, cutting each other's hair, posing with massive fish and docile lobsters simply grabbed from the barrier reef, hanging out in shacks with pinup girls on the wall. With fresh water rationed for brushing teeth and drinking, showers and clothes-washing had to wait till rainfall, "so it was reasonable that we became a nudist colony," George Kahanu recalled.

In 1937, the men on Howland got a new assignment: Amelia Earhart was coming. The aviator planned to stop at their island during her circumnavigation of the world, which the United States used as an excuse for building a runway; the Navy denied any connection to war planning, though this was the long-term objective. On July 2, 1937, Earhart and her navigator, Fred Noonan, departed the Pacific atoll of Lae, bound for Howland. The men were eager to welcome their guests. They'd built an oil-drum shower for them to use and cleaned up a bedroom for Earhart, hanging "the first curtains on Howland," sent by one of the colonizers' mothers.

They waited.

They waited.

They waited.

Earhart and Noonan never arrived. Somewhere, somehow, on their way to Howland, they disappeared, their fate a mystery that is famously unsolved even today. The men on Howland were distraught.

Still, the Hui Panalā'au program on Howland, Baker, and Jarvis Islands was going well enough that in 1938, colonists were sent to two more islands, Canton and Enderbury. By 1940, Japanese ships began passing through the nearby waters, and the islanders filed reports. The Pacific was a sea of tension, war creeping ever closer.

On December 8, 1941, one day after the attack on Pearl Harbor, two waves of Japanese planes bombed Howland Island. "There was a formation of twelve planes," said one colonist, Elvin Matson. "They had big bombs that left craters about ten feet deep." Two of Matson's fellow colonists were killed. In the ensuing weeks, Howland, Jarvis, and Baker were all attacked repeatedly, while their food supplies dwindled quickly, the *Itasca* unable to reach them. It wasn't until February 9, 1942, that the colonists were evacuated. They arrived back in Honolulu to no fanfare: *Don't say anything,* they were told.

In July 1943, the U.S. officially set up a military base on Baker Island. The war was in full swing, and these tiny islands in the Pacific were some of the planet's most valuable real estate.

• • • • •

I WANTED to know more about the war history, so I emailed the Veterans of Guam Motorcycle Club. Actually, I'll be honest: I was hoping for a ride on a Harley. I'd passed on the Rambo Package at the gun range, but this seemed to offer more accessible, nonviolent swagger. If it came with a bonus history lesson, all the better.

So you can imagine my reaction when Tony Duenas, the club's president, and Carl Blas, the vice president, roared up to my hotel in . . . Carl's shiny white Ford F-150. The only black leather was Tony's fanny pack. At least they were wearing Harley-

Davidson T-shirts.* I did my best to hide my disappointment, and my mood brightened after a round of handshakes. They were Chamorro, supremely friendly, with a low-key rapport; both were former cops. Carl, who now worked in IT for the Guam Department of Education, was nonchalant in denim shorts and a casual-yet-professional crest of graying hair. Tony, retired, had more of a free-spirit vibe—hair pulled back into a ponytail, scraggly goatee, tattoo on the back of his hand, a police-badge belt buckle—and was also Mr. Hospitality, silently opening the truck door for me, as I got into the backseat. Carl switched on the radio, settling on "Tiny Dancer," and off we went.

There was a big blue charter bus outside our first stop, the Pacific War Museum, when we arrived. A docent greeted Carl with a familiar wave before returning to her spiel, in Japanese, to her tour group. Glass cases displayed decades-old Coke and sake bottles; rusted machine guns and bazookas and centuries-old samurai swords; forks and knives and bento boxes; landscape drawings sketched by Japanese prisoners of war on threadbare pieces of fabric.

As I looked at the exhibits, Carl excused himself—he wanted to find his grandfather's name on a list of prisoners of war. A minute later, as I studied a wall of historic photos, Tony appeared by my side and pointed to a grainy image of a young priest with glasses and a half smile, staring right at the camera. "That's my uncle," he said softly. The placard said his name was Father Jesus Baza Duenas.

On Guam, the legacy of war is personal, recent, and omnipresent.

* By Carl's estimate, there were more than a dozen motorcycle clubs on Guam, including "the Hogs, the *Hawgs*, the Legends, the Warriors . . ."

The United States has a general dearth of fresh battlefields, for which I'm truly grateful, but this can make it difficult for us to understand the full impact of war. You can tour Gettysburg or Fort McHenry; you can trace your fingers over a small-town plaque honoring the soldiers who didn't come home. But the horrors they commemorate are so distant in time or geography that they can feel like abstractions, with only metaphorical impact on here and now. We remember, then we move on with the day's agenda.

All of Guam was a battleground. War's sear is inescapable, its wounds not fully healed.

There are official markers across the island, even in the parking lot outside the strip-mall coffee shop where we'd had breakfast. "There used to be a couple of tanks next to it," Carl said, "but someone stole them and sold them for scrap metal." And there are unofficial reminders in the hidden stories all around you. At the War in the Pacific National Historical Park, a ranger warned me not to venture off-path, because there's still unexploded ordnance lying around; he handed me a brochure featuring a cartoon icon of an angry-faced bomb, with the caption "DO NOT TOUCH, KICK OR MOVE." Over the years, Carl and Tony have found swords and machine guns and other war relics in the jungle. As we drove, they swapped stories, until Carl said, "One time, I found a skeleton with a bullet hole through the skull." Thus ended the one-upmanship.

The Japanese gave Guam a new name, Omiya Jima, and instituted martial law. They cut off access to outside news, including details of the war, banned U.S. dollars and the use of English. They forced the Chamorros to sing patriotic songs praising Japan, and to dig tunnels and build fortifications. The new troops overwhelmed the island: six thousand soldiers needed to be housed (so they simply claimed every building in Hagåtña) and supplied (leading to shortages for the local residents of food and other basic needs, including shoes, meaning they had to go barefoot and rates of hookworm infection spiked).

The war in the Pacific shifted in momentum, beginning with the Americans' victory at Midway in June 1942 and then at Guadalcanal in February 1943, and continued as they seized more islands, with the critical addition of Saipan—Japan's colony about 140 miles north of Guam—on July 9, 1944. Knowing an American invasion of Guam was imminent, the Japanese forced some 80 percent of Chamorros into concentration camps in the jungle, with no buildings, not even an outhouse. Others were simply massacred; in the villages of Faha and Tinta, forty-six Chamorros were killed with hand grenades.

The Japanese feared that the Chamorros would help the Americans, and with good reason. They'd been resisting their occupiers all along, including passing along war news in soap-paper wrappers. A popular Chamorro ditty, banned by the Japanese, was called "Uncle Sam, Won't You Please Come Back to Guam?"

Father Duenas, Tony's uncle, was the acting head of the Catholic Church on Guam and a prominent leader of the Chamorro resistance, proclaiming, "I answer only to God, and the Japanese are not God." He was one of several people who helped six U.S. servicemen in hiding, most famously Radioman First Class George Tweed, who survived thirty-two months in the jungle.* For this, Father Duenas was tortured and then beheaded, along with two other men, on July 12, 1944.

Eight days later, the liberation of Guam began when Chamor-

* Tweed recounted his experiences in his memoir *Robinson Crusoe, USN,* which was adapted into the 1962 film *No Man Is an Island*—which was shot in the Philippines, with Filipinos speaking Tagalog as the stand-in for Chamorros who primarily spoke English.

ros from the village of Merizo being held at a camp used a Springfield rifle they'd secreted away to kill six Japanese guards. One day later, July 21, 1944, Uncle Sam came back to Guam, in the form of fifty-five thousand troops. The Japanese had predicted that the Americans would arrive at Asan Beach and were well prepared when this turned out to be correct, setting up positions in fortifications and caves that they, and the Chamorros they forced to help them, had dug into the hills above the waterfront.

There's a monument on the top of those hills now. Carl, Tony, and I drove up there and silently surveyed the landscape. Even without mortars and machine-gun rounds raining down, this is tough terrain, hills on fractalling hills, a scrubland snapshot of a hurricane-churned sea. Plus, it was crazy-hot. I was wearing a quick-dry T-shirt and shorts, and *I* could barely move. I tried to put myself in the military-issue boots of the soldiers hunkered down in caves or arriving in amphibious vehicles, but of course I couldn't begin to imagine it—the uniform, the gear, the weapons, the weight of the world on your back as you scramble as best you can over this impossible terrain, surrounded by an apocalypse of explosions and carnage and expected to do your part to add to it, because the very fate of your nation depends on it.

Japanese Second Lieutenant Yasuhiro Yamashita was on a hill near where we were now, and later described the scene: "All over, bodies were being blown up as the cannon shells fell. The earth and sand buried the soldiers."

• • • • •

WAR WASN'T the only part of the day's agenda. We stopped for a leisurely lunch at Jeff's Pirates Cove, with a pirate-themed gift shop up front and postcard-worthy ocean views out back and a little history museum and what Carl claimed were the best burgers on the island. They came with a skull and crossbones branded on the bun. Carl's radio switched to "Piano Man" and then a somber announcement that a typhoon was heading for Guam in a few days, followed by a cheery ad for Chamorro immersion summer camps—from food to dance to language to the ubiquitous *latte* stone iconography, Chamorro culture was having a minor renaissance. We followed a convoy of tour buses to Two Lovers Point, an overlook with 340-foot cliffs, where Chamorro legend has it that a young couple with a forbidden romance once jumped to their deaths and where, Carl said casually, he used to practice rappelling when he was on the SWAT team. A beaming Japanese couple were taking wedding photos while dozens of their compatriots snapped photos of the view and bought souvenirs from the gift shop near the cliff's edge.

But the war always crept into the narrative. The museum at Jeff's Pirates Cove was largely dedicated to Yokoi. At Latte Stone Park, near a group of the eponymous columns, there was a low cliff with a cave carved into its base—yet another bunker dug by Chamorros ordered to work under threat of death. More than once, our tour took us along one of the island's main drags, Marine Corps Drive.

And, everywhere, planning was in full swing for the celebration of Liberation Day—the sixtieth anniversary was just days away. There would be a Liberation Parade featuring seven liberators—soldiers who'd been here in 1944—and a Liberation Queen. Out past the airport, the Liberation Carnival was already under way, with a Ferris wheel and a whirling "Super Twister" ride and aisles of games (the ring-toss, the pop-a-balloon-with-a-dart) and classic county-fair foods like corn-on-the-cob and barbecue and fish balls. Signs reading HAPPY LIBERATION! and GENERATIONS OF SERVICE AND SACRIFICE served as a constant reminder of the carnival's origins, and the site's temporary streets had occasion-worthy names: Courage Circle and Liberation Walkway intersected near the kiddie train. For their part, the Veterans of Guam Motorcycle Club always marked Liberation Day by helping to plant thousands of flags in the ground at Asan, honoring the American troops and Chamorros killed during the war.

As we drove, other wars, too, kept popping into the conversation, wars that didn't take place here but have left a lasting impact nonetheless. In the hills on the south side of the island, we stopped at a memorial plaque honoring the more than seventy men from Guam who died serving in the Vietnam War, including a buddy of Carl's named David Flores.

"I saw him at training in February" of 1972, Carl said as he ran his fingers over his friend's name. "He said, 'I'll see you over in Vietnam!' He flew over there in May and was killed on his very first mission."

Growing up, Carl watched lots of Audie Murphy and John Wayne movies and wanted to be a Marine. He enlisted and became a top sniper. All the other units would send their best men to compete against him, he said, and he always won. "I had to learn how to shoot when I was little," he explained. "My dad said, 'Go get a bird!' If I didn't get the bird, I didn't eat." Carl's mother died of tuberculosis when he was a kid, leaving his father to raise Carl and his four siblings. Before she died, Carl's mother made his father promise that their children would learn to speak English, not Chamorro.

Carl doled out the stories here and there, as I pieced them together to form a cohesive narrative—he may have seemed like a jovial sitcom dad but he was as close to an action hero as I'd ever met. He was also an expert welder, he mentioned in passing, so he made the SWAT team's big battering ram himself, with a smiley face on the end. Carl was proud of his family's history of U.S. military service: his grandfather served in World War I, his father in World War II, and now his son, Carl, Jr., lived in New Jersey and served in the Coast Guard.

All territories, not just Guam, have duel legacies as scenes of conflict and home to particularly high numbers of American troops. Charlotte Amalie on Saint Thomas and San Juan, Puerto Rico, were key refueling ports and bases for patrols combating German U-boats operating in the Caribbean. In American Samoa, U.S. Marines trained locals and set up huge guns (which are still in place) to protect Pago Pago Harbor, anticipating that the fighting might come to the island. There were no battles, but one Japanese mortar round landed on the island, hitting a store run by Japanese immigrants. And in terms of service, American Samoans may have the highest rates of enlistment and casualties, but the people of Guam, the Northern Mariana Islands, and the U.S. Virgin Islands also serve and die at rates higher than residents of any state. In Guam and American Samoa, the rate is *three times* higher than the states; in the most recent wars, in Iraq and Afghanistan, Pacific islanders' casualty rate was six times that of service members from the states. In each territory, when you ask if someone knows anyone currently serving, you don't just hear about a cousin here and there, but long lists of siblings, aunts, uncles, best friends. There are more than twenty thousand members of the United States Armed Forces from the territories, and for many it's not just about opportunity but something deeper—there's a true pride in being part of their island's legacy in the armed forces. (Meanwhile, one in eight Guamanians is a veteran but, as a recent PBS report noted, the island "ranks dead last in per-capita spending on medical by the U.S. Department of Veterans Affairs.")

Past efforts by Guamanians to lobby for true congressional representation have sometimes been rebuffed by Congress with an inversion of a familiar saying: "No representation without taxation." That is: *You don't pay federal income tax, so you don't get a congressperson*. But even beyond the fact that territory residents do pay various other federal taxes (Social Security, Medicare, import and export taxes, commodity taxes), "we also pay a blood tax," Carl said.

Carl's own service seemed to have made him all the more attuned to the pain of war for soldiers on all sides.

"If you think about it, Doug, the Japanese soldiers had mothers and fathers, too," he said when we visited the site of the Japanese last stand on Guam, which is now the South Pacific Memorial Park. It's a grassy expanse tucked between swaths of jungle and two white modernist structures: a chapel with a curved, pagoda-like roof, and a fifty-foot tower designed to look like two hands pressed together in prayer.

"Most locals don't even know about this place," Carl said. "I haven't been back here since I was a kid."

The Americans had reclaimed most of the island by the beginning of August 1944 and the Japanese set up one final defensive line here, in an area called Yigo, and forced Chamorros to dig a bunker. On August 11, the Americans used four-hundred-pound blocks of TNT to implode it, killing the sixty Japanese soldiers inside. Four days later Guam was officially back under American control. More than seventeen hundred American troops died during the twenty-six-day Battle of Guam, along with more than fifteen thousand Japanese. If you count Guam as still being part of the USA at this point (despite the Japanese occupation), it was the deadliest battle ever on American soil, with more fatalities than the Pearl Harbor attacks or the Civil War's infamously bloody battles at Antietam and Gettysburg. Nearly twelve hundred Chamorros died during the years of Japanese occupation and the Battle of Guam. (If you think about the standard narrative of the war in the Pacific, it's always USA versus Japan, with little acknowledgment that many of these islands were already *populated* by people caught in the middle.)

The South Pacific Memorial Park was established in 1970, a joint Japanese-Chamorro project. There's no ill will here, just a mutual sorrow. Carl pointed to the sharply curved base of the tower. "We used to bike up that slope. We didn't know what it was. We were just kids."

The air was still and there was no one else around and I was at a total loss for words.

"Just like these soldiers," Carl continued. "Kids. Their families never saw them again. They just know they're somewhere on Guam."

"A lot of them don't even know that," Tony said. "They just know their sons were fighting and didn't come back."

The ache in his voice was palpable. These two ex-cops, bona fide badasses, bike-club leaders, were on the verge of tears. From the jungle, I could hear what sounded like a dog barking. "That's a *frog*," Carl said.

One grave marker had a can of Budweiser and a can of Coke placed on its base, with a votive candle between them. The brass plaque on top had several divots.

"Someone must've done that with a pickax," Carl said.

There was a small fire in Tony's eyes. He shook his head. "Crazy people. Got no respect."

Carl slowly turned around, scanning the monument, the graves, the hillside that once held the Japanese bunker. "It's real sad," he said. "But it's good they keep the park up so nice so we can remember."

• • • • •

There was a question that was starting to bother me: How, when, and why did the issue of the territories fall out of the conversation back in the states?

Back around 1900, of course, the issue of overseas expansion, and the very existence of long-term territories, had been an issue of considerable national debate, at times the *central* issue of debate. Since then, from Guam's battlefields and beyond, the territories—even the tiny islands—had played an unmistakably important role in American history and in making the USA what it is today, a global power. An empire. And this empire had been assembled with purpose; contrary to what *Time* magazine publisher Henry Luce wrote in his seminal 1941 article "The American Century," it was not something that happened "blindly, unintentionally, accidentally and really in spite of ourselves." There was plenty of bumbling, to be sure, but also lots of planning and goal-setting, for the very reason that the territories were firmly on the national agenda.

Today, people in the territories still ponder their relationship to the United States, constantly. For them, the question of what it means to be American is not an academic abstraction but a matter of everyday import.

But for those of us back in the states, at some point, the territories seemingly just disappeared. In the introduction to his 2013 book *The Smithsonian's History of America in 101*

Objects, author Richard Kurin—the Smithsonian Institution's undersecretary for history, art, and culture—uses the steering wheel of the USS *Maine* to illustrate that sometimes an artifact's "meaning as a museum object changes." Kurin writes that initially the steering wheel "was put in a place of honor in the museum as a sacred, patriotic object. Over the years, the fervor that fueled its treatment subsided, and now it is relegated to distant storage." Unintentionally illustrating this point, in Kurin's own book the several pages of maps in the endpapers omit the territories.

So how did the territories go from a subject that was "impossible to avoid," as the *Atlantic* put it in 1898, to an utter afterthought? I was starting to develop an answer, or at least the *beginnings* of an answer. There were a few different factors on my list so far.

First, each territory, and even the Minor Outlying Islands, held some particular strategic importance for the U.S. military and commercial interests: coaling stations, plantations, other resources, control of the sea. But in large part, expansion was an end unto itself, a way of flexing the national muscles. When William McKinley won the 1900 election, granting a tacit approval for the nation to take the path of empire, he was given no particular mandate on what to *do* with that empire. The point was simply to create it, to check that box and say, *Yes, we are an empire, a global power,* without much concern of the follow-up question of, "Now what?"

But soon the United States did, in fact, have to consider what to make of its latest possessions, and here we come to the second factor: the Insular Cases. The Supreme Court took the American public's broadly held view of the territories' residents as "alien races" and put it into *law.* In doing so, the court applied this label not just to particular to ethnic groups (which would be bad enough) but to entire landmasses—*everyone* who lived in these places would be treated differently—which underscored the idea that the territories were, in fact, foreign rather than American. This designation largely continues today. To give just one example, *This American Life*, the popular public radio show, has very rarely seen fit to document *these* American lives; it has aired more than five hundred episodes spanning the globe while only touching down in a territory once, as part of a story about drug addicts from Puerto Rico living on the streets of Chicago.* Public radio's internationally focused show *The World*, however, has featured the territories many times.†

That categorization—"they are not us"—leads straight to factor three: competition for attention. The Spanish-American War had helped put the United States on the global stage, and soon there were much bigger battles, literally, than what was going on in these small islands. The United States became more deeply involved than ever before in goings-on across the globe, at the same time that the ever-growing mass media was covering ever more stories in ever more distant places. The territories were overshadowed by the competition. These "foreign" islands were no longer the most interesting foreign lands.

• • • • •

EVEN AS GUAM is often forgotten back in the states, its strategic importance for the United States hasn't waned.

More than three-quarters of the island's houses were destroyed in the war. Afterward, when rebuilding began in earnest, the

* The only other *This American Life* story I found with a territory connection was one about a family that moved from American Samoa to Alaska, where the story took place.

† The best source of information I've found for the Pacific territories, aside from their own media outlets, is Radio New Zealand.

U.S. military started claiming land (farms, homes, you name it) for building its own bases or just to hold in reserve for future potential use. This being a U.S. territory, regular federal laws didn't apply, a fact that confounded U.S. congresspeople in a 1946 hearing—"a very unusual thing," commented one.

In 1950—the same moment when Guam's lot seemed to be improving with its Organic Act and full citizenship—the Navy decreed that the whole island was effectively a base, and no one was allowed on or off without a security clearance. The war was over, yes, but the Cold War was in full swing—one of those new international distractions that overshadowed the territories, while also keeping the U.S. military on guard, eager to maintain its strategic outposts.

The travel ban was lifted in 1962, which was when tourism started to rise, but today the military still holds one-third of the land on Guam. Some of it is the Andersen Air Force Base and some is the Naval Base Guam at Apra Harbor, which includes the Polaris Point submarine base (along with the westernmost point in the United States, which is called Point Udall, just like the easternmost point on Saint Croix, although the two namesakes are not the same person but brothers Stewart and Mo, both former Arizona congressmen).* But much of this land is neither actively used by the military nor owned by it—the military simply *controls* the land, and no one else can do anything with it, because the military might, at some future point, want it.

* Aside from the USA's northernmost point, in Alaska, all extreme points are in the U.S. territories and, in their own way, fit their surroundings: the easternmost point, in the USVI, is a well-known tourist attraction; Tutuila's southernmost point requires bushwhacking on *'aiga* land to access; and the westernmost point, on Guam, is on a Navy base, off-limits to the public.

The connection to the land on Guam might not be quite as profound as in American Samoa, but it's still plenty strong. "When you meet people, they'll always ask, 'What village are you from? What's your last name?' And they'll try to create a connection," a woman named Regine Biscoe Lee told me when I met her and her friend Josh Tyquiengco at a Tumon coffee shop.

Josh's family had lived on the southern part of the island "for generations, and they've never moved. The idea is that this land belongs to me, but also I belong to the land. And eventually, when I die, I'm going to become part of this land."

When it comes to challenging military control of the land, Regine said, some people, especially *older* people, say, "'Oh, we don't really impose . . . we don't want to ask them for too much.' And you're like, 'No, we *need* to ask them, we need to tell them that these are rights that all Americans enjoy, and if we don't ask for it, then we're never going to get it!' But that's totally contrary to traditional Chamorro culture. But that's just embarrassing. It's called *mamolo*—like, you're embarrassed to ask for too much."

Land use is only going to get more contentious on Guam in the coming years, as the military prepares to move some five thousand Marines—along with an estimated thirteen hundred dependents—from Okinawa to Guam. Most local elected officials support it as a boost to a struggling economy reliant on the military and tourism. But it's a tenacious debate. Will the local infrastructure—the one hospital, the roads, the schools—be overwhelmed? If you add *more* infrastructure, how will that impact the environment? The island is not large; its land area is smaller than the city of Chicago.

"If you're an individual in the military, we'll welcome you with open arms, on a person-to-person basis," Regine said, adding that her husband was a Marine. "But the idea of hundreds and thousands of them, we're like, 'Sorry, we can't.' "

When the discussion started, in 2005, the plan was for eight thousand Marines and a new bombing range at the ancient village of Pagat, an important historic site. In 2009, a group of young Guamanians formed an opposition movement, called We Are Guåhan (using the Chamorro word for the island). I met one of We Are Guåhan's cofounders, a young lawyer named Ana Won Pat-Borja, for coffee near the end of my time on Guam, during an on-and-off pre-typhoon rain. She had long black hair and an air of apprehension about meeting with me, but Mars was a mutual friend and, it seemed, had talked her into it. We Are Guåhan, she said, had initial success with a lawsuit that pressured the military to do further studies on the impact of its firing range. Ultimately the military moved the location from Pagat to Ritidian—a wildlife refuge, another vulnerable place.

"It's really just this procedural dance," Ana said with a sigh. Time and again, "we're dancing around the same issue of whether or not we have a voice in [what happens with the land] and knowing full well that all we can do is respond and not expect particular action to be taken."

Environmental studies conducted by or on behalf of the military are so numerous that they have their own section at the public library. Studies don't mean change.

Ana felt the same way about the political status debate, which had heated up with the talk of military buildup but where change was also elusive. Completely severing ties with the United States was unlikely and had essentially no support, Ana said, but she favored becoming a separate, autonomous nation with strong ties to the United States, a so-called "freely associated state," which had some precedent in other Pacific islands. But overall, she said, altering the political status wasn't a big priority for most Guamanians. There was a political-status referendum in 1976, with "status quo with improvements" getting 51 percent of the vote, while statehood got 21 percent and independence got 5 percent.

"When the economy is hurting and people have other things to deal with, they don't want to talk about self-determination. They want to talk about how gas is almost five dollars a gallon right now," Ana said. We Are Guåhan had fractured, too, and she was no longer involved. "The thing is, it's rough running a movement," she said with a resigned laugh.

But the military buildup and land use were such widespread concerns that even Carl and Tony—hardly activists—had their reservations.

"Everything you see over here to the left is Tony's family's land," Carl said as we drove toward Anderson Air Force base at the northern end of the island. That is, they owned it but couldn't use it. President Obama told the military that they had to start returning any land they weren't actively using, but the order has been disregarded, Carl added.

"We're still loyal and grateful [to the United States]," Carl said, "because otherwise we'd be speaking Japanese or Spanish. But look over here." He pointed to the right. "All this used to be houses but the military kicked them off." A short distance later, he pointed out a McDonald's the Air Force was building on the edge of its base. "Why don't you give us our land and *we'll* build the McDonald's?"

Tony nodded toward to the edge of the base and said dryly, "But they do have a nice fence, though."

"This is why Guam is so important," Carl said. "You got the B-52s here. You can hit Japan, China, Afghanistan."

This was part of the reason for the buildup: the Department of Defense had recently announced an "Asia-Pacific Shift." Given the USA's long dealings with Europe and the political and cultural weight of the East Coast, it's easy to forget that, thanks in large part to the territories and Hawaii, the United States is a *Pacific* nation even more than an Atlantic one. But now the country's gaze is beginning to tack more firmly, more overtly, westward. There's one key reason for this: China. As an American official testified before the House Armed Services Committee in 2015, that nation's rising economy and military have "created a much more complex security environment in which we are now operating." At the same time, China's booming economy had expanded its middle and upper classes, and with these increased paychecks came, in part, a desire to travel—with Guam, USA, as an increasingly popular destination. Russian tourists, another up-and-coming market, had recently gotten visa waivers, and officials on Guam were talking about extending the same courtesy to Chinese tourists, too, in hopes of attracting even more. Guam was, in other words, simultaneously the USA's welcome mat and its heavily armed guardhouse, a tricky, burdensome dual identity.

• • • • •

The territories represent an offshoring of the American experience—recruiting soldiers, fighting battles, but also engaging in the soft diplomacy of tourism and greeting immigrants. Nearby countries look to the territories as a stand-in for the USA. That's the exact point of the Latte of Freedom: it is nothing less than a broadcast of American Exceptionalism and a representation of all the things the United States of America supposedly stands for. Representative democracy. Opportunity. Egalitarianism. Giant roadside attractions. Waffles with six inches of whipped cream on top.

This is the story we, as Americans, tell ourselves about Who We Are. It's a story to be proud of, a story with much truth. But as my travels through the territories were reminding me anew, you pull back the curtain on mythology at your own risk. The tourists and Americans who worship old-school cowboys would probably rather not know that these archetypes of ruggedness weren't as self-reliant or even as numerous as we like to think. As David Hamilton Murdoch details in *The American West: The Invention of a Myth*, Wild Bill was "a cold-blooded killer [and] Phoebe Anne Oakley Mozee was entirely the creation of show business," as was much of our modern-day conception of the Wild West. And even as I can't shake my fondness for Teddy Roosevelt—the Poe-quoting! the grizzled swagger! the national parks! the progressive reforms!—it's undeniable that his view of the territories was, well, racist: "The expansion of the peoples of white, or European, blood during the past four centuries has been fraught with lasting benefit to most of the peoples already dwelling in the lands over which the expansion took place." Roosevelt served as William McKinley's vice president until 1901, when McKinley was assassinated—and suddenly Teddy was the leader of the United States. When the time came to appoint a new Supreme Court justice in 1902, he had one specific litmus test: he would only choose someone who would uphold the Insular Cases. His appointee, Oliver Wendell Holmes, did just that.

"Myth cannot indefinitely act as a substitute for history," Murdoch says of the Wild West, arguing against the notion that "a democratic people's ability to order its society and government

. . . can only be managed by general subscription to a set of inventions."

Bit by bit, as a high-level picture of the territories had come into focus in my mind, a deeper, myth-busting reality was also taking form: First, the territories *matter*. You cannot write an honest master narrative of the United States of America without including the territories as key components. And you cannot write an honest master narrative of the territories without feeling acutely uncomfortable about the United States and its continuing struggles to live up to its own ideals.

In 1957, at the same time that Guam was off-limits for travel, a new case related to the territories, *Reid v. Covert*, came before the Supreme Court. And while the court's decision didn't overturn the Insular Cases, it chipped away at them, an acknowledgment of changing views about overseas possessions and colonialism. Justice Hugo Black, in his plurality opinion, undercut the very foundation of the Insular Cases:

> The concept that the Bill of Rights and other Constitutional protections against arbitrary government are inoperant when they become inconvenient or when expediency dictates otherwise is a very dangerous doctrine and if allowed to flourish would destroy the benefit of a written Constitution and undermine the basis of our government.

• • • • •

THE WARNINGS of the typhoon became increasingly dire and ubiquitous as the clock ticked down—it was just a day away. I stopped into a souvenir shop for some postcards, and paused for a moment to watch the television behind the counter; the chipper newscaster read a statement: "The governor's office advises that pregnant women at thirty-eight weeks or later should get admitted to Guam General."

The storm was expected to make landfall right around the time I was supposed to fly out to my next stop, Saipan, about 140 miles north and out of harm's way. I called the airline and got rebooked on an earlier flight, leaving late that night. I would beat the typhoon.

In the meantime, I had one last thing to check off my list. "Doug, you *have* to see a sunset here," Mars had told me. "I've seen my share of nice sunsets around the world, and Guam's are up there at the top."

I hadn't seen one yet—somehow I'd always been indoors or otherwise occupied—but now the skies briefly cleared up, giving me one last window of opportunity.

I drove over to a park in Hagåtña and parked by the Paseo Stadium, as two baseball teams took the field. High above the parking lot buzzed a drone with flashing red and green lights; nearby, five or six old men played cards in a little picnic shelter. I sat at the water's edge and a couple of long outrigger canoes glided by, each with five paddlers in perfect sync and corporate logos on the sleek hulls. Up the coast, the hotels of Tumon stood sentry on the waterfront, and I could picture the streets filling up with tourists, out for an evening of shopping or shooting, maybe both.

The sky churned through slow-motion pyrotechnics, swaths of gold, streaks of purple, and a diorama of clouds, one of each kind: the long, wispy ones; the perfectly formed claymation ones; the fuzzy balls sheared from a sheep. It was everything Mars had promised.

Far-off, unintelligible yelling broke my reverie. It got louder, closer, but I couldn't quite make out the words until I finally saw the source: a group of trim young men jogging through the park, belting out a call-and-response:

"HUH!"

"I can't hear you!"

"HUH!"

"A little bit louder!"

"One, two, three, four, UNITED STATES MARINE CORPS!"

Chapter 4

LAND OF OPPORTUNITY

The Northern Mariana Islands

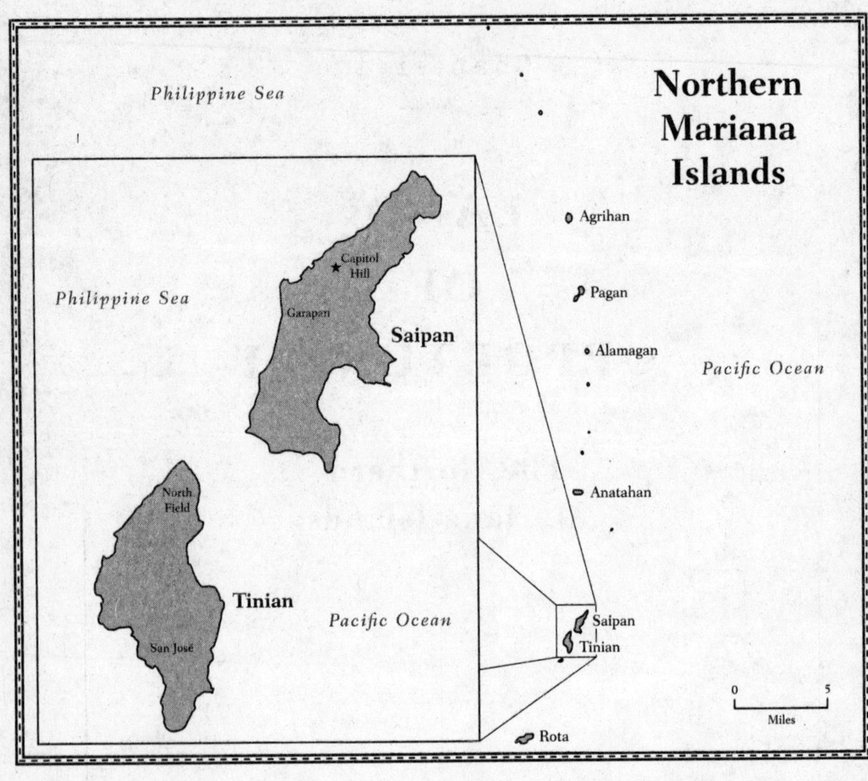
Northern
Mariana
Islands
Philippine Sea
Philippine Sea
Capitol
Hill
Garapan
Saipan
North
Field
Tinian
San José
Pacific Ocean
Agrihan
Pagan
Alamagan
Pacific Ocean
Anatahan
Saipan
Tinian
Rota
0
5
Miles

The U.S. territories attract a particular breed of outsiders: dreamers, dropouts, eccentrics, self-made men and women who find these places fertile ground for their schemes or their escapes. There are the community-oriented plotters like John Wasko in American Samoa, along with the straight-out-of-fiction types like the Contessa of Saint Croix. As Carl and Tony drove me around, Tony idly read the news on his phone and found a headline reading "Russian Hacker Found on Guam"—the man, it turned out, was "one of the world's most prolific traffickers of stolen financial information."

In my first few days on Saipan—the capital and largest of the Northern Mariana Islands—I met so many outsiders with big dreams that I began to wonder if there was some sort of governmental pitch: *Remake Yourself in the Northern Mariana Islands.*

There was a Jamaican named Walt Goodridge, a former civil engineer for New York City's Port Authority, who moved to Saipan somewhat impulsively in 2006. Trim and eternally smiling, he'd carved out a niche as a self-described "nomadic minimalist vegan" entrepreneurism coach, self-help author, and tour guide. Laurie Peterka, an energetic Californian in beaded flip-flops and a jade pendant, had lived here since 1993, when she was twenty-six. She belonged to the local Rotary Club and had built a career as a local business consultant.

"One of the great things about Saipan is the ability to keep reinventing yourself over and over," a man named Brad Ruszala told me when I met him for drinks one night at Godfather's, an agreeably divey bar in Garapan, Saipan's tourist district. Brad moved to Saipan from the states in 2003 to work for Homeland Security, before becoming a sports reporter for the local newspaper, a radio host, and then a television anchor. He looked the part, with short hair and a crisp collared shirt.

On Saipan, Brad said, "I don't feel like a fish being asked to climb a tree"—he felt free to be himself. "I live the life of a movie star here." For a while, he hosted Girls' Night Out at the local Hard Rock Café. Brad met his wife on Saipan, and now, he said, beaming, they have two *awesome* kids. He leaned back in the booth, with the carefree air of a man fully satisfied with, and a bit shocked by, his lot in life. For a few moments, he looked around the room, soaking it up. Godfather's was decorated with an Al Capone poster, newspaper clippings on the wall; there was a rock band playing in the corner and a full house of mainlanders.

The Commonwealth of the Northern Mariana Islands (everyone just says "the CNMI") is the least populous of all the territories, with some fifty-four thousand people, about 90 percent of them on Saipan, and nearly all of the rest on neighboring Tinian and Rota, with just a handful on the eleven northern islands. Because the territory is so small and close-knit, Brad said, one person can have a huge impact on the community. Heck, he and the governor were connected on LinkedIn, he added with a touch of amazement. Brad had organized a triathlon, so now he was the triathlon guy. His friend Angelo Villagomez was "the Beautify the CNMI guy," thanks to an environmental cleanup program he'd initiated. If you want to get civically involved, you can do it here, Brad said. "I came out here and learned how to be a better American."

A lawyer Brad knew stopped by the table. She twirled a string of pink plastic beads, casually mentioned a case she was working on, then threw back a vodka shot with a whoop.

The new arrivals who thrive—in the territories as anywhere—are the ones who immerse themselves in the community and the culture, like Brad and Walt and Laurie.

If you're an outsider moving to Saipan, it's probably not going to work out if you "come expecting to change the island," Angelo Villagomez later told me. You have to just go with the flow and let the island change *you*. "Most of the people who do come are either saviors or savers," hoping either "to convert people to Christianity or save the environment or rescue the puppies . . . or they're there for the hookers."

Angelo laughed ruefully. He had a mop of black hair that fell over his ears and a tattoo on one of his thick forearms, with several bands of geometric patterns. He'd already told me about one of Saipan's most infamous arrivals, billionaire Larry Hillblom, the *H* of the shipping company DHL, who moved here to avoid federal income tax, got himself appointed to the CNMI Supreme Court, and—as detailed in James D. Scurlock's 2012 book *King Larry*—used Saipan as a jumping-off point for his trips to brothels in Vietnam and the Philippines, before dying, in 1995, when he crashed his vintage Seabee into the ocean. Not all self-made men have triumphant endings.

"A lot of people move to Saipan and Saipan burns them, hard core," Angelo said. He, Walt, Laurie, and many others with whom I spoke bemoaned a blog published in the early 2000s called Saipan Sucks. Its initially anonymous author was eventually revealed to be a commonwealth attorney general, a mainland transplant who only lasted a few years and whose writing painted a coarse, sarcastic picture of an incurably corrupt island. He got burned, Angelo said. "I don't know the story of what happened to him. Don't care." For a while, Saipan Sucks dominated the search-engine results for anyone looking for online information about the island; along with other local bloggers, Angelo made a concerted effort on his website, the Saipan Blog, to tout the island's natural beauty and hospitality.

"Saipan is the most welcoming place on the planet," Angelo had told me in an email before I arrived, and every day I met people who proved him right. And the landscape really was gorgeous, with a sky so pristinely blue that it felt manufactured and seemingly endless flame trees, ablaze with bright orange flowers.

But there was also an unmistakable sense that all was not well on Saipan, a disquieting feeling that the whole island had been burned, hard core.

• • • • •

Garapan was a smaller, more down-on-its-luck version of Tumon on Guam. There were places to rent a Mustang or shoot an M16 or buy a Rolex. There were duty-free malls and a high-rise Westin and the Hard Rock Café where Brad used to host Girls' Night Out. There were gift shops, a small wax museum, and a short pedestrian promenade called the Paseo de Marianas. And on posters and shop-window stickers around Garapan, a bit of whimsy: the local tourism logo, an anime-esque panda with a golden horn, called a Saipanda. (It's a punning nod to the Japanese visitors, who have long been vital to the local economy. Phonetically, "Sai" means rhino in Japanese and "panda" means panda, but split the word differently and it becomes "Saipan-da," or, roughly, *It's Saipan!*)

But for every Standard Touristville storefront, there were another one or two, or entire buildings, that were long-shuttered and starting to crumble. Even Club Happiness was boarded up. And many of the operating businesses betrayed a decidedly unsavory side of the island: sad-looking poker rooms with happy-sounding names (U Luck Poker, High Roller Poker), massage parlors whose signs advertised curiously late hours, karaoke clubs where, as in American Samoa, singing was not really the main attraction. Every evening, I took a stroll along the main streets, and every evening, I got propositioned more than once.

Saipan is twelve miles long by five and half miles wide, and my first morning, I rented a car and spent a few hours driving around, well, all of it. I headed north first, and for a mile or so a sheer cliff rose just off the road, the coarse rock an art-directed counterpoint to the flame trees and sky. There were villages with kids playing in yards and resorts with tour buses outside, but very little traffic. A quiet breeze rustled the leaves, and now and then I could hear a weed-whacker, that modern-day machete.

But the overall quietude wasn't always a bucolic stillness. It was often the stillness of abandonment: empty houses, empty shops, entire vacant factory complexes, with broken windows and the occasional tree growing out of a roof.

I pulled my Hyundai to a halt when I saw an entire abandoned mall. Two stories, two long wings, an open plaza with an amphitheater and a fountain. Sea-foam-green walls with pink accents—very early nineties, post–*Miami Vice*. Large letters lay scattered on the ground and in muddy puddles below the latticed entrance arch, like pieces from an upturned Scrabble board. They spelled out LA FIESTA. Laurie Peterka told me that when she moved to Saipan, her first job was as the head of the mall's tenants organization—back then, in the early 1990s, it was a lively place: Donna Karan, Tony Roma's, GUESS, Chanel, Rolex, more than forty stores in all. Now: an empty shell.

Across the street, the massive Palms Resort—313 rooms, I would later learn—also stood abandoned and deteriorating.*

The more modern the ghost town, the more disconcerting it is. Pompeii has a certain charm. Chernobyl does not. Recent ruins indicate recent, relatable failings: THIS COULD BE YOU. Here, not too long ago, were vigor and joy and laughter and big plans. And then something went horribly wrong.

• • • • •

IT'S BEEN a long-term struggle for the CNMI "to get its footing," Laurie told me, in part because the islands have been passed among five different overseers in just over a century, with not a moment of self-rule.

The CNMI, like Guam—their southern neighbor in the Marianas archipelago—have ancient Chamorro roots and a history of Spanish colonialism, but around 1815 a new group began arriving: native Carolinians (or *Refaluwasch*, "people of our land," in their native language), whose ancestral islands to the south had been devastated by a typhoon. They settled on Saipan, Tinian,

* In 2015, a new owner purchased the property and began a major renovation effort, with plans to reopen it as the Kensington Hotel in mid-2016.

and the smaller northern islands, including Pagan and Aguijan, all of which had been essentially uninhabited since the Spanish forced their Chamorro inhabitants to Guam and Rota between 1698 and 1730. The chief who led Carolinians here, Aghurubw, is buried on the islet of Mañagaha, just offshore from Garapan, where parasailers now buzz around the sacred site all day.

After the Spanish-American War, the United States took over Guam while the rest of the Marianas went to . . . Germany. Blame Captain Henry Glass for this unlikely plot twist. His specific orders were "to capture the port of Guam"—which he did, after some awkward missteps—and then, mission accomplished, sailed on to the Philippines, leaving no occupying forces in the rest of the Marianas. This meant that, by international treaty, the USA hadn't actually claimed the other islands, which gave the savvy Germans, themselves trying to build a Pacific empire, an opening to negotiate with Spain. And when Germany lost World War I, Japan took the islands as spoils of war, and started planning *its* empire.

The partition of the Marianas "cost America dearly" a generation later, observes Tinian-based historian Don Farrell. "With the Marianas fully fortified [by the USA], Japan might instead have turned its martial spirit toward its traditional enemy, Russia," in the run-up to World War II. Instead, Japan expanded into the Pacific, and the Mariana Islands were split between two soon-to-be combatants.

Before the war, Saipan, Tinian, and Rota were plantations for tapioca and sugar, with booming cities and military bases. In 1941, Saipan was home to more than forty-two thousand Japanese civilians and thirty thousand Japanese troops, along with four thousand Chamorros and Carolinians. As fighting advanced across the Pacific, the Americans employed an "island-hopping" strategy that came to the Marianas in full force in June 1944, beginning with the two-day Battle of the Philippine Sea, an aircraft carrier battle in which American pilots inflicted so much damage—sinking three carriers and destroying more than five hundred planes—that they nicknamed it "the Marianas Turkey Shoot."

On June 15, the Americans invaded Saipan. Eight thousand Marines landed in the first twenty minutes, another twelve thousand arrived by the end of the day. "Just as D-Day in Normandy broke Hitler's grip on Europe," Japanese Vice Admiral Shigeyoshi Miwa of the Imperial Navy's Sixth Fleet later recounted, "the battle for Saipan would unlock the door to Japan's defenses."

Saipan is the bloodiest twentieth century battleground anywhere in the United States—more people died there than on Guam, and war's sear is even stronger on Saipan than on Guam. Just offshore from a tranquil oceanfront park was a Sherman tank sitting, rusting in the water. One man told me that he swam out to it most weekdays during his lunch break. Outside the airport fence were more tanks, covered in pine needles and green shoots, and a cave-like bomb magazine, its inside cavernous and echoing. Near the north end of the island, the Japanese Last Command Post was hollowed out inside a cliff; I climbed around with a family of Russian tourists before we went back outside to buy water from a cart run by a young Japanese man.

"I was four years [old] when the war came," a Carolinian man named Lino Olopai told me. "We were up in the mountain, in the caves, running around trying to avoid all those things. I was on the back of my mom, crying, hungry, and thirsty. And it's a bad experience."

For many of Saipan's Japanese residents, it was even worse. Just past the Last Command Post, at the northern tip of the island, cliffs loomed a hundred feet above the ocean. The Japanese military warned their civilian compatriots that the advancing Americans had come to torture and kill them. *There is no escape. There is only one way out with honor. Take your own life. Take your family, too.*

And so they did.

Here at this prominence, now called Banzai Cliff, and a few miles away at Mount Tapochau, where the north face is an eight-hundred-foot sheer drop known as Suicide Cliff, two thousand to four thousand—perhaps more—Japanese civilians and troops leapt to their death.* Men. Women. Families. At the American Memorial Park in Garapan, a video about the war included a clip from Banzai Cliff. It was only a second or two, grainy, distant, black-and-white, but it's etched in my memory. A woman in a long black skirt, with a baby in her arms, stood at the edge, then jumped.

A U.S. military report described the scene in the roiling sea: "A commander of a patrol craft said that progress of his boat . . . was slow and tedious because of the hundreds of corpses floating in the water."

Today, dozens of stone tombstones and obelisks and statues stand along the edge of the cliff. Remembering, bearing witness, forming a dotted delineation between this world and the next. Stand there, looking out at the blank horizon a stiflingly hot day, and you'd swear you're at the edge of the world, the precipice of life. The air was calm. The waves below me were towering yet slow-moving, hypnotic, sirenic.

* That's according to Don Farrell, who was referred to me by officials at American Memorial Park. Other estimates—including signs at the site, government documents, and other official and unofficial sources—range from hundreds to ten thousand.

• • • • •

Saipan was an important acquisition, but the Americans had a particular interest in its smaller neighbor, Tinian, three miles away. The Fourth Marine Division invaded the island on July 25, 1944, and captured it a day later. Within a year, the USA had built six runways, four of them on the North Field, which quickly became the busiest airfield in the world.

To get to Tinian from Saipan today requires a flight of less than ten minutes, but multiple locals warned me away, including a burly Navy vet who said he'd never made the trip because he didn't trust the planes. But on a clear morning, I decided to chance it—most flights didn't crash. Just in case, I left a gooshy note for Maren in my hotel room. At the airport, I was not reassured. The thirty-dollar fare was cash-only. There was no security check, not even real tickets: the agent simply handed me a dark green strip of plastic. One of the three other passengers—I swear this is true—was wearing Mickey Mouse swimming trunks and a life preserver. Our shoe box of a plane clattered up and then plunged down, yo-yo-like, and soon we were on Tinian, alive and dry. In a gate area smaller than a two-car garage, Fox News blared on a wall-mounted television, above shelves holding perhaps a dozen baseball trophies.

I rented a beat-up Yaris with a Natural Fresh Coconut air-freshener swinging from the mirror, and drove into the main town, San José, population two thousand or so, of whom there were just a handful out and about. It was a quiet place in the midday heat, and I was in my own pleasant daze, looking around—the ruins of a Spanish-era church steeple in the middle of one block, a couple of old boats beached by the waterfront—when I spotted something that jolted me upright, something that underscored just how far I was from home, because if it were somewhere even slightly more accessible, there would be tour buses lined up for miles: the House of Taga, *latte* stones on steroids.

Guam's *lattes* max out at seven or eight feet, but here were a dozen *lattes* at least sixteen feet tall and, according to an explanatory sign, twelve to fifteen tons each; their *tasa* capstones were the size of hot tubs. Only one was upright and intact—the rest were scattered like toppled rooks from a Brobdingnagian chess game—but the impact was no less stunning, like stumbling upon Stonehenge, minus the crowds and visitors' center.

What? I sputtered to no one. *How* . . .

Even more gobsmacking than the stones themselves was the fact that they were erected as the foundation for a structure perched *on top* and built, according to the legend told on the sign, by a chief with "superhuman strength." I looked around, instinctively wanting to share this with someone, but there was no one to be seen at this little-known national treasure.

So I drove on, passing streets named during the war: Broadway, Riverside Drive, Canal Street, Wall Street, Lenox Avenue, an alternate-universe Manhattan. After about fifteen minutes, the jungle started to close in. Starting in 1926, the Japanese sugar company Nan'yō Kōhatsu Kaisha (NKK) converted 80 percent of Tinian into a sugar plantation, and here and there paths, roads, and even abandoned rail lines, all covered in tall grass, led into the trees, where crumbling villages and shrines still stood, even more ubiquitous than on Saipan, and more haunting for the simple fact that there was no one else around, not a living soul.

Along the main road were administrative buildings built by the Japanese, with thick concrete walls. The Radio Communication

Building was the largest, two stories and quite wide—hundreds of people must have worked there. Now: empty. The hulking shell looked like something out of a post-apocalyptic video game. Farther north were air-raid shelters, with buttressed walls. The afternoon sun was casting shadows everywhere, adding a bit of atmospheric creepiness. I kept driving, following wooden signs to Runway Able, and suddenly realizing with that I was *on* the runway, its entire length empty but for me and my Yaris. The accelerator suddenly begged to be pushed to the floor—the car-rental agent had assured me that "all tourists bang this thing up"—and I obliged, watching with nervous glee as the speedometer ticked upward.

My heart was racing when I finally slowed and turned off Runway Able. I pulled into a broad, paved square flanked by flame trees, where there were two pits topped with glass pyramids. There was another car at one pit, a dinged-up white sedan with two middle-aged men from the states, one in green surf shorts, one in yellow, both wearing white sunglasses. They were as surprised to see me as I was to see them.

The North Field was built to accommodate the new B-29 Superfortress long-range bombers, two of which were taken to these isolated pits to prepare for especially top-secret missions. On August 6, 1945, a 9,700-pound, ten-foot-long bomb known as Little Boy was loaded from one pit into a B-29 called the *Enola Gay*, and then dropped on Hiroshima. Three days later, in the other pit, the even larger bomb Fat Man was loaded into a plane called *Bockscar*, then dropped on Nagasaki. They were the first atomic bombs used in warfare. On August 10, the emperor of Japan surrendered.

In the immediate aftermath, for most Americans, the narrative was straightforward as this: bombs drop, mushroom clouds rise, war over, we win. It was not until August 1946 that many Americans understood the rest of the story, not just the sheer numbers—150,000 killed in Hiroshima, 80,000 in Nagasaki—but the unimaginable on-the-ground details, which first reached a wide audience with a John Hersey piece to which *The New Yorker* devoted an entire issue, with page after vivid page of reporting on the human impact:

> There were many dead in the gardens. At a beautiful moon bridge, [Father Kleinsorge] passed a naked, living woman who seemed to have been burned from head to toe and was red all over. . . . [As] he looked for his way through the woods, he heard a voice ask from the underbrush, "Have you anything to drink?" . . . When he had penetrated the bushes, he saw that there were about twenty men, and they were all in exactly the same nightmarish state: their faces were wholly burned, their eyesockets were hollow, the fluid from their melted eyes had run down their cheeks.

This was the toll of Little Boy and Fat Man, we now understand. A faded memory flashed in my mind: A peace rally my parents took me to when I was a child, at which one of the speakers was a Japanese man who had survived one of the bombings; patches of his face and hands, too, were maimed, the skin shiny and warped. His tone conciliatory, as Carl and Tony's had been when they took me to the park on Guam.

"Such a serene environment," Green Shorts said softly as we looked at the pit and the flame trees surrounding the paved square. "You'd never expect a place like this would be the start of something that would wreak such havoc."

I nodded.

He continued, "All because of some Pearl Harbor bullshit. You *did* wake a sleeping giant."

He snapped a photo with his phone, grinning, then walked over to his car. Just before he slammed the door shut, he yelled enthusiastically, "MAN, THAT'S COOL SHIT!"

• • • • •

AFTER THE war ended, the USA controlled the Northern Marianas. They weren't yet *part* of the United States—and wouldn't be for another three decades—meaning the Americans were, officially, an occupying force. For two years, while they cleared unexploded ordnance and started setting up their own facilities on Saipan, they forced all the island's civilians—Chamorros, Carolinians, Japanese, Koreans—to live in camps, removed from their villages.

On July 4, 1946, the people of Saipan were finally allowed to go home. Liberation Day is still celebrated every year, Angelo told me, but "the meaning has been muddled, because we are now American, we watch baseball." Even among locals, the camps don't fit the preferred narrative of what the USA stands for, particularly since Liberation Day also happens to be the Fourth of July. "So in essence," Angelo said, "in the CNMI, we celebrate our liberation *from* and our relationship *to* the United States on the same day."

The newly formed United Nations took control of eleven former Axis possessions; they were called the Trust Territory and were administered by specific nations. New Zealand oversaw Western Samoa (now Samoa), Britain ran the show in Togoland (now Ghana), and the United States took responsibility for a scattering of Micronesian islands formerly controlled by Japan, among them the Northern Marianas, the Marshall Islands, Chuuk, Palau, Pohnpei, Kosrae, and Yap. The Trust Territory of the Pacific Islands' capital was Saipan.

It was a happy place, said Lino Olopai, the man who had been a four-year-old when the Americans arrived in 1944. After the war, "us kids, we don't worry. We were having fun watching the GI driving the big trucks and they'd throw candy and bubblegums to us, which was a new thing to us." Americanization had begun in earnest. School lessons were taught only in English, and from 1950 to 1962—the same time that civilians couldn't travel to or from Guam—the United States blocked off areas of Saipan as secret CIA training grounds for insurgents fighting communism in China and Southeast Asia.

Walt Goodridge introduced me to Lino. We arrived unannounced one morning at Lino's small house just off the beach and next to a high-rise hotel, and he appeared at the door shirtless and understandably surprised to see us. After a brief explanation from the ever-cheerful Walt, Lino gestured to a picnic table shaded by pine trees, and popped into the house to get a coffeepot and mugs.

When he was seventeen, Lino lied about his age to get a job as a security guard for the CIA site. A few years later, he got a job as a language teacher on the island, working for the Peace Corps, which was established by President John F. Kennedy in 1961 as part of the USA's postwar image-softening efforts to show that it was powerful *and* benevolent. (Think also of the Marshall Plan and the founding of the United Nations.)

"I think that's when we started looking into bringing back our way of life," Lino said, pouring himself a mug of coffee. "They say, 'Yeah, your [traditional] ways are also very important, too,'" Lino said. He was surprised to hear this seemingly subversive message from the young Americans. "'You mean I can speak up against my government?' They said, 'Yes, it's a democracy.'"

Lino spoke methodically, with a soft gaze accentuated by bushy eyebrows. Before the islands formally joined the United States, he said, "I can already see the impact of the giant that was coming."

The Trust Territory was, by design, a temporary setup. The United Nations' very charter had emphasized the importance of self-government and the UN got even more serious when it established its Special Committee on Decolonization in 1961. In 1945, there were ninety-seven "non-self-governing territories"—colonies—with a combined population of some 750 million: about one in three people on the planet at the time. Two years later, after a long independence movement, the world's largest colony, British India, became the sovereign nations of India and Pakistan. By 1965, more than sixty onetime colonies had been removed from the UN's "non-self-governing" list; within another decade, all of the Trust Territory except for the Pacific islands had become independent.

The Americans had never really considered themselves colonizers, of course. More like liberators, and noble overseers of "effective poorhouses" constructed by others. But the fact remained that, by UN standards, the United States controlled several colonies at war's end: Alaska, Hawaii, the Panama Canal Zone, Guam, American Samoa, Puerto Rico, the U.S. Virgin Islands, and the Trust Territory of the Pacific Islands. The anticolonial movement put the United States in a bind: we still wanted to hold these territories, and relied on them in the Cold War (particularly Guam's military base and Saipan's CIA training ground). But this empire was becoming a problem for the national brand; as early as the 1950s, the State Department itself noted "the importance of colonialism and imperialism in anti-American propaganda."

Most people in the Northern Marianas wanted to become part of the USA. In four separate referenda—1958, 1961, 1963, 1969—they voted to incorporate with Guam, only to have Guam voters reject the proposal. In the early 1970s, a new idea was proposed: the islands would join the United States on their own terms.

Lino, for one, wasn't interested. In 1974, the year before the referendum, he hopped aboard an outrigger canoe with his cousin and set sail for the outer Caroline Island of Satawal, more than 450 miles south. The whole island is less than one square mile; at the time, Lino told me, the buildings were all made with thatch, except for the clinic. He set out to rediscover his roots, as the Peace Corps volunteers had encouraged. The old ways were alive and well on Satawal, including dancing, massage, and his particular interest, navigation—sailing guided only by stars, currents, cloud movement, and other cues from nature. Lino and the other men learning the techniques of traditional navigation were isolated from the rest of the village and sat on special mats, called *sághi al palu*, while they learned to count and name each star in the night sky, "like ABCs," Lino said.

"You name all the stars, backward, forward, you get to know which is the opposite of another. The opposite of the North Star is the Southern Cross. And then you recite in the canoe, out in the ocean, which island is under which star."

This is how the Pacific was settled—Satawal, Saipan, American Samoa, Guam, all those dots in the ocean. Hawaii, too. Lino's teacher, in his three years on Satawal, was a man named Mau Piailug, who in 1976 helped teach native Hawaiians traditional navigation, a skill that had been lost on the islands.

Today, thanks in part to Lino's own teaching, there are still some young navigators learning and practicing the craft. Walt, who had been quietly listening, raised his hand. "Including one Jamaican!" We made an unlikely trio: a bare-chested Carolinian, still strapping in his seventies; a Jamaican in a white linen shirt that he self-deprecatingly called his "guru gear"; me in crumpled clothes dug from the bottom of my backpack, weeks into my trip.

Lino told a story about Mau Piailug going out in a boat with a nephew who was showing off his brand-new navigation gadget. "Yeah, you can program it and find out where you are going and punch this and punch that," the nephew had said.

"Let me see it," Mau had replied. "Ooh, so this what you call GPS, yeah?" Then he'd thrown it in the water.

Lino chuckled and added: "You are not gonna be brave if you have these things."

Here was a true experimenter, a man who remade himself to be as rugged and self-reliant as they come, as a direct rejection of the United States and its political experiments and cultural trappings. That's not to say that he shunned modernity. He ate at McDonald's, used email. It was, as so many people had told me across the territories, all about finding a balance, and holding on strong to your roots even as you accept some changes. At the high-rise hotel next door, power saws whined and hammers pounded, renovations in progress.

A key factor, for Lino, was the government—he thought it had become too intrusive and people had, in turn, become too dependent on it.

The people and the government "are into this together, but I have a system," he said. "Let me work it through. If I cannot, I'll call on you. But the way you're doing it . . . you're not helping us look back into how we survive on this grain of sand in the middle of the ocean over ages. Help us look back into that as we fit into modern time. Modern time is coming whether we want it or not. That's my personal opinion. Stay back there for a little while. I'll call on you."

At the same time, Lino hoped for more government support to help maintain key cultural traditions. The local Indigenous Affairs Office and Carolinian Affairs Office, he said, "can really play a big role if our leadership truly wanted to protect our language and our culture . . ." But he wasn't optimistic about the chances of this actually happening. In elections, he said, "they'll talk about 'We must protect our language' and this and that. But when it's over, they're not gonna fund any of that."

• • • • •

THE CNMI's founding document, which set the groundwork for its relationship with the United States, was called the Covenant. It was intentionally not called a treaty, said Angelo, whose father was instrumental in writing it. "A covenant is a sacred agreement," Angelo told me. "I don't have proof of this, but I think the word was chosen because of the strong Catholic presence in the country." Like many people, here and in every territory, he used the words *country* and *nation* to describe both the territory and the USA interchangeably.

The framers of the Covenant—which would become the basis for the local constitution—had a pointed lack of trust in the American federal government. In some ways, the Covenant emulated American Samoa's cultural protections, including a provision—which would become Article 12 of the CNMI Constitution—stating that land could only be owned by persons of Chamorro or Carolinian ancestry (though others could lease it for fifty years, hence the high-rise hotels like the one next to Lino's house).

The key predecessor, though, was Puerto Rico, which had gotten off the UN's "colony" list in 1953, after its affiliation with the United States changed in the process of becoming a commonwealth rather than a territory. It's a nuanced, nebulous difference.*

Kentucky, Massachusetts, Pennsylvania, and Virginia all call themselves commonwealths, as did the Philippines, which was never a happy, status-quo-loving territory, and after much petitioning and fighting was granted commonwealth status in 1934, as a transition period before gaining independence in 1946. In that case, "commonwealth" meant, *This place is on the path toward independence*. But none of these are the same sort of commonwealth that applies to Puerto Rico or the CNMI.

Here is the official, current United States government definition of a *commonwealth*:

> The term "Commonwealth" does not describe or provide for any specific political status or relationship. It has, for example, been applied to both states and territories. When used

* Today, in addition to the three American territories, the UN lists fourteen colonies: Western Sahara, Anguilla, Bermuda, British Virgin Islands, Cayman Islands, Falkland Islands (Malvinas), Montserrat, Saint Helena, Turks & Caicos, Gibraltar, French Polynesia, New Caledonia, Pitcairn, and Tokelau. The great majority of these are held by the United Kingdom (the Falklands are disputed with Argentina), plus two for France, one for New Zealand, and one place, Western Sahara, where . . . it's complicated.

> in connection with areas under U.S. sovereignty that are not states [that is, Puerto Rico and later the CNMI], the term broadly describes an area that is self-governing under a constitution of its adoption and whose right of self-government will not be unilaterally withdrawn by Congress.

This version of *commonwealth* was dreamed up by Puerto Rican leaders, as the island's political status debate raged in the early 1950s. It offered—on paper, anyway—an upgrade from territory by providing more autonomy, enough to please the UN Special Committee on Decolonization, which considers the American territories to be colonies (the USVI, American Samoa, and Guam) but says the commonwealths (Puerto Rico and the CNMI) are not. This new designation allowed the United States to hold its power while showing the world it was a kinder, gentler, with-the-times sort of empire.

The Northern Mariana Islands' Covenant was put to a referendum in 1975 and passed with more than 78 percent the vote. On March 24, 1976, after congressional approval, the Northern Mariana Islands became a commonwealth of the United States of America. In the states, this went all but unnoticed. There was no collective discussion about the meaning and use of empire. It did not become a presidential campaign issue. There were no long articles and blaring headlines in the national media about the CNMI. In fact, the commonwealth status wasn't even fully official—and CNMI residents weren't American citizens—until 1986, when the Trust Territory was formally dissolved, with the authorization of the United Nations.

But even in this era of greater autonomy for the former Trust Territory of the Pacific Islands, this time when the territories seemed to be catching a bit of a break, the Insular Cases were still casting their long shadow. In the 1980 case *Harris v. Rosario*, the Supreme Court ruled that, even though the federal Aid to Families with Dependent Children Program provided lower reimbursements in Puerto Rico than in the states, this was permissible—Congress, the court decided, "may treat [the territories] differently from States so long as there is a rational basis for its actions." In other words: Congress can do what it wants in the territories, even if it seems unfair, as long there's a good-enough reason for it. The autonomy that came with the *commonwealth* label was, apparently, not quite as strong as originally advertised.

• • • • •

THE COGNITIVE dissonance of Saipan showed no signs of abating: warm welcomes, burned-out landscapes, stories of shady goings-on.

At a beachside café called Snack Shack, a cheery, laid-back place specializing in crepes, I struck up a conversation with the thirty-something proprietor, Glen Hunter, who turned out to be an anti-corruption crusader; the discussion quickly veered away from tourist small talk.

On a side street near the island's cockfighting stadium, I walked around an old Japanese jail, where thick trees had overgrown the walls and cells. It felt a bit eerie, though not *sinister* like Banzai Cliffs or Tinian, until Walt told me, while we sipped smoothies at a nearby health-food store, that according to one theory about Amelia Earhart's ill-fated trip to Howland, she crashed in the Marshall Islands, where she was captured by the Japanese, who brought her to this jail.

One day, I got back to my hotel to discover that I'd lost my new hat, the one from the world's largest Kmart. I hate losing things. I never lose things. And now, since the *aitu* in American Samoa, two different hats had disappeared. I checked my email and found a note from John Wasko telling me that the hat I'd lost on Aunu'u had just appeared in his pickup cab. He added, *I'm not touching it.*

Even Saipan's innovations were unnerving. All around the island was a business model I'd never seen before: a combination Laundromat and poker room, open 24/7. My first instinct was to laugh—*Ha ha, maybe I'll wash some clothes and play a hand of Texas hold 'em at three a.m.!*—but this was chased by the realization that this wasn't Monaco. There are no tuxedoed dealers, just rows of poker machines and a miasma of misery and aching hopes for quick success and all the trappings of the American Dream on the next hand or maybe . . .

Each day, I awoke with a gambler's optimism: *Today will be my lucky day!* My goal was simply a flicker of uplift, evidence that Saipan didn't *suck*. There were countless small moments, enough to keep me going, but I never seemed to hit the jackpot until I got an invitation from a friend of Angelo's, a lawyer and politician named Cinta Kaipat, to attend a small family party. It took some doing to find her house, since buildings on Saipan have no address numbers. (Until recently, many streets didn't even have names, aside from the two main drags, Beach Road and Middle Road; you can guess where they are.) But after several U-turns, I arrived at a small white house with black trim and lots of plumeria flowers. I walked around back, where several picnic tables were set up on a covered concrete slab; about twenty people were sitting around chatting and drinking Fanta and Bud Light.

They might not have recognized me, but I was fairly certain they had an idea of who I was: the Writer from the States, a latter-day Margaret Mead come to observe them. Saipan residents are well aware that various scribes have written not-so-flattering reports about their island. I gave a shy wave. A lithe middle-aged woman waved back, beaming. "You're in the right place!" She introduced herself as Emma. She had sandy hair and a necklace made of chunky, colorful disks cut from seashells.

Another woman emerged from the house. "Hi, Doug!" she called. This was Cinta, a head shorter than me, with a broad, beaming face framed by dark brown hair. She embraced me in a firm hug, then pointed me to an empty spot at a picnic table, next to a balding, mustachioed man named Desi. "He helped write our constitution!" Cinta said, and so it was that I had a Fanta with a Founding Father. Soon it was time for prayer, and we all gathered around a table covered with platters of food. After "Amen," the room stayed quiet and no one moved. Everyone stared at me. My mind raced: *Am I supposed to give a speech? Is my fly down?*

Desi stepped to my side and said, in a low voice, "You're the guest. They're not going to get in line until you're at the head." I grabbed a plate and mounded it with barbecued ribs, fried chicken, octopus, rice, and an extra-large serving of chicken *kelaguen*.

I met aunts and uncles and sons and daughters; an old woman, the family matriarch, clasped my hand with a bony, kindly shake. At times, I struggled to understand the web of family. "I'm Cinta's sister," Emma told me, although she meant it in the local way—they didn't have the same parents, but here, those closest to you are your siblings, no matter what bloodlines say. Emma was Chamorro—"part of the first Chamorro team to swim the English Channel," she said. Cinta was Carolinian, originally from the remote island of Pagan, near the north end of the Marianas, which was evacuated in 1981 when Mount Pagan erupted. She attended law school at the University of Minnesota, in the very building where Maren worked. We compared notes on Minneapolis winters. Cinta had loved the snow.

Cinta's brother, Gus, pulled out a ukulele and started noodling. He wore a red T-shirt and glasses, and he was a beefy guy, the instrument cartoonishly small in his hands. His son, Kyle—who wore a thick necklace like Emma's, a trademark of Pagan, where the shells showed off the bravery of the men who dove deeply to collect them from the ocean floor—picked up another ukulele and balanced his own toddler son on his knee.

Gus's playing streamlined into a distinct melody and he started singing, with Cinta harmonizing on the chorus, their voices crisp and balanced. They sang a traditional song from Pagan and then an original composition called "Two Lovers Point," telling the story of the site on Guam, and performed in honor of me and my distant wife. I felt a pang of homesickness, followed by a rush of gratitude for the hospitality. When they finished, Cinta said, "Now we're going to do 'Marianas,'" which she'd written when she was in Minneapolis, missing *her* home; it was a love song for the islands. Nearly everyone in the room harmonized, dulcet and warm. The fluorescent lights above us seemed to delineate all the known world, as everything else faded away.

Just before I left, I met another relative, a middle-aged woman in a black blouse. She said, in a tone that was at once friendly and wary, "I hope you got all you wanted here." It was the only time anyone directly acknowledged that I was here to write about them.

I assured her I'd had a lovely evening. I meant it.

Cinta walked me out to my car, accompanied by a young girl,

perhaps seven years old, of unknown relation. Cinta gave me a big hug and then another, and the girl silently handed me a can of Fanta for the road.

• • • • •

YET EVEN at Cinta's house, in the course of a delicious meal and rousing conversation, the underlying problems came up again and again. I asked Desi and Emma about local political issues, and Desi said, "There are none! . . . Well, politicians don't *talk* about them." A typical political campaign speech, he said, goes something like this: "My name is ———. My parents are ———. My grandparents are ———. Vote for me!" In this newest of territories, Laurie Peterka had told me, there's a "village mentality now with this other structure"—the American government system—"laid on top of it."

Each territory has close-knit communities, rich in what the sociologists call social capital, a strong network of friends and families and acquaintances, but within each territory there's also a strong sense of disparate and often *competing* communities. In the CNMI, cultural identity is so split that there's no broadly used word for someone from Saipan or from the CNMI. Anyone from Guam is Guamanian, but in the CNMI you're Chamorro or Carolinian or Filipino or Chinese or white (or haole). Local politics, multiple people told me, were dominated by a few families, mostly Chamorro; everyone else was struggling to make their voice heard, as Lino had said.

There's no getting around Saipan's problems, even beyond what I could see with my own eyes or what directly affected the people I met. "You know, *Breaking Bad* could've been filmed on Saipan. Meth is bad," Angelo said, adding that in the local government—the territory's largest employer—nepotism was common and generally considered no big deal, and what most statesiders might see as corruption was considered here simply *patronage*. Of course, there was still outright corruption, some of it genuinely jaw-dropping in its brazenness and absurdity, like the 2013 incident that caused then-Governor Benigno Fitial to be impeached and subsequently resign: his crime was illegally releasing a federal prisoner who happened to be his personal masseuse.

"The territories are like laboratories for the United States," one Chamorro man on Guam had told me. His words echoed the bromide that the states are laboratories for democracy—meaning local experimentation will lead the way toward a more perfect union—but his statement was less optimistic. He meant that the United States sees the territories as a place to mess around, mix elements indiscriminately, and experiment just to see what happens, without regard for what might blow up. And as I drove back to Garapan from Cinta's house, I passed one of the most damning case studies, the reason former United States Speaker of the House Tom DeLay, Republican of Texas, once called Saipan "my Galapagos Island": a hulking, sprawling garment factory, now shut down, with broken windows and an ominous air.

• • • • •

As the CNMI officially joined the United States, the experimentation began in earnest.

Among the Covenant's special provisions were one that the commonwealth would regulate its own immigration and another that it would be exempt from federal minimum-wage laws. (In 1979, federal minimum wage was $2.90; in the CNMI, it was $1.35. By 1998, federal minimum wage was $5.15 and in the

CNMI it was $3.05.) In practical terms, these two provisions meant that employers could easily import workers who would be willing to toil for low wages.

Imagine that you used a Club Med brochure and *Atlas Shrugged* as your manuals for constructing a new economy in a place with a long history of insularity and colonialism. What's the worst that could happen in this laissez-faire Shangri-la?

There were early, significant dividends, including a tourism boom. Japan Airways built hotels and malls, including La Fiesta, which opened in 1990, and hired Greg Norman to design a golf course, Lao Lao Bay. And then there were the garment factories. The first opened in 1983; at their peak in the late 1990s, thirty-six operated on Saipan, with nearly a billion dollars in annual exports. They employed between 20,000 and 35,000 workers (estimates vary widely), most of them young women from China. In 1983, the population of the CNMI was 24,308. By 1998, a congressional report estimated the island's population at 70,000, of whom 42,000 were foreign workers, largely in the garment factories and tourism industries.

Since the factories were on American soil, they could avoid import tariffs and sew "Made in USA" labels on the clothes, helping mainland consumers feel better about their purchases, never mind the fact that, since Saipan was not *quite* full-fledged American soil, the pay and factory conditions were also not *quite* up to mainland standards. Saipan's garment industry made clothes for brands including Ralph Lauren, the Gap, Tommy Hilfiger, Calvin Klein, Donna Karan, Liz Claiborne, Banana Republic, Old Navy, Champion, High Sierra, the Dress Barn, Gymboree, J. Crew, Oshkosh B'Gosh, Cutter & Buck, Nordstrom, Sears Roebuck, JCPenney, Lane Bryant, the Limited, Levi's, Talbots, Abercrombie & Fitch, and Brooks Brothers. If you wore clothes from any of those brands between the mid-1980s and the mid-2000s, it's possible they were made on Saipan.*

• • • • •

WALT TOOK ME to a neighborhood dense with onetime garment factories, all corrugated metal roofs, broken windows, and tall chain-link fences. As we passed one, windowless and yellow and with a broken-down minivan out front, Walt said, "This is one of the places where Chun worked."

Walt befriended Chun Yu Wang shortly after he moved to Saipan. She was from Wuxi in China's eastern Jiangsu Province and came to Saipan in 2000, when she was twenty-five. She recounts her experiences in her memoir *Chicken Feathers and Garlic Skin*, which she wrote with Walt. The title comes from a Chinese idiom; it's "the rubbish left when cooking a chicken. . . . Being worthless, they attract little attention." Chun still lived on Saipan and she said she'd be willing to talk to me. The three of us went to American Memorial Park, where we sat on a low wall at the edge of an amphitheater. Chun had black hair pulled back into a ponytail, and a professional outfit: maroon blouse, thin gold necklace, black slacks. As I started to ask her questions, she fidgeted and offered only short answers.

Chun had worked in garment factories in China, but she'd heard that on Saipan "in three years, I could make almost thirty thousand dollars . . . It might take me ten or twenty years to make that much money in China." To get a placement, she had

* This list comes from a 1998 report by California Congressman George Miller, along with reporting by the *New York Times*, the *Washington Post*, and the *Los Angeles Times*, although these documents do not specify the years during which each individual company was using manufacturing facilities on Saipan.

to talk to a recruiter in Jiangsu, take a test, do an interview, and pay about $3,500, which she borrowed from friends and family.

She expected the USA of movies—tall buildings, bustling cities—and arrived disappointed; Saipan was less developed than Jiangsu. The factory was also a letdown—no, more than that, a nightmare. It was called Mirage. There were eight other women in the room, with no air-conditioning, beds consisting of bamboo mats laid on wooden frames, and the occasional rat scampering by her head.

"In China it's hard, but not hard like Saipan," Chun told me.

Her first job was sewing hems on blouses, with a quota of one thousand every day and "cruel" monitors who would shake down workers for bribes of as much as $500. Accidents were common; scammers were rampant, like one who took $3,000 from Chun with the false promise of getting her a green card; debt bondage—workers having their wages garnished for recruitment fees, plane tickets, room and board—was a fact of life. CNMI work permits were contingent on a contract with a specific employer. To quit was to jeopardize your immigration status. To file a complaint with local labor officials, as Chun found out the hard way, was to navigate an unsympathetic bureaucracy that typically sided with the employers. To go home, for many workers, was to face loan sharks who had fronted the placement fee, and disappointed family.

All of this had been *even worse* before a 1998 congressional report by California Democrat George Miller. In addition to the garment factories, Miller found Indians who worked in stores and "were not allowed out of sight of their employer," and Chinese men lured with false promises of construction jobs; one politely asked Miller, "Could you help us arrange to sell one of our kidneys so we could have enough money to return home?"

Chun was paid minimum wage, $3.05 an hour. After taxes

and deductions for room and board, she earned about $412 per month, after working sixty to seventy-hour workweeks.

This is where things get complicated. To me, those hours are exploitative, the pay criminally low. This was a key point of the news coverage about Saipan's garment industry in the late 1990s—*20/20* came here, the *New York Times*, *Time*, *Ms.*, the Associated Press. But to Chun, it was very good money. This was why she was here: to earn more than she could in China. Here, unlike there, overtime meant time-and-a-half pay, and she wanted as much of it as possible. The mantra was, *Work and save, work and save.*

Part of me cheered, *Such stoic self-sacrifice! Eyes on the prize!*

But mostly I felt slow-burn outrage. What we had here was not just strivers hoping to improve their lot but rampant exploitation of that desire—abuse of strivers' bodies and dreams by the people who controlled their destiny. Based on all the other accounts I heard and read—the most thorough is John Bowe's 2007 book *Nobodies*—Chun's experiences were typical. And as Bowe writes, "the fact that workers wanted more hours needed further parsing: if they were paid a higher wage, they could work forty hours a week and still have a decent life."

Chun sat perfectly upright as she spoke, clutching her designer leather handbag. There was an unmistakable weariness to her voice as she talked about the six factories in which she'd worked. A pair of joggers cruised by, not even noticing us.

It wasn't all bad, she said. She enjoyed the warm weather and the exotic flowers; also, "I like the freedom."

The latent patriot in me perked up. Like, freedom of expression? Political freedom?

No. "In China, you have family, you have to call, you have to buy food every day, you have to take care of them. Here, I don't have to, right?"

I tried to formulate a question that circled back to the American Dream and whether she thought she'd found it. It was, admittedly, abstract and probing. By this time, Chun had started to warm up, but now I'd taken us right back to awkwardness. She looked at Walt.

"Here's what I think is important," he said. "When she came, it wasn't, 'Go to America and succeed and become wealthy.' It was specifically to work at a garment factory, specifically to make *x* dollars an hour, for a specific period of time"—a contract was typically three years—"and then go home."

After Miller's report and further congressional study, the CNMI garment industry was officially an embarrassment to the United States. In 2000, the U.S. Senate unanimously voted to extend the federal minimum wage to the CNMI. But when the bill moved over to the House of Representatives, Speaker of the House DeLay blocked it from reaching a vote. DeLay had been to Saipan a couple of times, at the invitation of lobbyist Jack Abramoff, whom the CNMI government paid more than $7 million. DeLay played two rounds at Lao Lao Bay and called Saipan "a perfect petri dish of capitalism." If you're looking for insular communities with rampant cronyism and a stubborn resistance to change, you'll find a prime example in Washington, D.C.

The CNMI's minimum wage didn't budge from $3.05 until 2007, when Congress—in its power as ultimate ruler of the territory—moved it to $3.55, with a mandate that it increase every year until it reaches parity with the federal minimum wage, which is all well and good except that the timetable has been pushed back multiple times. And after the 2005 elimination of the worldwide General Agreement on Tariffs and Trade (GATT), "Made in USA" no longer had the same tariff-avoiding economic advantage. Factories on Saipan started to shut in 2000, anticipating the end of GATT, and the last closed in 2009. Simultaneously, the commonwealth's tourism industry had been hit hard by the reeling Japanese economy, starting in the late 1990s, leading to the empty hotels, the abandoned Fiesta. It was a one-two punch of an economic hit. The last population figures, from 2013, show 53,855 people living in the CNMI, though it's well known that there are many more—perhaps tens of thousands more—uncounted immigrants.

Federal officials took over CNMI immigration in 2007, but they made things even more complicated. Chun had a contract worker visa, which the government was, as we spoke, planning to phase out. Anyone who had arrived using the contract worker visa could stay, but if they ever left for any reason they'd have to reapply for a new, more restrictive visa, shelling out $300 or more just for the opportunity.

"So people are trapped here," Walt said. "They can't visit their family in the Philippines or China because they don't have enough money to fly and to apply to come back."

At this particular moment, in Washington, D.C., there was a debate about granting amnesty to undocumented immigrants, especially those from Mexico, Central America, and South America. Lost in that discussion, Walt pointed out, were the immigrants on Saipan, who'd come legally but were trapped in a limbo state, the laws under which they had emigrated soon to be changed. They seemed like good candidates for permanent-resident status—or even a clear path to citizenship—given their circumstances, but the precedent this would set for *other* immigrants, back in the states, made it a long shot in Congress. And locally, Walt added, "indigenous politicians here will rarely favor a move that favors a path to citizenship for the contract workers, and the reason for that is the fear of loss of control." Add a critical mass of new citizens and you've got a bloc of people with newfound power and political voice—they might well come out of the shadows.

Chun quit the garment industry for good in 2008. Now she works two jobs, at a nutritional supplement store and at the Fiesta Resort. About eleven and a half hours a day, six days a week, with shorter days on Fridays. The long hours are her own choice.

"For me, I think I am happy," she said.

"Do you still want to go to America?" Walt asked, meaning the states.

"Maybe. I just want to see," Chun said. "But I heard it's not all good."

• • • • •

THE TERRITORIES are a geopolitical personality test: Is the glass half full or half empty? Are they lands of opportunity or disappointment?

When you compare them to other countries in their own regions and look purely at cold, hard figures, things appear pretty good: higher incomes, better infrastructure, longer life spans, higher literacy, better health outcomes. If you compare the territories to the states, by the same measurements, the outlook is much more bleak. Then again, if you're measuring collective well-being by considering what places have maintained longtime traditions and distinct cultural identities, well, the ones without American oversight appear to be in better shape. In American Samoa, the comparisons were always to (Western) Samoa; about half the people with whom I spoke were wistful about their independent neighbor's "more intact" traditions—more *fales*, more ceremonies—while the other half boasted of the American territories' better roads, cleaner water, and access to American brand-name goods.

Do you accept the argument that everything is awesome in the territories for the simple fact that, regardless of whether the glass is half full or half empty, at least the tap water is potable?

By the way, on Saipan, the tap water for most residents *is not* potable.

On my way back to my hotel one night, I stopped by the I ♥ SAIPAN duty-free store. Out front, four young Chamorro men, shirtless and in red wrap skirts, danced for a gathered crowd in the glow of tiki torches. They slapped their chests and waved for the cameras. It felt like an elegy for a culture.

For the longest time, Angelo said, retirement age in the CNMI was thirty-eight, because people would get a government job at eighteen, work for twenty years, get their pension, and that was it. (Which is to say that the territory is a cautionary tale of *both* laissez-faire capitalism and big, stagnant government bureaucracies.) Angelo was in his mid-thirties, "and I feel like I'm just *starting* to have an impact." A few years earlier, he had been instrumental in advocating for the creation of the Marianas Trench Marine National Monument, which George W. Bush established in the final days of his presidency, protecting more than ninety-five thousand square miles of land and ocean.

But Angelo still had big plans. In fact, he had to leave the island to take the next step in his career in marine conservation. Though some outsiders come to the territories to prove themselves, far more locals leave to do the same. The Saipan Blogger now lives in Washington, D.C., where he works for the Pew Charitable Trusts. I met him in person only after our paths happened to cross when I left the Northern Mariana Islands to check in on the rest of the former Trust Territory of the Pacific Islands and see how it measured up.

• • • • •

WHILE THE CNMI became part of the United States, the other islands comprising the Trust Territory opted for independence, becoming the Federated States of Micronesia (or FSM), the Republic of Palau, and the Republic of the Marshall Islands. Each continues to have a strong relationship with their onetime overseer, having set up a Compact of Free Association with the USA. Technically speaking, their connection to the United States is as "freely associated states" and they're insular *areas*, even though they're not insular *possessions*. They're sovereign nations with their own seats at the United Nations, where they are among the USA's most reliable allies. But they're also served by American domestic programs including the Federal Communications Commission, the Federal Emergency Management Administration, and the National Weather Service. They use the dollar and their residents serve in the American military, also at higher rates than any state. Their residents don't need visas to visit or work in the United States.

It was the Marshall Islands that most interested me. After an early morning flight to Guam, I boarded a United route known as the Island Hopper and bounced two thousand miles east by southeast before arriving in the nation's capital, Majuro Atoll. It's a curving ribbon in the ocean, twenty-six miles long and typically no more than a quarter mile in width; at the airport, the atoll has been bumped out to accommodate the width of the runway. Like the CNMI, the Marshalls were settled by outrigger-sailing ancient mariners—two of the most popular tourist souvenirs sold on Majuro are traditional stick charts, the stick-and-shell guides that navigators used to learn the locations of atolls and islands; and replicas of the famously speedy Marshallese outrigger sailboats. The islands were briefly claimed by Germany (in 1884), taken over by Japan after World War I, and invaded by the United States in 1944.* American GIs named the areas at either end of Majuro: Rita, after Rita Hayworth, lies to the east, in the densely developed area where most of the atoll's twenty-seven thousand residents live, while Laura, after Lauren Bacall, is the pastoral western point.

Today, Majuro is a developing-world small town of the twenty-first century, with a couple of big-box (well, like, *medium*-box) all-purpose stores called Payless, a concrete rectangle of a courthouse, a small but busy port. In downtown Majuro, such as it is, the buildings span practically edge to edge; parts of the atoll appear from the air to be a mass of pixels floating in the sea. Majuro didn't make me perturbed in the way that Saipan did (though I suspect I would have found it more melancholy if I'd been coming from nearly anywhere else). There were no poker rooms; no sprawling, abandoned malls; no scantily clad women beckoning to me on street corners; no sense that the place had fallen on hard times, so much as a reality that the good times had never come at all.

Near my hotel, a two-story turquoise building stood out. A

* The islands that now comprise the Federated States of Micronesia were also claimed by the Japanese before World War II and were the site of much fighting. The Chuuk Lagoon was the primary base for the Japanese Imperial Navy fleet until the Allies sank dozens of the ships in a series of air attacks in February 1944. Today the lagoon is a popular scuba diving spot that the *New York Times* has called "the biggest graveyard of ships in the world."

large sign read BIKINI ATOLL TOWN HALL. Bikini and Majuro are more than five hundred miles apart, so this was like seeing Detroit City Hall in New York. It's a result of the fact that the Marshall Islands were for decades the subjects of one of the most ambitious and deadly experiments in American history.

In 1946, the American Navy forced residents of Bikini, Rongelap, Enewetak, and Wotho Atolls to evacuate their islands—their ancestral homelands—to make room for nuclear testing. It was, they said, "for the good of mankind and to end all wars." This was a new generation of firepower: the March 1954 Bravo test, at Bikini, was fifteen megatons, *a thousand* times the explosive force of Little Boy. In all, there were sixty-seven detonations, and taken together, they were equal to "1.6 Hiroshima bombs being detonated *every day*" over the twelve years of testing, writes *Marshall Islands Journal* editor Giff Johnson in his insightful report *Nuclear Past, Unclear Future.*

The fallout drifted far from the evacuated areas, and people on every atoll in the Marshall Islands were exposed to high doses of radiation, many suffering skin burns, vomiting, and diarrhea; their hair and fingernails fell out. The long-term effects were far worse: a 2004 study by the U.S. National Cancer Institute found that, all told, the testing would likely result in 532 cases of cancer among the Marshallese, to say nothing of the impact of having their communities uprooted. Even today, Bikinians are Cold War refugees, living on Majuro and Kili Atoll; the people of Rongelap also continue to live in exile.

Just outside the Hotel Robert Reimers, where I was staying, was one of Majuro's busiest spots, the Te-Eak Im We-Eak Snack Shack, where old men played checkers, using washers and bolts as pieces. Across the street was a U.S. post office storefront (Majuro's zip code is 96960; postage rates are the same as in the states, but the physical stamps say "Marshall Islands") and next door to this was a clinic where anyone can walk in and get free radiation testing. This was a provision of the Compact of Free Association that the Marshall Islands negotiated when it became independent in 1983. The U.S. agreed to pay a total of $270 million, spread out in annual payments from 1986 to 2001, as "the full settlement of all claims, past, present, and future" for the effects of the nuclear testing. Specific claims would be awarded by a Nuclear Claims Tribunal.

One afternoon, I met a former chairman of the tribunal, an American named Jim Plasman, with khaki pants and a white mustache, in his office as he shuffled papers while the atoll's power was out. "[People] would be awarded a set amount depending on the type of condition," he said. "For instance, a benign thyroid nodule would be paid much less than lung cancer." The awards ranged from $12,500 to $125,000, and added up quickly; before shutting down in 2001, the tribunal had awarded "over ninety million dollars for personal injuries and over two billion for damages to property." But *awarded* doesn't mean *paid*, and the USA hasn't budged beyond its "full settlement" of $270 million, despite lawsuits and requests, including Plasman's own testimony before Congress in 2007 that this amount was insufficient. No Marshallese received their full award. (In comparison, at the Nevada Test Site, where exposure was lower, paid compensation totaled around $1.2 billion.)

"Legally, there's probably no more obligation for the United States to do anything here," a man named Jack Niedenthal told me. "But morally there's still a huge deficit." Bikini Jack, as he's sometimes known, was an American who first came to the Marshall Islands with the Peace Corps in 1981. His scruffy goatee and tattooed knuckles belied his stature as the trust liaison for the people of Bikini Atoll. We met for lunch at the Hotel Robert Reimers' restaurant, Tide Table, a generic-feeling room that seemed to be the crossroads of the island. Just sitting there, I met ambassadors and government officials and missionaries and NGO workers and plenty of locals, everyone at once cultivating the grandest of plans and hanging on for dear life, commiserating over Filipino beer, chicken teriyaki pizza, and sumo wrestling on the bar TV.

"We've got about a forty percent unemployment rate, and people are working for two dollars an hour; that's the minimum wage," Jack said. Diabetes rates were among the highest in the world, but there was no dialysis on the island. Infrastructure was crumbling. The National Gym, opened in 1997, was now permanently closed due to termite damage and general neglect, although kids routinely broke the locks to go in and play basketball. At the national capitol, a twenty-one-year-old building with the glass curtain walls of a corporate headquarters, the offices of the president and the cabinet minister were uninhabitable due to structural damage; the root cause, according to recent report by a consultant from Honolulu, was a lack of "any apparent concern" on the part of the Marshallese government.

As part of the Compact of Free Association, Marshall Islands citizens can travel and move freely to the United States, and, in search of better job prospects, many have done just that—about a third of the nation now lives in the USA (roughly 22,400 people, according to the 2010 Census, up from 6,700 ten years earlier). There's a particularly large community in Springdale, Arkansas, working at the Tyson chicken plant. Notably, although other immigrants are eligible to receive Medicare and Social Security after five years in the United States, residents of the freely associated states are not—ever.

"I group the Pacific Islands into three levels of situation," an American named Gary (who asked that I not use his real name) told me. "There's developed, dependent, and life support." Gary put the Marshalls in the second category, having seen far worse situations—like Kiribati and Tuvalu—in his years of working and living across the Pacific.

There's significant investment in the Marshall Islands' infrastructure, Gary pointed out, including by many other countries. The National Gym had been funded by the government of Japan, the airport security system by "the people of the United States." Walking around Rita, past well-kept houses holding garage sales and shanties formed of Jengaed piles of cinder block and scrap metal, I saw dozens of water catchments given by the European Union, a medical van donated by India, and countless signs, including outside one of the municipal city halls, reading GIFT FROM THE REPUBLIC OF CHINA. The last was particularly curious, because the government based in Beijing is the *People's* Republic of China. The signs, Gary explained, represented *Taiwan* and its attempts to assert its own independence from China (which claims Taiwan as its own). Taiwan even had an embassy here, one of its twenty-one on the planet; most are in cash-strapped island nations, some of which, Gary said, essentially sell embassy rights to the highest bidder, Taiwan or China. For Taiwan, the point is recognition on the world stage. For China—which between 2006 and the beginning of 2015 donated $1.5 billion to eight Pacific Island nations, according to a Lowy Institute study—the aim is "to help demonstrate that it is a responsible power that supports other developing countries." In other words: to expand China's influence while softening its image.

As an independent nation, even a tiny one, the Marshall Islands has a place at the international table in a way that the territories do not. "I think the CNMI has lost a lot by not being an independent country," Angelo Villagomez said when I met him at Tide Table one day; he was on Majuro to give a presentation about marine conservation. "To have your own nationality . . . I think a strong case is to be made for actually being a country and not being a territory."

But the gains in international standing come with the tradeoff of less leverage in Washington, particularly with regard to nuclear compensation. "Guys like my father argued against the compact," a middle-aged man named Ben Chutaro told me. "Why would you, as a negotiator, compromise that leverage?" We sat on Ben's deck at the edge of the Majuro Lagoon, where a couple of catamarans bobbed in the water, with the shell of an old ferryboat rusting nearby. His father, Chuji, who shuffled outside to greet me at one point, was a Marshallese leader in the early 1980s. Ben looked the part of a businessman off the clock, in shorts and a T-shirt. At the time of the compact referendum, which passed with more than 60 percent of the vote, becoming a commonwealth instead of a freely associated state wasn't a clear option, Ben said, "but I think if the Marshall Islanders were given a choice of becoming a U.S. commonwealth, *clearly*, my suspicion is that they probably would have."

If you're going to be dependent on outside help, would you rather have one benefactor or many? Better the devil you know or the multitudes you don't? Better to manage a single big check, and the gamesmanship that comes with it, or a fistful? If you don't trust the USA—and, really, not many people in Micronesia do—is the solution to make your relationship to Uncle Sam stronger or to cut ties?

In 1951, the USA built a base on Kwajalein Island, forcing the Marshallese who lived there to move to the nearby island of

Ebeye, one-tenth the size. The Island Hopper had stopped on Kwajalein, where passengers were warned not to take photos out the window. (I hope I'm not revealing any national secrets when I say that there was a golf course on one side of the runway and there were some domed structures on the other, and it all looked rather pleasant, like a forgotten Florida Key.) Ebeye, Ben said, is bursting with overpopulation and a "raw-sewage smell and constant blackouts." Days earlier, a restaurant had burned down in part because the island had no fire truck. But the base was still active—when Maren and I were departing MSP Airport, a headline had scrolled by on CNN: "Missile defense system passes key test in the Marshall Islands." The Marshall Islands had no intention of kicking out the Americans, because they counted on the lease payments and, for that matter, many of the goods available at the base. At the Majuro airport, a young Marshallese man in a navy blue track suit pushed a cart with large boxes full of sandwiches, easily a hundred of them, fresh (or at least fresh-ish) from the Subway on Kwajalein. His expression was triumphant.

But it's hard to see a bright future for the Marshall Islands, in large part because, on top of everything else, the nation is facing a genuine existential threat from climate change. The official highest point on Majuro is twelve feet, on a bridge between two of the atoll's islands. A bit farther west, the distance between ocean and lagoon is merely the width of the two-lane road. I threw a stone across Majuro, watching it *plunk*. Soon, that stone-toss will be even shorter. The extra-high king tides were already coming more often, Jack Niedenthal told me said. "It's just mind-blowing, people running from their houses with their goods." And on Kili Atoll, the Bikinians were preparing to move yet again, due to increased flooding. From one man-made calamity to the next.

Ben hadn't given up hope for the Marshall Islands. He was working on increasing tourism, using the remoteness as a selling point, along with the crystalline waters and world-class diving and surfing. Big-wave surfer Kelly Slater had been out a few times.

"It's a nice place. I mean, I like it," Ben said, looking out at the lagoon, where raindrops were starting to fracture the glassy surface. He had gone to college in the USA and expected his children would do the same. "Maybe not in my lifetime, but hopefully my kids will be able to come back here," he said.

He paused for a second. "If we haven't overfished it or if the islands are still around."

• • • • •

AS I CHATTED with Angelo at Tide Table, the two of us reflecting on Saipan from afar—as so many have done before—he said, "My father was not born an American citizen but he died one. And he was able to take advantage of the American educational system. He went to law school in Washington, D.C. He came back and he helped write the constitution that was modeled after the United States Constitution. You know, he was able to live the American Dream. He was born a poor fisherman and the relationship with America provided opportunities for him that wouldn't have been available otherwise. At the same time, he was also very critical of America."

I told him about my conversations with Lino and Chun, and how, in their own ways, each had felt left out of the broader conversation on the island, and how no one on Saipan or in Washington seemed to have a good handle on how to set the territory on a better path. The CNMI's problems defied easy solutions or standard political party-line answers; in *Nobodies*, John Bowe writes that "my most conservative friend on the island . . . was all for [federal] takeover [of the CNMI]. As he put it, 'This place has to decide: Do you want to be part of the United States, or not?' Liberal Pam Brown, on the other hand, was largely against the idea. She, like others, felt skeptical that federal officials could ever do a good job of making decisions regarding a complex, faraway place about which they knew little."

At Tide Table, Angelo put it this way: "You're Spider-Man and Venom at the same time, the United States. Two different feelings, but it plays out every single day in every way of your life."

It reminded me of something Foster Rhea Dulles had written back in 1932, in his book, *America in the Pacific*: "It has always been difficult for the United States to know just where it stands, with principle ever warring against expediency, protestations of altruism denied by an aggressive nationalism. . . . [The USA has] always decried imperialism while creating an empire."

The story of the U.S. territories is the story of a nation that really, truly believes itself to be exceptional but also can't make up its mind what, exactly, that means. More powerful or more just? Ever more culturally diverse, the definition of "American" constantly expanding, or increasingly assimilated around a specific set of static cultural norms? How do you strike the right balance? And who gets to make the judgment?

Empire-building is easy enough: you just keep acquiring new lands, setting up additional outposts. Building a functional, cohesive nation—trying to form all those lands into one coherent, truly egalitarian body—that's much harder.

Chapter 5

BE TRUE TO YOUR HOME

Puerto Rico

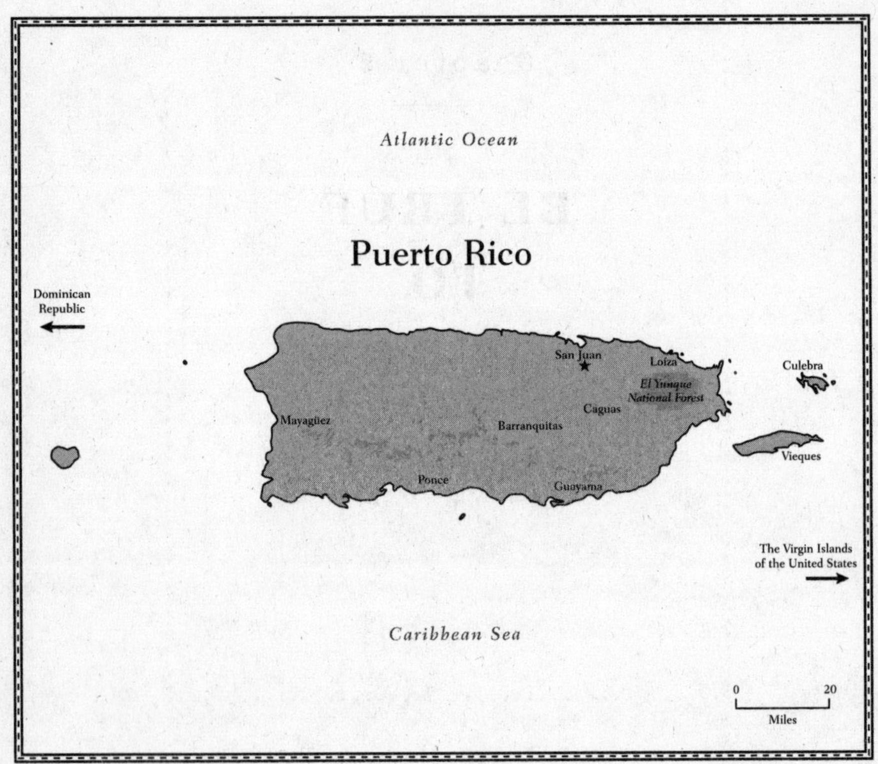
Atlantic Ocean
Puerto Rico
Dominican Republic
San Juan
Loíza
Culebra
El Yunque National Forest
Caguas
Mayagüez
Barranquitas
Vieques
Ponce
Guayama
The Virgin Islands of the United States
Caribbean Sea
0
20
Miles

Five months later and nearly half a world away, I was in a light- and art-filled home on Puerto Rico's northeast coast, considering the question of balance in a different, more concrete context. In front of me, a woman was levitating. Her bronze-toned body was arched, her arms outstretched. A long strip of turquoise fabric draped between her bare breasts and twisted loosely around her thigh, hanging so it just grazed the floor. She was a sculpture, called *Levación*, created by the artist I'd come to see, Samuel Lind. And even though I knew her every inch had been calculated, I couldn't figure out how she managed to stay upright, ascending from her base at a sharp angle.

Samuel's two-story studio/house/gallery was down a long driveway in the town of Loíza, about fifteen miles east of San Juan and known as the heart of Puerto Rico's African heritage, founded by escaped slaves who hid in the mangroves. I'd been brought here by a man named Jesus Ayala, a native Puerto Rican, Vietnam War vet, and retired NYPD cop, who was dressed smartly in slacks and a tucked-in polo and a red MARINES baseball cap. Samuel wore rectangular glasses and a brown shirt with the sleeves cut off, looking more like a trim computer tech than your wild-haired stereotype of an artist.

As my unofficial tour guide for a few days, Jesus was adamant that I understand the depth and complexity of Puerto Rico's cultural roots, and in Samuel's home, where we'd come less than twenty-four hours after I touched down in San Juan, there were ample lessons. From the impeccably lit main gallery area on the ground floor, we moved to a small, windowless studio. On a pedestal was a bronze statue, a couple of feet tall, of a woman dancing the bomba, for which Loíza is known, and which dates to the days of slavery. Women dancers traditionally wear white dresses, long and modest, as required by the slave owners, Jesus said, but their movements tell a different story, energetic and flamboyant. In the bomba, there's just one dancer at a time, accompanied by three or four drummers, one of whom has to match the dancer's movements. "The dancer leads the beat—you understand?" Jesus said.

Upstairs was more gallery space, more studio space, and Samuel's living area. We stepped into the kitchen and he took a peeled orange off the countertop as a tabby cat brushed against his legs. It was airy up here, with high ceilings and lots of natural light and a balcony. On one side of the room was a table with a scattering of prints: salsa and bomba festival posters, and scenes of *jibaros*, Puerto Rico's iconic field-workers of the mountains, with straw hats and white work shirts with the sleeves rolled up. Samuel explained what I was seeing, pausing to nibble on orange sections while Jesus offered his own commentary. The bomba is still popular here, he said—he even knew a guy who teaches a bombaerobics exercise class.

"And, um . . . *Que es eso?*" I asked, pointing to a wooden purple forearm standing upright on the table, with an eye in the palm of the hand.

"That's the Power Hand," Samuel said, a symbol of Espiritismo, a belief system that, like Santería, mixes elements of

Catholicism and the Yoruba mythology of Western Africa—plus, Jesus added, books by a nineteenth century French mystic.

"So it's a synthesized, crazy version of everything," Jesus said. As the stories continued, this was his refrain: Puerto Rico is many cultures, united. Samuel nodded.

But as in any history with two tellers, the versions didn't always line up. At one point, Jesus and Samuel disagreed about the precise way that Moorish traditions had filtered, via the Spanish, into modern Puerto Rico. There was a momentary pause and Samuel said, "You are with me but no . . ."

Jesus chuckled and turned to me: "He believes in independence; I believe in statehood."

"The most important thing is, Puerto Rico is very different," Samuel said. "Puerto Rico has . . . I don't know, Puerto Rico has a different history, no?"

"America wants diversity," Jesus countered. "Texans are Texans, Floridians are Floridians . . . My point is, we could become a state with our own identity."

"But we are another thing here!" Samuel said. "We are a nation like you! When the United States came, we had already made everything for hundreds of years. We have our own culture, our own history, no?" He touched my arm slightly, familiarly, speaking more to me than to Jesus.

The conversation had veered, abruptly and conclusively, becoming a verbal tennis match between two longtime, friendly rivals. *Independence, statehood, independence, statehood.* They agreed that the status quo was unacceptable, and in their deep-seated pride in being Puerto Rican. For twenty minutes, and backed by a soft chorus of birds on the balcony railing, Jesus and Samuel traded points in English and Spanish.

Basically: *We're financially better off as a state, and though it'll be a struggle to keep our cultural identity intact, we'll figure it out.* Versus: *We're culturally better off independent, and though it'll be a struggle to keep our already-faltering economy intact, we'll figure it out.*

They both anticipated every volley, prefacing every point and counterpoint with knowing smiles and small sighs that said, *Well, I've heard* that *line a thousand times.* They seemed to enjoy the conversation, the camaraderie of the debate, and their tone was consistently warm if sometimes impatient or sarcastic, a collegial urgency in their voices as they detailed their own hopes for Puerto Rico's future.

Finally, Samuel looked at me and laughed. "Sorry for the politics."

He plucked a print off the table. It depicted five *jibaros* having a late-night jam session around a lantern, each playing a different instrument. Jesus explained: The *güira* (a gourd scraped with a metal comb) and maracas originated with the indigenous Taínos. The handheld drum, a *pander*, came from Western Africa; the drummer kept a particular beat, called a *clave—"bumbum bum bum bum,"* the root of Puerto Rico's native music. The last two *jibaros* held a guitar, from Europe, and a *cuatro*, "our own local guitar." The heyday of the *jibaro* had come and gone by the early twentieth century, Jesus added, as industrialization took off, but they still made for a popular local legend.

"You like this?" Samuel said, pointing to the print. I nodded.

He smiled. "I give to you."

He signed it and added the title: *Tertulia Borincana*, which he translated as "Puerto Rican Talk-Together." Given Jesus's brief history lesson, and the conversation that had just unfolded between Jesus and Samuel, I imagined the *jibaros*' song to be a lament: *From this rich, proud history, what comes next?*

• • • • •

IN THE WEEKS before I flew to Puerto Rico, the island was suddenly in the national headlines—not front and center, but more prominent than the back-page sidebars where I'd usually tracked down the latest territory information. The news wasn't great: Puerto Rico was facing an economic crisis, its government more than $70 billion in debt; people were moving to the states by the thousands; there was a worrisome crime wave (one Puerto Rican friend-of-a-friend offered to accompany me for my entire trip, because she was so concerned for my safety); and, most recently, there had been an alarming uptick in the mosquito-borne chikungunya virus. Meanwhile, there was the percolating hot topic of an upcoming referendum on Puerto Rico's political status—it wasn't on the election schedule yet but maybe, possibly, would be sometime soon-ish . . . whatever that meant.

Uncertainty shapes the everyday mood in the territories in subtle but undeniable ways. Sometimes it translates into a sense of despair. Sometimes it hardens into cynicism or a dark, brooding shrug-and-carry-on fatalism. I arrived in San Juan, on a warm winter's day, to a different sort of vibe, a fatalism with a live-it-up edge. The atmosphere was at once electric and anxious, underscored by a restless bohemianism manifest in graffiti (a stylized Virgin Mary, a big-eyed purple cat, a stenciled #STOPTHENSA) and in the salsa and hip-hop blasting from clubs and cars and apartment windows.

I spent my first few nights in Old San Juan, a one-square-mile peninsula jutting into the ocean. The rest of San Juan, a regional capital of four hundred thousand people (two million in the metropolitan area), is sprawling and modern, with ever-clogged freeways, a small subway system, and vast stands of high-rises: banking headquarters, luxury hotels, workaday apartments, decrepit public housing. But Old San Juan is all hilly cobblestone streets and wedged-together houses and storefronts in a rainbow of edibly vivid colors (so European!). In the mornings, I ate guava-filled pastries and brioche-like Mallorca buns* in genteel plazas, with fountains and landscaped grounds and old men reading the newspaper. My evening itinerary was a drink—my hotel was next to a bar called Douglas, which I was duty-bound to patronize—and an hour or so wandering the streets, peeking past curlicuing iron gates into houses, and strolling past bars and cafés spilling outside, with tables taking over parking spots, snug between SUVs (so American!). At all hours, well-fed cats loped along the curbs, Old San Juan's unofficial mascots and catchers-of-rats. I'd promised Maren more text messages—now that I was back in what Verizon considered to be the United States—and San Juan offered plenty of fodder.

Old San Juan was something of a world apart from the rest of the island—tidy, safe, literally walled-off—but even here the anxieties were evident at every turn. The restaurants at nighttime were beckoning and beguiling but mostly empty and lonely, Edward Hopper's *Nighthawks* in the tropics. The street smelled, somehow, of caramel corn and turmeric, with an ever-present hint of cigarette from the police officers standing watch on seemingly every corner.

The nervous energy built as Old San Juan prepared for the Fiestas de la Calle San Sebastián, the island's biggest street festival. Painters touched up trim and deliverymen in sunglasses

* Mallorcas are so intrinsic to Puerto Rican life that they even have them at McDonald's.

delivered pallets of Heineken and a drink called Gasolina ("Party in a Pouch" read the boxes). Workers built stages in seemingly every plaza, dwarfing the statues of Very Important Men. For days, the anticipation was growing.

• • • • •

From my first gray-matter-pulsing night in the USVI, I'd been propelled along—across months of travel and a year of research and rumination—by the hope and assumption that a Grand Unified Theory of the United States' Insular Possessions was within reach. My head was overstuffed with information, yet I felt irredeemably clueless, forever tumbling down the rabbit hole, discovering new offshoots to explore, new tidbits and perspectives I'd somehow never seen before.

Now I was tumbling once again. For starters, I had to recalibrate my conceptions of territory size and scale. Puerto Rico has ten times more people than all the other territories combined, and the island itself, an almost-rectangle of 110 miles by 40 miles, also dwarfs its insular compatriots (and is also larger than Delaware or Rhode Island). It's big enough that there are tangible, stereotyped regional differences: San Juan, on the north side of the island, is the bustling capital; Ponce, to the south, is the haughty second city; the central mountains are the home of the *jibaros*; the eastern islands of Vieques and Culebra are former military bases with small, laid-back towns. Puerto Rico was simply larger and—amazingly—even more complicated than the other territories.

But even as I was ever-adjusting my understanding of the territories, it was increasingly clear that there were many shared traits. These included, for starters: polyglot cultures proud of being distinct from the states; close-knit, insular communities; a history of colonialism followed by parallel improvements and declines in the American era; messy (and often just plain corrupt) local politics; heavy reliance on tourism and a general lack of stable investment and economic diversification outside this fickle industry (the USVI's economy was long based on tourism plus Hovensa; American Samoa was pretty much just tuna; Guam was tourism plus military; the CNMI was tourism plus the garment industry); and perpetual frustration with the ever-shifting nature of the local and federal laws and the relationship to the USA.

And on the issue of political status, even in the territories where this hadn't been a major topic of discussion, when it did come up, there was common ground on the primary talking points:

The Change-Averse, who support the status quo, say: *It's not perfect, but we're better off partly with the United States and partly on our own. We have more economic opportunity than our regional neighbors and more cultural independence than the states. We just need to do a better job within the current setup.*

The Nationalists, who support independence, say: *We have a separate cultural heritage, which is threatened by Americanization. We should fight colonialism and become our own country. The economics might be tricky, but we'll make it work; we'll attract investors from the whole world, not just the few people in the USA who are paying attention.*

Then you have the statehood supporters, who take two different approaches to reaching the same conclusion:

The Melting-Pot Optimists say: *The United States, for all its flaws, has brought a lot of good things here; we're proudly Americanized, and the United States is a diverse place, with plenty of room for us to keep aspects of our culture if we become a state. It's not too late for the nation to live up to its ideals of pluralism and equal opportunity for all, and to give us a stronger political voice without imposing cultural domination.*

And the Jaded Realists say: *Like it or not, we're dependent on the USA, and that won't change at all if we're our own nation—we'll just lose what little voice we have because we're no longer part of the USA. We might as well stick with them. Besides, there's no stopping cultural change at this point; globalization is the new Americanization.*

Underpinning each of these views is a general feeling of being in a limbo state and trying to find a way out. More often than not, the outlook was not especially optimistic, because uncertainty—political, economic, cultural, and otherwise—was so long-standing, with no real signs of abating. Though each territory has followed its own path, they share a fraught, bumpy common ground, and a sense that it's getting bumpier all time. In the territories, the trajectory of history trends not toward justice or coherence but toward confusion and chaos.

• • • • •

ONE AFTERNOON, I walked to the eastern edge of Old San Juan. Wedged in the hundred yards or so between the thick stone wall and the crashing Atlantic was La Perla, a famously rough and ramshackle neighborhood that my *Lonely Planet* guidebook cautioned even the most intrepid travelers to avoid. I followed the wall to the tip of the peninsula, and suddenly I was in front of a broad green space, at least a quarter mile long, that stretched to one of the most recognizable symbols of Spanish colonialism and the American Imperial Moment: Castillo San

Felipe del Morro (commonly called simply El Morro), a sort of early colonialism Death Star, with walls 140 feet tall and up to 25 feet thick.

For nearly three hundred years, starting in the mid-1500s, Spain dominated the Caribbean, thanks in part to El Morro; its even larger sibling, Castillo San Cristóbal (a short walk away); and (Old) San Juan. Christopher Columbus came to what's now Puerto Rico in 1493, and Ponce de León founded the first European settlement, called Caparra, in 1508. Jesus took me to the Caparra's ruins, which stand discreetly along a stretch of urban highway, near a pool supply store and a veterinary clinic. Out front, a sign said that the structures were built to "protect the settlers from Indian attacks," though in truth it was the Taínos who were in danger.

The Taínos called their island Borinquen (or Borikén) and called themselves *boricua*, terms still in common use; the commonwealth's anthem is called "La Borinqueña."* There were more than ten thousand Taínos when Ponce de León arrived; within ten years, a third of them died of smallpox. Many of the rest were enslaved to build cities and mine gold and silver. In the 1530s, officials in Spain asked the governor how many Taínos still lived on the island. The answer was none.

The Spanish brought in thousands of new slaves, from Africa, who constructed much of what you see in Old San Juan today and worked in the sugarcane fields that, as in the USVI, made this an economically important colony, envied by other Caribbean colonizers. The English bombarded El Morro in 1595, 1598, and 1725, in an attempt to take the city and the island, and

* Incidentally, it is also from their language that we get common words including *hurricane*, *canoe*, *tobacco*, *hammock*, and *barbecue*.

the Dutch tried in 1625. (The English actually took the fort that second time, but left after six weeks because so many men got dysentery.) By the early 1800s, the Spanish Empire was facing an even bigger test, as independence movements swept through its South American holdings, and in 1868 the fervor spread to Cuba and Puerto Rico. On September 23, more than six hundred Puerto Ricans marched into the mountain town of Lares and decreed the island an independent republic. The next day, the Spanish military quashed the rebellion. Brief and unsuccessful though it was, El Grito de Lares ("The Cry of Lares") looms large in Puerto Rican pride as the day when the island became not merely an outpost but something unto itself, a culture tied to this specific land rather than to a far-off ruler.

As ripples of unrest continued, El Morro came to symbolize not so much security from invaders but the Spaniards' heavy hand. It was a dungeon for dissidents.

As you walk around El Morro today, it's hard to figure out what's dungeon and what's everyday quarters—it's all dark, dank, a little bit spooky. The tunnels and stairways keep going down and down and down. Near the bottom, I found myself in a cavernous room. The air was cool and silent but for a buzzing floodlight. My eyes traced the curve of the mottled stone wall, all greens and whites and browns, and stopped on a menacing protrusion midway up one side, a rusty hunk of metal that looked like a petrified railroad tie. It was part of a shell from the last bombardment of the fort, on May 2, 1898, by the United States, during the Spanish-American War.

The shelling that hit El Morro, at the beginning of the Puerto Rican campaign, didn't result in a full takeover of the city, but it did allow the Americans to set up a blockade, cutting off San Juan's harbor. (By the way, don't go looking for San Juan Hill here. As the website of the San Juan National Historic Site—

which includes El Morro—dryly notes, on the Frequently Asked Questions page, "The famous hill which Teddy Roosevelt and the Rough Riders charged up . . . is in eastern Cuba, 500 miles away.") In Cuba and the Philippines, fighting was in full swing, steadily ticking up through May and June 1898. On June 10, the United States Navy, along with Cuban independence fighters, captured the Cuban harbor of Guantánamo Bay. It was a critical gain, positioning the Americans for the Battle of Santiago de Cuba, on July 3, when they all but wiped out Spain's Caribbean fleet.

On July 25, 1898, American troops from Guantánamo landed at Guánica, on the south side of Puerto Rico. "The Spaniards were completely taken by surprise," the *New York Times* reported, before describing the bucolic meadows-and-mountains scenery and adding, with a vacationer's breeziness, "Guánica is the most delightful spot yet occupied by our forces."

The Americans were largely welcomed by Puerto Ricans, and for a brief period after the war, it seemed as though their island was on the fast track to become a full-fledged part of the United States. The island's Organic Act—the Foraker Act—established the local government and courts in 1900, seemingly the start of a path toward statehood. It followed the same general principles and guideposts as Organic Acts of prior territories but, Christina Ponsa explained to me, in earlier instances there was "this sort of pro forma language in the Organic Act that says, Congress hereby extends the Constitution and laws of the United States. And the Organic Acts for Puerto Rico and Philippines left that out." The one prior instance of this omission had happened two years earlier, with the annexation of Hawaii, but Congress had quickly extended the Constitution to those islands, as a virtually automatic act—which is to say, Congress incorporated Hawaii before the term existed. Ponsa added: "Once the Supreme Court invents all this business [of incorporation]" with *Downes v. Bidwell* in 1901, "Congress never does this again."

During the American invasion in 1898, Carl Sandburg (then an American soldier, later an acclaimed poet) reported, "On roads and streets as we marched were barefooted men and women smiling and calling us '*Puerto Rico Americano.*'" The Insular Cases, however, quickly undermined this feeling of common ground, not least by confirming that Puerto Rico had taken a step backward, rights-wise. Near the end of its colonial run, Spain had sought to temper Puerto Rico's independence movement by granting island residents Spanish citizenship and representation in the Spanish Parliament, and most Puerto Ricans expected equivalent rights under American rule. Yet it would take nearly two more decades, until the 1917 Jones Act, for Puerto Ricans to finally gain American citizenship—just in time for eighteen thousand territory residents to be drafted into World War I—along with the right to elect their own (nonvoting) congressperson, known here as the resident commissioner.

It was a slow process, but bit by tiny bit, Puerto Ricans seemed to be making headway in becoming more equal Americans.

• • • • •

Parts of Puerto Rico reminded me of Tumon on Guam, in the sense that they felt not just American but *extra*-American—but in Puerto Rico it wasn't a matter of tourists' taste but locals'.

Jesus was eager, in his stoic way, to show me his hometown of Caguas, the Creole City, a mixture of the territory's Taíno, African, and European roots. And so, one morning, he picked me up and we got on the freeway heading south. We whizzed past the

Hiram Bithorn baseball stadium and a cockfighting arena, and trucks parked on the shoulder selling bananas, and the Plaza de las Americas, a three-hundred-store shopping mall with a Cheesecake Factory and the first Macy's outside the continental states.

As we entered Caguas, he said with delight, "We have six Walgreens!" and I later learned that, in fact, Puerto Rico has the highest concentration of Walgreens in the United States, and the highest concentration of Walmarts in the world.

Jesus grew up in a poor section of San Juan—he showed me a photo of houses connected by a haphazard plank boardwalk above the swampy ground—in a neighborhood that was later leveled to make room for a freeway interchange. Now, having retired from the NYPD in 1995, he lived in a gated subdivision called Mansiones de Bairoa, where, he said, houses sell for $250,000 to $300,000. His house, where we joined his wife for lunch, was even tidier than most model homes I've toured, the tile floor spotless, the yard immaculately buzz-cut.

All of this is essentially what Puerto Rican and American leaders had in mind in their postwar development plans, as highways and malls and industrialization and tourist infrastructure came in, and agriculture went out.

It had been a rough few decades. After the American takeover, Puerto Rico's coffee, tobacco, and, especially, sugar industries had flourished, thanks in large part to free trade with the states, but the prosperity was selective. In 1899, a hurricane wiped out almost the entire coffee crop, forcing many farmers to sell their land to banks; they and other famers were hit two years later by a substantial property-tax increase. By 1930, absentee owners—corporations—controlled more than one-third of the island's land in use. Everyday Puerto Ricans felt left out. In the middle of this epochal transition, in 1912, a Puerto Rican delegation traveled to the White House to discuss their concerns with President Taft; during their post-dinner conversation, the president fell asleep and started snoring.

But in 1948, the American and Puerto Rican governments developed a new initiative to modernize and jump-start the local economy: Operation Bootstrap, which focused on increasing manufacturing and tourism. The results were immediate: by 1952, Puerto Rico had 150 new industrial plants in production, and some 100,000 tourists. In 1958, Puerto Rican Governor Luis Muñoz Marín was featured on the cover of *Time* magazine, under a headline "Democracy's Laboratory in Latin America."

But again the success was selective. Between 1950 and 1960, factory jobs rose from fifty-five thousand to eighty-one thousand, but in the same period, as César J. Ayala and Rafael Bernabe write in their book *Puerto Rico in the American Century*, sugarcane-industry employment dropped nearly in half, from eighty-seven thousand to forty-five thousand, and needlepointing, a once-thriving in-home industry, fell from fifty-one thousand workers to ten thousand. All told, "The 'golden age' of Operation Bootstrap was actually characterized by a shrinking economy in terms of employment."

On the other hand, agriculture and needlepoint almost certainly would have declined even without Operation Bootstrap, in parallel with the trend elsewhere. "Progress" is always in the eyes of the beholder, as I'd been reminded constantly on this Territories Tour.

In Caguas, Jesus pointed out a Sam's Club, a Costco, and two malls. Where slaves once worked the sugarcane fields, there was now a Macaroni Grill and a Caribbean Cinema. We passed a university, which provided Jesus the opportunity to boast of Puerto

Rico's many institutions of higher education. (I later looked up the numbers and the territory has seventy-four accredited four-year colleges and universities. In comparison, Iowa, which has a similar population, has forty-seven such schools. Jesus was right to be proud.) Then Jesus took me on a whirlwind tour of the town's cultural highlights: a performing arts center; a tiny but genuinely impressive history museum; and a sprawling botanical garden, with separate sections showcasing plants from the town's Taíno, African, and European heritage. (The garden was closed for the day, but Jesus insisted I needed to see it and, much to my chagrin, badgered the local tourism officials into opening it up for the Important Writer from the States. The officials also gifted me with a blaze-orange, Caguas-branded insulated lunch bag and a beige Caguas-branded hat. What the Pacific territories had taken away, again and again, the Creole City had returned.)

In the center of Caguas, Plaza Palmer was a town square to make all other cities jealous, with a carousel and a floral clock and a snack kiosk. Jesus beamed as he told me the history. As we looked across the street at vacant storefronts, he noted that the historic downtown, like many around the USA, was struggling in the shadow of the big boxes on the highway.

There was only the slightest hint of wistfulness in his voice. It was all part of the path of progress.

At Casa del Trovador (House of the Troubadour), a group of perhaps twenty children were trying their hand, one by one, at singing ballads of the *jibaros*. Operation Bootstrap pretty well wiped out the real-life *jibaros*, but the archetype has remained essential to Puerto Rico's identity, something like a *Grapes of Wrath* meets Will Rogers figure, with dirt on his hands and a song in his heart. There's a monument to the *jibaro* up in the mountains, next to the tollway that connects the island's north and south coasts and is itself a symbol of the modernization that relegated the *jibaro* to the realm of lore.

But at the Casa del Trovador, he lives. To one side of the stage stood a man who looked like Benicio del Toro, the Puerto Rican actor, playing Huck Finn. He wore a straw hat and introduced himself to me as Don Chema, and spoke animatedly as he explained *jibaro* music's defining elements: the mix of instruments, as I'd seen in Samuel Lind's prints; the *decima* lyrical structure of ten lines with a specific rhyming pattern, which the best singers improvise on the spot; the *cuatro*, similar to a guitar but with five sets of paired strings.

Don Chema mimicked playing a *cuatro*: "*Ting, ting, ting, ting! Es la parte mas romantic.*" Out on the stage, a man in his thirties was accompanying the kids on a *cuatro*, its twinned strings creating a twinkling, haunting backdrop to the ballads.

This sort of music was "dying out," Don Chema said, but then gestured to the students. A young man in a wheelchair and a fedora was singing, his voice crisp and passionate. "At the same time," Don Chema added with evident pride, "coming back."

A boy who couldn't have been more than six stepped onstage, in a blue American Eagle shirt and with a terrified expression. An accompanist played some opening notes, *ting, ting, ting, ting*! and the boy took a deep breath, clenched a tiny fist at his side, and began singing.

• • • • •

As Operation Bootstrap left a broad swath of Puerto Ricans out of its vision for the future, the Gran Migración—Grand Migration—began. Almost 530,000 people, more than a quarter of the island's population, left between 1950 and 1970, tacitly encouraged by the commonwealth government. The Gran Migración was also assisted by the fact that, in the mid-century, air travel was starting to open up to the masses—moving to the mainland was easier than ever. Today, there are more than five million people of Puerto Rican descent in the states, only about a third of whom were born in the commonwealth itself. (Incidentally, it's important to note that people moving from Puerto Rico are not "immigrants" any more than someone moving from Minnesota to New York; it's all the same country.)

Now, as Puerto Rico's economy struggled, a new Gran Migración was under way: in the last four years, more than 170,000 people, almost 5 percent of the island's population, had moved out of Puerto Rico. The outflow was especially pronounced among professionals, including doctors—in early 2016, according to a National Public Radio report, doctors were leaving the island at a rate of one every day. The commonwealth's largest pediatric hospital had to shut down two of its wings. More than 10 percent of the commonwealth's schools closed.

Many Puerto Ricans, particularly those who supported statehood, tied the exodus to the commonwealth's political status. "Every month, thousands of island residents vote for statehood with their feet, in search of political rights and economic opportunity," Puerto Rico Resident Commissioner Pedro Pierluisi said in an official press release. He added: "There is no better evidence that the current territory status has failed, and that statehood is the right status for Puerto Rico, than these stunning numbers."

Before I'd departed for the USVI, a year earlier, I'd expected that the political status would be the most fiercely debated issue in every territory, but that hadn't been the case at all. I usually had to drag opinions out of people. In Puerto Rico, I just had to wait a moment. The topic seeps into unrelated conversations, blares across the front pages of the newspapers, and forms the key platform planks for the island's two main political parties, the pro-statehood Partido Nuevo Progresista (PNP) and the pro-status-quo Partido Popular Democrático (PPD). (Neither has any specific alignment with the main national parties of the United States—you'll find plenty of Democrats and plenty of Republicans within the ranks of both the PNP and the PPD.) The status debate "trumps the issues that really ought to be debated day to day," Christina Ponsa, who is originally from Puerto Rico, told me. You might like one candidate's overall platform—economic development, educational improvements, filling potholes—but if you don't agree with his or her position on Puerto Rico's political status, then never mind. The status issue is like the bomba dancers that Jesus and Samuel had told me about, sneakily dictating the rhythm of everyday life.

While we were in Loíza to call on Samuel, Jesus took me to the town's city hall. In the lobby was a photo of the mayor—a youngish man with braces that made him look even younger—and a Puerto Rican flag.

"Look at the shade of the blue," Jesus said, pointing. The left side of the Puerto Rican flag features a white star inside a blue triangle. To my eye, it was royal blue, Crayola blue, standard-issue blue.

"It's *dark* blue. That means this town is pro-statehood." Many pro-status-quo towns, he said, fly flags with a lighter shade. In the San Juan suburb of Guaynabo, Jesus said, the mayor, as a signal of his support for Americanization and statehood, had mandated that in the square mile around city hall, all stop signs had to be in English: STOP rather than PARE.

For Jesus, statehood represented the ultimate progress—though, of course, Samuel and many others would have disagreed.

• • • • •

PUERTO RICO'S LOSS, in the Gran Migración, was the states' gain. Puerto Ricans formed substantial communities in cities including Miami, Chicago, Philadelphia, and, most of all, New York City, where by 1970 more than eight hundred thousand Puerto Ricans lived.

They quickly made their mark on the landscape, politics, and culture of the city, notably in the Nuyorican movement of writers, artists, and musicians. Though the names of certain Nuyorican luminaries, like the poets Miguel Algarín and Miguel Piñero (who also founded the Nuyorican Poets Café in the East Village), may be familiar in select quarters, it's salsa—which has roots in Puerto Rican plena and bomba music—that has found the largest stage and has proven resilient and adaptable, working its way into the DNA of the modern American pop canon. And this, too, is progress of a sort. Just as Jesus welcomed elements of Americanization, the growing Puerto Rican population in the states is a boon to their new neighborhoods, adding new people and perspectives, in the same way that the outflow of residents from other territories also enriches the American cultural fabric.

Salsa and its relatives—merengue, bomba, plena, and the newest cousin, hip-hop-inflected reggaeton—were inescapable. I heard the music in restaurants, from passing cars, on seemingly every radio station, floating in the air from unknown sources. Jesus took me to a salsa dance lesson (where I impressed everyone with my ability to inadvertently stomp my partner's toes perfectly in time with the *clave* beat) and to the gentrifying Santurce neighborhood, where the evening scene around the public market was lively with people eating and drinking at everything from literal food counters to the internationally acclaimed restaurant José Enrique, to salsa karaoke bars. At one, a pair of yellow maracas sat next to the mic stand, just in case singers wanted to accompany themselves.

Back in Old San Juan, the Fiestas de la Calle San Sebastián had started up and nearly every plaza hosted a band with horns blaring, drums *clave*-ing, and crowds throbbing, where seemingly everyone was dancing brilliantly, all twirls and dips. One guy had brought his own *güira* and was playing along.

Once the party started, it didn't stop. Even away from the stages and the sea of vendors' tents—ceramics with Taíno petroglyph motifs; driftwood furniture; T-shirts that read NO HABLO INGLES BUT I FUCK VERY WELL—the frenzy was unavoidable, pulling me from one wave of sound and mass of revelers to the next.

At the edge of one crowd, fast-buck hopefuls sold selfie sticks and T-shirts. A group promoting AT&T paraded by carrying orange weather balloons, followed by an ecstatic trio in green top hats, guerrilla marketers handing out Tic Tacs. I'd heard rumbling that the festival was getting too corporate, and hand-wringing that the enthusiasm would be dampened by the island's myriad woes: the mosquitoes, the economy, the crime, the new *migración*. But as the merrymakers downed their breath mints and their Heinekens and Gasolinas, the general mood was: *We know we should be worrying. But for now, let's party.*

• • • • •

I POKED AROUND the island's eastern side for a couple of days, hiking in the El Yunque rain forest and eating inadvisable quantities of *alpacurrias* (fritters made with taro and green banana and filled with meat) and *lechón* (roasted pork) before heading south, to Guayama.

"Why you going there?" Jesus had asked, incredulity in his gravelly voice. The town is not on the standard tourist itinerary, meriting barely a mention in my guidebooks, but I had an invitation to spend the night with some locals, and I felt duty-bound to accept.

I guessed that Quique and Ana were in their early sixties, he slender, with glasses and a tendency to quote Marx with a friendly intensity, she with a short just-so hairdo and a quiet, maternal concern for my well-being; she had worriedly texted me several times while I was lost on my way to Guayama. I met up with them at a small art museum that they helped run. Their friend Jorge joined us to smooth over our otherwise highly imperfect grasp of each other's languages. Jorge was an architect, historian, and poet, with a casual intellectualism, citing architectural theory and Puerto Rican novelists in the humble, unaffected way that few people can pull off.

Guayama felt like a smaller version of Caguas: suburban bigboxes on the outskirts, a historic downtown that had seen better days. The art museum was only three rooms, but was recently opened, the building lovingly restored. After a brief tour, we drove to a seafood restaurant near the waterfront, austere but endearing, more like a church fellowship hall than my stereotype of the sort of place where you can order lobster. The catch was as fresh and tasty as at any seafood restaurant in the states, which wasn't a shock, but the prices took me by surprise: twenty to thirty dollars for an entrée, not what I'd expected from the surroundings.

As we were leaving the restaurant, Quique told me we needed to go see Bob the Gringo.

"Bob . . . the Gringo?" I asked.

Quique grinned.

So off the two of us went to the next-door town of Arroyo, where we drove along the oceanfront main drag and turned left at an obelisk commemorating Samuel Morse, who came here to set up the first telegraph lines in Latin America. We parked and entered a small corner store—a *colmado*—where most of the floor space was given over to a handful of black patio chairs and a plastic table with dominoes awaiting players. There was a diagonal counter cutting off one corner, where the owner, César, greeted us and asked me a question I've never heard at a bodega back in the states: "What do you want to drink?"

César had a few shelves full of goods behind the counter—steel wool, toothpaste, cans of Goya beans—but I quickly gathered that this wasn't a store so much as an unofficial community center. Jorge was already there. I got a can of Medalla Light and took a chair at the table while Quique and César started chatting and César's black cat came over to inspect us. As I told the men about Caguas and the *jibaros,* César cocked an eyebrow and smirked at something over my shoulder. I turned to find an elderly man with lean, wrinkly arms and a hunched posture—plus a strut in his slow step and a spirited, high-pitched Texas drawl.

Bob the Gringo had arrived. The energy of the room shifted, all eyes on him. He spoke not in sentences but in smiling decrees.

"I've been here for eighteen years," he said, opening a can of Budweiser.

"Why here, why *Arroyo*?" I asked. It wasn't exactly your typical retirement community. Most of the buildings near the store were run-down, if not actually falling down.

Bob pointed a long, bony finger. "I'll tell you! It's simple! I just found a town where the people are as crazy as I am!"

"Ask him what he thinks about the political status," someone said, to a chorus of muffled snickers.

Bob pointed again. "When I came down here, I thought Puerto Rico should be a state, but now I've changed my mind completely! We can't afford to be a state or independent! We should stay *exactly* the same!"

"That's the view from a gringo," Quique countered.

"It's true!"

Like every iteration of this debate I would hear in Puerto Rico, there was no animosity or surprise in anyone's tone; the points were passionate but the edge was dulled by their predictability, their familiarity.

"The president and Congress have been saying for years that Puerto Rico can't make up its mind," Bob said. "People can't figure it out!"

César chimed in. "Doug, independence is stronger than you think." He had a buzz cut and round John Lennon glasses and a small stack of books sitting on one side of the counter: one about the philosopher Epicurus, another titled *Puerto Rico: Una Historia Contemporanea*. "We have a joke here," César continued. "Do you know that it is against the law to sell or even to drink alcohol on Election Day here?"

This was news to me.

"Do you know why?" César stared at me deadpan, waiting. Bob the Gringo sipped his Bud.

"No," I said.

"Because when we're drunk, we're all independents!"

The store erupted in laughter, although for Bob it was more of an eye-rolling, *I-saw-THAT-coming* chuckle.

• • • • •

WHAT BOB was getting at was this: Puerto Rico has voted on its political status four times—1967, 1993, 1998, and 2012—and the results have been all over the board. The first two times, the voters favored commonwealth status. In 1998, the preferred choice was "none of the above," because of disagreements over what, exactly, the other options actually meant. In 2012, there was a two-part ballot. First: *Should Puerto Rico continue its current territorial status?* Most voters, 54 percent, said no. Second: *Which non-territorial option do you prefer?* Statehood received 61 percent of the votes, free association (like the Marshall Islands) got 33 percent, and full independence got 5.5 percent. People who supported the status quo, however, pointed out that even if they voted "Yes" to continuing things as they were, they still had to vote on the second question. And when it comes to electing a governor and a resident commissioner, that unofficial barometer of public sentiment, voters go back and forth between the pro-statehood PNP and the pro-status-quo PPD. There's no clear, definitive answer to what Puerto Ricans want, although debating the options is something of a local pastime. (They turn out to elections at higher rates than the mainland U.S.; it helps that Election Day is a territorial holiday, with businesses and schools closed.)

Part of the issue is disagreement about what, exactly, *commonwealth* means and what improvements are possible within the constraints of this designation. "Nobody knows what a commonwealth is," Christina Ponsa told me, "and that was pretty much on purpose." For starters, the very label is misleading. As discussed, there are myriad definitions of "commonwealth," but that's not what they call it in Puerto Rico. Here, the political status is known as Estado Libre Asociado (or ELA), a term dreamed up to sell the idea of this non-statehood, non-independence compromise designation in the first place. Translate Estado Libre Asociado directly into English, though, and it's *free associated state*, which implies that the island has entered a compact of free association, which it has not. Legally, "freely associated state" applies only to the Republic of the Marshall Islands, the Republic of Palau, and the Federated States of Micronesia—not to Puerto Rico.

The ELA/commonwealth status was proposed by Luis Muñoz Marín, the president of the Puerto Rico Senate, and set up in 1952. Even beyond the name, this new status was an optical illusion of a policy change, its meaning depending on your view. It offered an apparent increase in autonomy, promising a divorce from congressional oversight, and for the optimists among the local statehood and independence movements, this seemed to be a step toward their differing desired outcomes. But the new status actually changed very little in everyday terms, much to the delight of Puerto Ricans who favored the status quo.

Today, most people who support the status quo—with the possible exception of Bob the Gringo—believe it should be "enhanced," with more local rights but no change in the overall setup. Most people who support independence or statehood note that various "enhancements" have been proposed over the last fifty-plus years, but none have accomplished much, and there's no reason to believe more minor tweaks will help. Real change, they say, will require the setup itself to be overhauled. As numerous legal scholars have pointed out, Congress still holds plenary power over the commonwealths, meaning it can unilaterally withdraw their right of self-government at any time. This requires a few more hurdles than in the territories, but, from a constitutional perspective, it remains an option; the commonwealths are still, like the territories, under congressional control.

What César, Quique, and Jorge were getting at was this: Sure, the Puerto Rican Independence Party (PIP) hasn't done so well at the polls. But the Grito de Lares has echoed across the decades. In a tourist-town souvenir shop a few days later, I would even see it emblazoned on a T-shirt, along with the slogan VIVA PUERTO RICO LIBRE (and sharing shelf space with Che Guevara shirts). There's a baseline of Puerto Rican pride, nudging toward Puerto Rican exceptionalism—even Jesus and Samuel Lind had agreed on this—and this, nationalists say, is a tacit support of independence. For instance, at the 2004 Summer Olympics, the Puerto Rican men's basketball team beat the superstar-filled Team USA, and all of a sudden, César said, everyone was a nationalist. The British historian Eric Hobsbawm's comments about soccer are pertinent here: "The imagined community of millions seems more real as a team of eleven people." (According to the Olympic charter, "the expression 'country' means an independent State recognized by the international community," which is not to say that "countries" with Olympic teams must be autonomous or recognized by the UN.)*

Everything was cordial, even if it was Bob against the room, with smirks all around, on every topic, from the closure of the Navy base on the Puerto Rican island of Vieques ("A big mistake!" said Bob) to whether students should be compelled to say the Pledge of Allegiance in school ("Who do you think is *paying* for the schools?" said Bob).

The conversation floated between Spanish and English, with many clarifications and restatements to make sure we all under-

* The USVI, Guam, and American Samoa also field Olympic teams. Puerto Rico has won nine medals—picking up its first gold in 2016—and the USVI won a silver medal for sailing at the 1988 Summer Olympics. Interestingly, all four of these territories have even fielded *Winter* Olympic teams, including an American Samoan bobsleigh team, in 1994.

stood each other, although even this sometimes became genially contentious because, Quique said, "*Español es el idioma más fuerte*"—Spanish is the stronger language. It's the language of Puerto Rico's native songs and poems and literature and everyday life, intrinsic to the culture. Being forced to switch to English, as part of any changed political status, was to Quique a deal-breaker, a likely death blow to the island's heritage. After the Americans took over in 1898, César J. Ayala and Rafael Bernabe observe in *Puerto Rico in the American Century*, "Spanish acquired an added significance as it suddenly became available as the most evident marker of a distinct Puerto Rican identity, a role it could not play under Spanish colonial rule." In a 1990 referendum, Puerto Ricans voted to make Spanish the official language, though this was overturned two years later, and today English and Spanish share the title.

Every few minutes, someone came in and bought some candy or a beer from César, but most took one look at Bob and me and then went outside to socialize on the sidewalk. Quique later mentioned that he'd told a pro-statehood friend I was coming and the friend recoiled.

"*Yo quiero gringos pero no quiero gringo*," Quique said, summing up his friend's view. *I want the gringos—I want to become part of the United States—but I don't want to talk to any gringos.*

Bob stayed for two Budweisers. As soon as he left, César asked me, "So what did you think about Bob?"

I could feel everyone staring at me intently. My face turned red. César leaned on the counter. He wore a small peace-sign necklace that swayed slightly over his blue shirt. "I'll tell you what I think," he said. "Bob is my friend. But he's a fucking imperialist."

He walked around to the front of the counter as he continued, "Fighting against the American imperialism is harder than fighting against the Spanish imperialism. Because the Spanish fuck us *hard*"—he thrust his hips several times, laughing—"and the Americans fuck us *hard*, too"—more hip thrusts, with a delirious grin—"but they use Vaseline."

César stopped hip-thrusting and the smile disappeared. "*En serio*, the independence struggle is very difficult because the Yankees say they give us everything and without us you are nothing. They give us Pell grants and food stamps. The American imperialists are more smart."

"It's political hegemony," Jorge said. "People think it's all fine because it does not look like the Haitian standard here."

In the states, the economy was improving: employment rates going up, optimism coming back after a long slump. The USA's overall unemployment rate was at 5.6 percent. In Puerto Rico, it was 13.7 percent. In the Guayama statistical area, which includes Arroyo: 19.4 percent.

César had a bachelor's degree in history. He pointed to his stack of books and gave me one, a thick academic tome about the island's coffee industry. He used to work for Jorge, and Quique was trying to find him a job. But for now, he was here, running this little store, with his loyal cat, on a quiet corner of Arroyo.

"It's okay, but . . . I want to get out of here," César said. His tone was not despairing, just frustrated, tired, darkly amused. "It's the same shit every day. The same conversations, the same jokes, the same fucking shit."

• • • • •

The Puerto Rico Independence Party is a minor player today, holding just one of the twenty-seven seats in the commonwealth senate, and none of the fifty-one seats in the house.

Nonetheless, the independence movement is the strongest one you'll find in any territory, and with the deepest history.

The movement's most influential figure was Pedro Albizu Campos, who first came to prominence in the 1930s, as the leader of the Partido Nacionalista. With a thick mustache and an ever-present bow tie, Albizu Campos looked the part of the Harvard-educated lawyer he was, a dapper firebrand who advocated armed rebellion against American "plutocracy." In the midst of a series of incidents starting in 1935—Nationalists attacking police, police attacking Nationalists, each with deadly consequences—he was indicted on charges of "conspiring to overthrow the government of the United States" and sent to a federal penitentiary for ten years.

By the time Albizu Campos was released, in 1947, major political change had begun in Puerto Rico, but not the kind he had in mind. Luis Muñoz Marín, a PPD member who had long been an outspoken supporter of independence, had recently changed his mind, deciding that a total split from the United States was not, in fact, a pragmatic path forward. The ELA was his proposed alternative. In 1948, Muñoz Marín was elected the territorial governor, the first voted into office rather than appointed by the U.S. president. The ELA passed in 1952, along with the Puerto Rico Constitution (both of which required the approval of Congress).

To Nationalists, it was a step backward, and Muñoz Marín was a traitor who was undermining the cause of true sovereignty, not just through the ELA but also in his support, in 1948, of the Ley de La Mordaza, or Gag Law, which made it illegal to fly the Puerto Rican flag, sing patriotic songs, organize pro-independence events, or even write in support of nationalism. (The law was repealed in 1957.)

Of course, outlawing a point of view doesn't make it go away. In the autumn of 1950, while the ELA debate was in full fervor, Albizu Campos called for a revolt, and what followed was just that: the largest armed insurrection in modern American history and one that is curiously absent from the nation's collective memory.

On October 30, Nationalists in San Juan, Ponce, Peñuelas, Mayagüez, Naranjito, Arecibo, Utuado, and Jayuya held rallies and attacked police stations; in San Juan, they attempted to storm the governor's residence and to take over the federal courthouse. The United States government declared martial law, sent in five thousand National Guard troops, and deployed P-47 Thunderbolt airplanes to bomb Nationalist-held buildings in Utaudo and Jayuya. The uprisings lasted just a few days and left twenty-eight people dead, including sixteen Nationalists. (The story is well documented in Nelson A. Denis's 2015 book *The War Against All Puerto Ricans.*)

In the states, two Nationalists living in the Bronx, Oscar Collazo and Griselio Torresola, traveled to Washington, D.C., where President Truman was staying at Blair House while the White House was being remodeled. On November 1, 1950, Collazo and Torresolo attempted to storm the residence. In the ensuing gun battle with police and Secret Service agents, Torresolo and a police officer were killed, while Truman—who was napping when the shooting started, and initially got up to look out the window—was unharmed.

Four years later, another headline-grabbing act in Washington, D.C.: On March 1, 1954, four Nationalists, Lolita Lebrón, Rafael Miranda, Irving Flores Rodríguez, and Andrés Figueroa Cordero, entered the visitors' balcony overlooking the floor of the House of Representatives, and opened fire with automatic pistols. Five congresspeople were hit, though none were killed. Lebrón was the group's leader, and although she later claimed to have fired at the ceiling, it is she—"dressed stylishly with high heels and bright red lipstick"— who has entered the lore. "She emptied the chambers of a big Luger pistol, holding it in her two hands, and waving it wildly," the *New York Times* reported. "Then she threw down the pistol and whipped out a Puerto Rican flag."

Remarkably, the four shooters were arrested, not killed in a shoot-out. Lebrón, Miranda, Flores Rodríguez, and would-be Truman assassin Oscar Collazo were granted clemency by President Jimmy Carter in 1979. When they returned to San Juan, "5,000 Puerto Ricans gathered to welcome [their] American Airlines jet," *Time* magazine reported.

What's especially notable about Carter's action is that it came at the same time that a new group, called Fuerzas Armadas de Liberación Nacional (FALN)—Armed Forces of National Liberation—was carrying out attacks in New York and Chicago, calling the acts statements "against Yanki colonial domination." Over the course of a decade, starting in October 1974, FALN bombed Department of Defense offices, military recruiting stations, banking headquarters, restaurants, and other military and civilian locations—in all, seventy-two bombings and forty incendiary attacks. The acts injured eighty-three people and killed five, including four in a 1975 bombing of the Fraunces Tavern in Manhattan.

Before she died, in 2010, Lolita Lebrón came around to a more nonviolent point of view—independence, yes, but through civil disobedience and activism. At my hotel in El Yunque, the pro-statehood owner told me that he used to cross paths with Lolita Lebrón now and then, and "she was a real nice lady."

Quique emphasized that the days of violent action were over. "We have a political struggle, but no *bombas*."

• • • • •

I woke up early to a horse clopping by on Ana and Quique's subdivision street. Ana packed me a bag of fruit for the road and Quique pulled out a map and showed me how to get to Barranquitas, about an hour's drive away, where I had a date with Luis Muñoz Marín's father, Luis Muñoz Rivera, one of the early leaders of the Puerto Rican autonomy movement. The house in which he was born is now a museum, showcasing family history and his death mask.

The route wound along mountain passes and through the town of Aibonito, whose name means, literally, "Oh! Beautiful"—before arriving in Barranquitas, which means, somewhat more unnervingly, "Little Mudslides." I gulped the crisp high-altitude air and strolled around the central plaza before heading up the block to Casa Muñoz Rivera. It was a beige, one-story wood-frame house hard against the street, with closed-up shutters and a thoroughly locked front door.

It was twelve-thirty p.m. I had nowhere else to be today; I'd already booked a room at a nearby guesthouse. On cue, a man walked by wearing houndstooth pants and a gray button-up shirt with pens tucked neatly inside a little pocket on the sleeve. A chef.

"*Perdóneme*," I began, and asked him in Spanish if the museum was just closed for lunch.

He answered in English: "No, it's closed today." His name was embroidered on his shirt: CARLOS.

"Where you from?" he asked.

"Minneapolis," I said. "In the middle."

His eyes lit up. "Prince!"

"Yeah!" I said. "And Bob Dylan!"

Carlos gave me a sideways look. He had closely trimmed short hair and a probing gaze softened by a quick if gruff smile.

"What are you doing right now?" he asked. "You got time?"

I nodded, laughing. Carlos led me down the block, to a door with a sign reading CAFÉ LUCIA. Inside were ten or twelve tables with red tablecloths covered in plastic, black-and-white photos on the wall, and no one else around but a sous chef chopping vegetables in the open kitchen. Carlos grabbed a guitar from below a kitchen counter and walked me over to the bar.

"You want a shot?"

My plans for the day were changing with remarkable velocity.

Carlos grabbed a bottle of dark rum and motioned over the sous chef, a young man named Emanuel. We toasted and Emanuel gave a friendly nod, then went back to the kitchen. Carlos stared at me for a moment, as though trying to make me flinch, then grinned and started playing "Knockin' on Heaven's Door." He paused every few measures to remember the words, then continued in a Dylan growl.

Carlos had opened Café Lucia six months earlier, he said. His specialty was Puerto Rican–Asian fusion. He showed me a menu, everything written out in a red script: egg rolls with Puerto Rican beef, chicken with a mango-ginger chutney, tempura shrimp.

"I trained at the Culinary Institute of America," Carlos said. "Then I worked at the InterContinental in Panama, the Caribe Hilton in San Juan. I was Emeril's sous chef in Orlando . . ."

He could cook anywhere, he said, but he decided to come back home, settling down with his wife to raise their two young daughters in a familiar place. Carlos pulled out his iPhone to show me photos of his daughters, and regaled me with stories about Barranquitas. There were the gregarious blind brothers who walked around selling lottery tickets, asking people what number they wanted and somehow always knowing what number was on each ticket. The guy who made a living handing out flyers for businesses but spent most of his days in the library, studying Ph.D.-level textbooks. The amusement park with a vaguely Wild West theme, costumed cartoon mascots, a small shop selling cheese imported from Paris, and a main attraction of helicopter rides over the valley.

"It's like a comic book or a movie, man," Carlos said. He paused and smirked. "You gotta be true to your home, you know?"

Business was okay, but he'd put a lot of money into this place, and just since he'd opened, he said, "We got hit with eighty-seven new taxes." He held up a plastic cup. "Four percent gas tax on everything, including this. How the *fuck* we gonna survive?"*

Some nights, restaurant owners in Barranquitas would call each other. "Hey, man, you got anyone? No? We're all coming over."

"I gotta help people," Carlos said. "It drives my wife and my mother crazy: 'Think about the money!' I don't need a dishwasher, but this guy, he needed a job and some help, so I hired him."

Carlos rapped his knuckles on the counter. "We touch wood so all the spirits hear us and give us a chance. It's not about busi-

* While I couldn't verify all eighty-seven, I did confirm that the Puerto Rican government had, indeed, recently instituted more than a few new taxes, including raising the sales tax to 11 percent, higher than any state's rate, and increasing the tax on gasoline and petroleum-based products, among them certain types of plastic goods.

ness—it's about love, man." He reached under the counter and pulled out a can of beer. "You want a Medalla Light?"

• • • • •

I WENT OUT to the plaza and sat there enjoying the cool, sunny afternoon. After a few minutes, a pair of twenty-somethings came by taking pictures of the plaza, and we started talking. David, wearing a Spanish soccer jersey and red Toms shoes, was an architecture student working on his master's degree at Cornell; Edda was a photographer, in a black shirt and tight jeans. After some introductory pleasantries, David said that they'd just heard about a historic house on the hill above town, where there was evidently some kind of garden party going on. They were going to try to talk their way in—would I like to join them?

It was that kind of day. Up the hill we went, past gates reading EL CORTIJO and up a driveway winding around manicured grounds with a massive Spanish villa set in the middle. The party was winding down, the tents being dismantled, but David charmed the owners with a bashful student-of-architecture plea, and soon we were inside for our own private tour. In all my travels in the territories, I'd seen countless shacks and set foot in many middle-class houses and gaped from afar at the occasional oceanfront villa. But this was something else entirely. Here, in a little-known town in the mountains of a struggling island, was the most opulent house I'd ever entered.

It was the sort of place where the guest room has a full coat of arms with swords and an honest-to-goodness suit of armor in the corner. The open stairway to the second floor had a custom-made Tiffany chandelier and, progressing up the stairs, around eighty handmade tiles telling the story of *Don Quixote*. The rest of the tile, on the floors and halfway up the walls in nearly every room, had Moorish patterns with intricate, delicate, repeating forms modeled, the home owners said, on the tile of Alhambra in Grenada. There were paintings by Spanish masters and tall lamps imported from Italy and carved wooden tables that you could probably trade for a decent car. David asked a torrent of questions, the home owners happily answered, and Edda and I merely gaped.

By the time we left, it was after seven p.m., and we were hungry. We parked at the plaza, where teenagers were filming each other break-dancing, and speed-walked to Café Lucia. I'd told David and Edda the whole story: how I'd met Carlos on the sidewalk and he'd poured me a shot and sung me a song, how it turned out he was a seriously pedigreed chef and this meal was gonna be *epic*, and—

The door was locked.

I couldn't believe it. I *refused* to believe it.

We walked down the alley to the back door and peered in. Carlos and Emanuel were talking at the bar. The kitchen lights were off. Carlos looked at me like I'd let him down.

"The restaurant is closed."

My heart sank.

His expression softened. ". . . But I will cook for you. No menus! Just what I want. We had no customers and so I said I just wanna go out. But now you're here."

Carlos switched on the kitchen light and pulled out a cutting board, holding it up with obvious relish, as if to say, *Watch this.*

Another couple of customers appeared, and then another, and a friend of Carlos's named Leo wandered in and invited himself to join our table, telling us stories from their childhood and boasting, repeatedly, of the view from his house, overlooking a valley. Soon the conversation was spanning across the tables, an impromptu dinner party in an officially closed restaurant. And then the food came. I'd been a touch concerned that, after all this, it wouldn't live up to my hype, but from my first bite of delicate tempura, it went above and beyond. David and Edda and I exchanged approving mumbles as we tucked into egg rolls with Puerto Rican beef and succulent, fall-apart ribs with a luscious tamarind sauce. As we licked our fingers, more plates arrived, with grilled chicken with a ginger-mango chutney that prickled my mouth in an oddly satisfying way, sweet and spicy. Everything was served with a modern flourish, on broad white plates with squiggles of sauce. Carlos was having fun, showing off.

As we finished up, he got out his guitar again and played some Hendrix as a digestif.

I looked around the room and saw that everyone else was looking around, too. Exchanging glances. This place *was* like a movie. *Fucking crazy, man. But we're all in it together. You gotta be true to your home, you know?*

• • • • •

SEVERAL TIMES during my travels in the territories, I heard state-dwellers ask locals why they stayed, or why they'd come back. It was meant as idle small talk, but the underlying condescension was tangible: *We've got it better back in the states.*

The locals heard it. There was always a pause, and for the briefest of moments their muscles tensed before they answered, "Because it's *home*." As dysfunctional as the territories can be—and I met no one who disputes that they can be tremendously dysfunctional—their residents are still proud of their homelands and have no interest in your pity or your patronizing.

Every time I heard someone like Carlos tell stories of struggling through, I thought, *These places are cool. These people are wonderful. Why the hell doesn't anyone in the states know anything about them?* This, in turn, led to the question that had long been nagging me: When did Americans in the states stop caring about the territories? When and why did they drop out of the national discourse?

My list still started with the factors that I'd been thinking about since Guam:

1. The primary purpose of the USA's nineteenth century expansionist push was to show the world that we were a real-deal power. Acquiring an empire was an end unto itself, the geopolitical version of buying a Ferrari or a flashy Rolex. What *happened* to the places, and their people, was beside the point.
2. The Insular Cases, in setting up the "foreign in a domestic sense" label and the legal difference between *incorporated* and *unincorporated*, added more steps to the statehood process and also set into law the idea that the people of these islands were alien, not true Americans. It set them apart from the rest of the nation, not just legally but psychologically.
3. The United States moved on to bigger battles (literally) around the world, battles that overshadowed the territories in the realm of foreign affairs, even though the territories are actually a *domestic* issue.

To these three factors, I now had more to add:

4. During the rise of postwar decolonization movements, empire became toxic to the national brand, opening

the USA to Cold War propaganda that it wasn't the beacon of democracy it claimed to be. The federal government didn't want to get rid of the territories (hence the "commonwealth" label) but it also tried not to talk about them too loudly. Out of sight, out of mind.

5. In 1959, we hit fifty states. In the process, we stretched the nation beyond its sea-to-shining-sea identity—we fulfilled our Manifest Destiny assignment and got extra credit by doing a bit more. The nation felt complete, numerically and geographically. Today, we have gone the longest stretch in our nation's history without adding any new states; less than a quarter of Americans were alive when Hawaii and Alaska got the promotion. We're no longer accustomed to this change occurring.
6. As the territories have faded from view, ignorance and silence have bred more ignorance and silence. It's an inertia of awareness: a discussion at rest tends to stay at rest.
7. As Bob the Gringo would be happy to tell you, the territories haven't been able to make up their own minds, collectively, about their preferred political status (or, in the case of American Samoa, birthright citizenship). Most territory residents agree that the status quo is not satisfactory, but the solution is in dispute. As people told me time and again, there's a profound feeling of unsteadiness. And when your footing's already precarious, every potential major change can seem like a mountain, every slope slippery. With the notable exception of Puerto Rico's independence movement, there have been few highly visible acts of protest or of political pressure from the territories regarding the political

status or, for that matter, any other issue relating to the territories, such as funding disparities in comparison to the states. None of the territories have yet put Congress on the spot and requested statehood or independence. You don't hear stories of pro-independence sit-ins on Guam or mass marches demanding voting rights in the U.S. Virgin Islands. The status issue is not a celebrity cause, has no series of 5K runs, no annual telethons, not even a social-media hashtag. The lone organization advocating for the rights of the territories, collectively, is the We the People Project, with one employee, founder Neil Weare—and even he has critics in the territories, people who disagree with his court-oriented tactics or, even if they agree, see him as yet another outsider meddling in their local affairs.

8. Those rare times when the territories do come to the attention of people in the states, we almost always talk about them separately: *Here's something that's happening in Puerto Rico or on Guam or in American Samoa.* That's true even in the territories, even among people who are the harshest critics of the political-status setup—there's an oddly myopic lack of acknowledgment of the parallel histories and shared concerns. In every territory, discussions about political status and its consequences happen in a vacuum (with the exception of Guam and the CNMI, where there's typically a nod to the Marianas neighbor). Even at the federal level, the territories are treated in a piecemeal fashion. There's been no single act or piece of governance that lays out an all-encompassing policy for the present-day territories. The Office of Insular Affairs—

part of the Department of the Interior—is the official federal overseer of the Virgin Islands, Guam, American Samoa, and the Northern Mariana Islands, as well as the American-administered programs in the freely associated states. Puerto Rico, however, is under the purview of the Puerto Rico Federal Affairs Administration. But it's only by considering the territories as a whole that we—and they—can see the damning common ground: the comparative lack of federal investment or concern, the frequency of local corruption, the ways the early decades of U.S. power follow the same exact template. One instance is a fluke, two a coincidence . . . but five? Five's an outrage.

9. Finally—and I think this may be the most significant—we forget about the territories because, quite simply, they're not states. This puts them immediately outside the collective conversation, because our concept of ourselves is that of a nation of states—that's what's on the flag, in the maps, in the songs, in our very name. In 1900, we talked about the territories because they had the potential to *be* states, but when the Insular Cases effectively shut that door, and they continued to be *not-quite* states, our attention waned.

The territories are neither united nor states nor part of either American continent, which makes it hard for them to assert their legitimacy as part of the United States of America. It's understandable that so many people think of them—implicitly or explicitly—as foreign. But when you consider everything tangled up in the territories—issues of basic human and political rights, issues of immigration and military readiness, issues of regional politics and our reach in the world—it's clear that they are integral to our national story, even today. And there's the rub: The territories are the most important domestic-policy issue Americans aren't talking about, precisely because we don't think of them as a domestic-policy issue at all.

• • • • •

My plan for the next day was to drive La Ruta Panorámica—the Panoramic Route—a two-lane-at-best byway both scenic and treacherous, spanning the east-west width of Puerto Rico's mountainous middle. The route is steep like a roller coaster, coiled like an old-school telephone cord, with mountain vistas that you can't really enjoy because to take your eyes off the road is to miss the oncoming propane-tank delivery truck that just barreled around the blind curve.

But it turns out Monday morning is a good time to drive crazy, dangerous roads. The weekend traffic was all gone, the hauling-stuff traffic hadn't yet begun. It hadn't previously occurred to me, but Puerto Rico has not only the most urban setting of any territory, but also the most rural—it's big enough to have wide-open spaces and lonely expanses where you only see one house in your field of vision. At one overlook, near the middle of the island, I could see the Atlantic, the Caribbean, and much of the island; with the aid of one of the requisite scenic-vista telescopes, I spotted a broad plain with perhaps forty wind turbines in the compressed foreground, and, far to the east, the island of Vieques.

I'd expected La Ruta Panoramica to have road-blocking scrums of goats and shells of burned-out cars and more signs of economic catastrophe, visual evidence of the fact that per-capita income in Puerto Rico was half that of the poorest state,

Mississippi; and that 37 percent of households received food stamps. But while there were mountain shacks and cinder-block ruins, they were far outnumbered by hale, two-story, freshly painted abodes—many of them just inches off the road—with gleaming Honda Fits and Ford pickups in the driveways. It was a lovely drive.

And then I got to Ponce.

On the drive into the city center, I passed countless once-proud Neoclassical manors, their plaster and red tile now crumbling and overtaken with tufts of weeds and bushes and even small trees, more small-scale nature preserve than human habitation.

"Ponce is Ponce and everything else is parking," goes the local saying, and the city has a reputation as being proud, even stuck-up. The central plaza—one of the most famous on an island full of them—bore a lingering air of grandeur, housing a church, a historic firehouse with a striking red-and-black-striped exterior, and a large fountain with spitting lions, moved here from the New York World's Fair in 1939. But the plaza was strikingly empty of foot traffic—no break-dancing teenagers, no intertwined couples on the benches—while on the surrounding sidewalks, I had to step into the street two or three times per block to get around clusters of people surrounding lottery-ticket vendors. There were countless vacant storefronts with signs reading SE VENDE, For Sale, and a rainbow of graffiti tags on most windows—pink on the onetime law office, white at the former sandwich shop—while others were simply boarded up.

The roots of Puerto Rico's economic skid were something of a Greatest Hits of Territorial Dysfunction. They were not a freak convergence of problems so much as the inevitable if especially vicious result of several broader trends that have been occurring in all the territories for decades. Ineptitude and mismanagement at the federal and local levels, narrowly focused economic development efforts built on shaky grounds, issues relating to the political status—it's all here.

One of the early cracks in the foundation began to form in 1996, when Congress decided to repeal a set of tax breaks it had set up in 1976 to lure corporations to the U.S. territories. One industry that took advantage of this was pharmaceuticals, with companies such as Pfizer opening manufacturing facilities in Puerto Rico; at their peak, nearly ninety such plants dotted the island. But, just as corporations left other territories once their specially tailored economic incentives dried up (such as the garment factories in the CNMI), Big Pharma didn't linger in Puerto Rico after the tax breaks were all gone in 2006. Two years later, the Great Recession hit the entire nation. This one-two punch wiped out around half of the island's manufacturing jobs.

The Puerto Rican government had a tried-and-true plan for raising funds, though: *Let's sell some municipal bonds! Lots and lots of bonds! Make it rain!* As it happens, these bonds were especially enticing because, unlike bonds sold by states, those sold in the territories (which you can buy no matter where you live) are exempt from all local, state, and federal taxes. "It was a lot easier to go out and borrow, as opposed to making tough decisions," Luis Fortuño, the commonwealth's governor from 2009 to 2013, said in remarkably clear-eyed (if not quite contrite) hindsight. The result of all this was that, as *Bloomberg View* observed, "the competitive advantage made it easy for Puerto Rico to double its debt in 10 years by selling bonds to plug annual budget deficits and pay for operating expenses—the combination that brought New York City to the brink of bankruptcy in the 1970s."

As bills started to come due, there was another matter that compounded the problems: the Puerto Rican Constitution contained a mandate that, as the commonwealth made payments, bond holders were first in line, even before funding for the basic services that are, really, the government's core function. This, predictably, meant that problems with those basic services kept spiraling downward, along with the economy. The commonwealth's government and utilities amassed more than $73 billion in debt by 2015.

When states have similar crises, they can restructure their debt through Chapter 9 bankruptcy. The territories? Read the fine print: *Not applicable.* Chapter 9 rules *used* to apply to Puerto Rico (though not the other territories), until 1984, when a one-line provision was stuck into a congressional bill, eliminating the commonwealth's access to this protection. Why, precisely, it was added is something that no one seems to be able to identify (not Congress, not various news outlets that have investigated), though it was hardly the first territory-related law to be cloaked in mystery and confusion and to pass without any say from the people of the affected islands. It was also, of course, not the last.

In late 2015 and early 2016, as Puerto Rican leaders worked with Congress to help the commonwealth restructure its debt, secretive opponents emerged from the woodwork. Two groups, one called Main Street Bondholders and another called the Center for Individual Freedom, lobbied Congress *not* to assist Puerto Rico. Both were generally believed to be the work of the so-called "vulture" hedge funds that held around 30 percent of Puerto Rico's debt and were known for their aggressive efforts to extract profits from faltering economies—they thrived on instability. The *New York Times* reported that the Main Street Bondholders were connected to DCI, "a Republican public relations firm that specializes in 'AstroTurfing'—orchestrated lobbying campaigns designed to look like grass-roots efforts. DCI's clients include the hedge fund BlueMountain Capital, which has been one of the most aggressive opponents of federal intervention in Puerto Rico."

In the meantime, Puerto Rico had tried a few other tactics to bolster its economy, using methods that had also been tried in other territories: increase certain everyday taxes (as Carlos the chef had lamented) but offer tax breaks to rich people. The tax breaks came in 2012, through Acts 20 and Act 22, and were intended to woo investors. Act 22 offered full tax exceptions on capital gains, dividends, and interest to anyone who lived in the territory for more than half the year. Supporters of the laws boasted that that would bring fifty-five thousand new jobs to Puerto Rico. Reality, however, missed the mark: according to later assessments, the true number was around fifty-eight *hundred* jobs. According to some observers, Acts 20 and 22 also increased income inequality, which was already higher than in any state, according to U.S. Census data. (The rates in the other territories were not measured, but it's safe to assume they were also quite high.)

A subtler and more long-term issue was the 1920 Jones Act (the law that Mars had told me about during our barbecue-feasting on Guam), which mandates that to deliver goods directly from one U.S. port to another, a ship must be American-built, American-crewed, and sail under an American flag. Almost all ships do *not* meet this criteria, so they can't go straight from the U.S. mainland to Puerto Rico. Inefficient routes lead to higher prices, including an extra fifteen cents per gallon of gas, according to a 2015 Manhattan Institute report. Eliminating the Jones Act wouldn't be a panacea—the USVI, the CNMI, and American

Samoa are exempt, but prices are high on those islands, too—but it would be a start.*

Back in Ponce, there were some signs of hope. My hotel, a colonial-era classic, had recently been refurbished, as had the Museo de Arte de Ponce, the latter to the tune of $13 million. An architecture school buzzed with students working on models in a streetfront workshop; their brightly colored fixed-gear bikes were locked out front. A few doors down, there was a long line every night for the sublime fruit ices at King's Creams on the plaza.

And right outside King's, every night, sat a gregarious disabled military veteran named Felix, who was adamant that he didn't want money, just a meal. He went to the Veterans Affairs clinic for diabetes treatment every day, he told me, and he was happy with his care. But he couldn't work, didn't have a home, couldn't travel in search of other opportunities elsewhere.

"When the United States gets a cold, Puerto Rico gets, like, double pneumonia," one longtime Ponce resident, an academic, told me. "Here [in Ponce], maybe triple." He sighed. "People in the government here have not been doing a very good job."

As in the CNMI, the situation made for unexpected political positions. In Washington, D.C., many congressional Republicans wanted the federal government to simply take over the commonwealth's finances, while Democrats favored letting Puerto Rico work it out on its own, including allowing bankruptcy restructuring without conditions. Puerto Rico's government, for its part, won no new fans when, in early 2016, it failed to reach an agreement with lenders, and the power company "warned that failure

* Technically, Guam is also exempt from the Jones Act, but because it's on a natural shipping route with much-larger Hawaii, the law is in place, for all practical purposes.

to make payments on that debt could lead to delays in fuel shipments and blackouts across the island."

As a *New York Times* editorial put it, Puerto Rico's financial problems are "a reminder that benign neglect has terrible consequences for millions of Americans." What the editorial didn't note was that, although these consequences have been particularly acute for Puerto Rico and affect an especially large number of people there, the problems and their roots are similar across the territories.

• • • • •

After two days in Ponce, I pressed on. Although there were entire regions of Puerto Rico I hadn't visited—*another trip,* I promised myself—there was one place I needed to see *now,* a place that seemed to call me with a particular urgency: the island of Vieques. It's a "double territory," as César in Arroyo had put it, not quite part of Puerto Rico, which is not quite part of the United States. Vieques has a population of nine thousand on its twenty-one-mile-wide landmass—twice the land area of Saint Thomas, a fifth of the population—with two small towns, Isabel Segunda and Esperanza, and a scattering of other houses and developments. Some 70 percent of the island is a U.S. Fish and Wildlife refuge. Wild horses roam about and a traffic jam is one other car ahead of you.

In part, my reason for ending my trip in Vieques was purely selfish. I'd enjoyed my travels around Puerto Rico, but I was also exhausted, and here was a chance to relax. Esperanza, where I was staying, is a barefoot-living sort of place, and I was looking forward to lazily strolling along its two-hundred-yard-long waterfront *malecón,* before settling in for a rum punch at one of the intriguingly named bars across the street, like Belly Buttons, Lazy Jack's, Bananas, or Duffy's. (The last dates to the 1960s, when Dennis Duffy, a close friend of the Mamas & the Papas, started the hippie-tourist trend here.)

But I had more on my mind than cocktails and beaches. Vieques was undergoing its own reboot, and offered a case study in a territory transforming itself from a military zone to a tourist playground. Here was a chance to see many of the issues I'd observed elsewhere, playing out in real-time and at a small scale. More than perhaps anywhere else I'd been, change was in the air.

The U.S. Navy first set up shop on Vieques in 1941, holding it as a secure port for the British Navy; should their homeland fall to the Nazis, this would be their refuge. When the war ended, well, the *Cold* War was just beginning. In the 1940s and 1950s, the U.S. Navy took over a chunk of the island's western side and all of the eastern half, giving some residents a day, a week, or no advance notice at all. "They gave us a paper that said we had to leave within twenty-four hours," recalled one resident quoted in a locally produced history titled, simply, *Vieques*. "Everyone was in a state of panic, taking down their houses before the bulldozers came and left us with nothing."

One of the Navy's primary plans for this land was the creation of a bombing range. Once the residents were gone, the bombs rained down—tens of thousands every year, during runs conducted 180 days a year. The residents of Esperanza and Isabel Segunda were caught in the middle, access to much of their own island cut off, their water and soil contaminated with nitrates. In 1978, Viequense fisherman, angered by naval vessels destroying their fish-trap buoys, set up a blockade to prevent the Marines from conducting exercises. The so-called "Fishermen's War" catalyzed more protests against the Navy, which continued the bomb tests throughout the 1980s and 1990s, without gaining much broader notice. But in 1999, an errant five-hundred-pound bomb killed a civilian guard named David Sanes, sparking international attention and drawing bold-name outsiders, including Reverend Al Sharpton and Robert F. Kennedy, Jr. (While Kennedy was in jail for his action, he missed the birth of his son Aidan Caohman Vieques Kennedy.) The United States finally relented, and the base was shut down in 2003.

It didn't take long for magazines and newspapers to take note of this largely undeveloped Caribbean island, and soon they were touting Vieques as the next hot spot, an undiscovered gem, off the beaten path.

"It's like the rest of the Caribbean used to be before the resorts and cruise ships arrived," said a woman who'd moved from the states twelve years earlier and now ran a gift shop. This was a common theme among locals I talked to, one that echoed Tisa in American Samoa and Lino in the CNMI: *We're wary of what will happen if more people come here. We like it quieter—not "simpler," necessarily, but calmer.* A local conservationist named Mark Martin told me that thirty television shows had come to Vieques in the last decade to document this island in transition. A W Retreat & Spa had opened in 2010, and now, the W's parent company wanted to build a 150-acre resort with a golf course and maybe a casino. "The consequences of such rapid growth could be really great," he said (meaning *significant*). "The question is, who's benefiting?"

These questions weren't abstractions: Environmental impact studies were already well under way, the development plans beyond mere concepts, even while the onetime naval bombing range was still being cleaned up—the military-to-tourism timelines of the other territories was highly compressed in Vieques.

On Calle Flamboyan, Esperanza's restaurant-filled oceanfront main drag, there was a new boutique hotel, El Blok, with a restaurant headed by Jose Enrique, whose eponymous restaurant in San Juan's Santurce neighborhood had garnered him a James Beard Award. At four stories, El Blok was the tallest building on the street, and the most strikingly modern, with white walls and long rows of shutters formed of concrete punched out with a pebble-like lattice. By the time I got there, less than a year after it opened, it had been written up in the *New York Times*, *Travel + Leisure*, and *Architectural Digest*, all of which cropped out the scrubby vacant lot across the street, where a wild horse sniffed an empty potato chip bag as I entered El Blok for dinner one evening.

I was the lone charge of the bartender at my end of the football-shaped bar, and we got to talking while he mixed me a cocktail called Sahumerio, with rum, coconut ice, cinnamon, and rosemary. Jose wore tight jeans and curving spikes in his earlobes. He was soft-spoken and patient as I asked him about the island's history while half eavesdropping on the conversation among the cashmere-and-loafers group at the other end of the bar. ("I had four flower girls at my wedding," said one woman.)

Jose spoke with a shy enthusiasm, and seemed to know a bit about everything on Vieques. When the subject turned to the protests against the Navy, his eyes gleamed. "I was part of that." Jose's friend, he said, once shot a flare off a boat and hit a military helicopter; he got two years in prison for it. Jose didn't do anything that wild but did trespass on military property, as part of a mass protest effort, and was jailed for two days.

Maybe it was the Sahumerio getting to me, but I started to view Jose as my personal guru, and began to feel hopeful that here, finally, I would find concrete answers that would tidily sum up my year of research, ideally packaged in a Teddy Roosevelt-esque bon mot, wise yet direct, somehow quintessentially American.

I asked him: "So, what's next for Vieques?"

I leaned in, awaiting my answer.

Jose offered a tight chuckle. "Well . . . here we are," he said, and turned to make a cocktail.

• • • • •

What remains to be seen is whether and when Puerto Rico's next referendum will happen. If Puerto Ricans vote conclusively in favor of statehood, the matter would still have to go to Congress, thanks to the Insular Cases. What that august body would do is hard to say. It would hinge on a political calculation that Foster Rhea Dulles would have predicted nearly a hundred years ago: *How do you weigh principle against expediency, altruism against aggressive nationalism?* It would also come down to a simple matter of whether or not Congress is actually paying attention to Puerto Ricans, in all their complexity.

At the present population, Puerto Rico would get five representatives in the U.S. House, along with two senators and thus seven electoral votes. This is not insignificant political clout. Some 83 percent of Puerto Ricans on the mainland United States voted for Barack Obama in 2012, according to exit polls, a fact of which Republicans will surely be aware. This alone may be enough for some afraid of a Democratic shift to get on their soapboxes and scrounge up some seemingly noble excuse to oppose this fifty-first state, never mind what Puerto Ricans want. In his keynote address at the "Reconsidering the Insular Cases" conference at Harvard Law School in 2014, Juan R. Torreulla, a judge on the

United States Court of Appeals for the First Circuit, recalled that, years earlier, then-Senator John Chafee, Republican of Rhode Island, had told him:

> I come from one of the original thirteen colonies. We have two Senators and one Congressman. If Puerto Rico becomes a state, you'll have two Senators also, and seven or eight Congressmen, and they'll probably all be Democrats! I don't know if I can go for that.

Beyond the appallingly antidemocratic idea of shutting people out of the political process because you don't like their views, this is a simplistic calculation, one you'll also see in assorted think-pieces mainland commentators have written over the years. It's based much less on hard evidence of a Democrat-embracing electorate than on a gut feeling that *of course* people in Puerto Rico and any other territory will vote Democratic because they're not as economically well-off as the rest of the United States and because, well, they're not *white*.

It's an Insular Cases sort of perspective, troubling in its archaic assumptions about homogenous, predictable populations. In Puerto Rico and the other territories, the Christian faith that forms a cultural bedrock also creates a strong strain of cultural conservatism. Guam's presidential straw poll has accurately reflected the national results for decades. The territories all present an interesting mix of views that don't neatly fit with the Republican or Democratic platforms.

But Congress's understanding of the territories has always been spotty. The representative from American Samoa was once introduced, before speaking on the floor of the House, as hailing from "American Somalia." Congress even had a hard time approving the quarters that had piqued my interest in the territories on that cold November day: the first four efforts to approve quarters for the territories and the District of Columbia didn't even make it out of the Senate committee, after an anonymous, unexplained "hold." It wasn't until the fifth try that the bill passed, in December 2007, after Representative José Serrano, a Democrat from New York who was born in Puerto Rico, tucked it into the federal budget bill at the close of the session.

All of this speaks to an important, troubling fact: even our nation's leaders in Washington, D.C.—in theory, some of the foremost experts on How America Works and What It Means to be American and, more important, the people with ultimate say over every facet of life in the USVI, American Samoa, Guam, the CNMI, and Puerto Rico—don't have much of a clue about or a concern for the United States territories.

• • • • •

My last activity on my last day in the territories was pure pleasure: a kayak tour around Vieques' Puerto Mosquito at night. The bay's off-putting name belies the joy it holds: bioluminescence. Every sudden movement in the water—a dragging hand, a gliding paddle, a swimming fish—makes it light up, briefly, in a brilliant, otherworldly green.

There are only a handful of bioluminescent bays around the world and the *Guinness Book of World Records* certifies this as the brightest, offering ideal conditions (small size, the right nutrients) for microscopic organisms known as dinoflagellates, specifically a genus called *Pyrodinium*, which comes from the Greek words for fire and whirling.

Stir them, splash them, or scoop them and you activate a biochemical process that makes them spark like teeny-tiny fireflies. Multiply that by a bajillion, and you've got something that looks like the force field in a science fiction flick. Contrails traced the lines of my paddle strokes, and every drip of water onto the kayak was like glowing glitter. Once I got up a good pace, even the wake of my boat pulsed, and it looked for all the world like I'd installed neon lights in the hull.

Above me, another brilliant show: the night sky, a million pinpoint twinkles, not quite as stunning as at Tisa's, but pretty damn close. My guide, Julia, pointed out Orion and apologized for not knowing much else. Except, ah, there was Polaris.

A wave of homesickness washed over me. After all these miles, it was almost time to follow the North Star back to my own home, this time to stick around for a good while with Maren and our soon-to-arrive baby girl, our own marvel. There was a pulse of light across the sky and I made a wish, the first time I'd done that since I was a little kid myself. I wished the world for my daughter, health and happiness for her, for Maren, for us. My heart was overflowing and, suddenly, I was a quietly bawling mess. I figured I might as well keep wishing, since I had a decades-long backlog. I wished for more customers for Carlos the chef, a permanent-resident visa and a trip to the states for Chun, more whales (but not tourist influxes) for Tisa, sweet new Harleys for Carl and Tony, a full generation or two of stability for the Bikinians, all the best for everyone I'd met in the territories.

"Ooh, we've got a hot spot over here!" Julia called, snapping me out of my thoughts. The bay's bioluminescence isn't entirely consistent, she'd explained—better in some places some days, worse in others. The lights went out entirely for a while in 2014, for unknown reasons—a shifting wind might have altered the conditions or maybe it was pollution. But now the glow was back.

Things were in order. There were many factors, so many things that could go wrong. And what the future held was anyone's guess. Everyone was holding their breath. For now, all you could do was try to appreciate the beauty and wonder in this moment.

I pulled my paddle in a long stroke, scattering a school of fish into liquid fireworks. A grand finale.

Epilogue

THE FUTURE OF EMPIRE

On a clear January evening, I boarded a plane in Puerto Rico and flew across the sea and halfway across a continent, home to Minneapolis. In the coming weeks and months, the territories followed me. When I saw them, they were no longer confusions but delights, a welcome part of the fabric of everyday life in Middle America.

I noticed, for the first time, a small section of West Indies food at my local grocery store (no *mauby*, alas), and thought of it not as exotic but as American regional cuisine. I heard salsa's *clave* beats drifting in the air, and saw Head Start buses puttering around the city, and remembered that, as Jesus had told me, this national program of early childhood education was modeled on a program initiated by former Puerto Rico Mayor Felisa Rincón de Gautier. At a Super Bowl party, someone brought up the topic of Samoans in the NFL, and we all spent some time studying the teams' rosters, surprised and disappointed to find no players from the territory. In the headlines, Puerto Rico's financial crisis was soon inescapable (the *New York Times*, the *Economist*, Minnesota's *St. Cloud Times,* even the television show *Last Week Tonight*), as was the Zika virus making its way across the tropics. The *New York Times* ran a long feature about the virus in Puerto

Rico, failing to mention that it was in the USVI, too, as well as American Samoa.

I kept in touch with many people I'd met. Emanuel, the sous chef at Café Lucia, had friended me on Facebook the day after my dinner in Barranquitas, and thereafter my news feed was filled with a steady stream of photos: salmon fillet with Thai sweet chili, garlic chicken breast with mushroom risotto. John Wasko sent photos of a new house he and his family were building, and gave updates on his efforts to raise money to start a new university in American Samoa; last I heard, he was excited about a new potential investor in Chicago. Over the summer, Walt and Cinta sent emails about new U.S. military plans to turn all of Pagan—Cinta's beloved home, in the remote northern islands of the CNMI—and two-thirds of Tinian into a large-scale war-training ground, with live-fire exercises and thousands of troops coming in to scurry around the beaches and trample the undergrowth, as part of the Asia-Pacific shift. And as the 2016 presidential primary season dragged on and became ever more combative, the territories crept into the national consciousness as candidates battled for each and every delegate, even in these islands most people had forgotten even *had* delegates. Marco Rubio, Bernie Sanders, and Hillary Clinton all campaigned in Puerto Rico, and a group of mainland Republican activists moved to the USVI just in time to become the territory's official slate of delegates.

I kept pondering the territories—how they fit into the American Story, what their future might be. There were more rabbit holes, endless hours in the library. I daydreamed about finagling my way to one of the Minor Outlying Islands. About a week after my flight from Honolulu to Guam, another plane on the same route had mechanical problems along the way and had to make an emergency stop at Midway Atoll, a key World War II battleground and present-day national wildlife refuge. I cursed my misfortune for missing out on this experience (while understanding that for all the other passengers, this side trip would have been harrowing, not a delight). But maybe I could get there, or to Howland Island, or to incorporated Palymra Atoll, or to Johnston Atoll, although the last quickly went to the bottom of my list when I learned that for decades it was a storage site for leaky Agent Orange containers. I spent a day trying to figure out if it was feasible to get to Wake Island, and several more days exchanging emails with a man who, in the 1990s, joined with a friend to claim that the island was a sovereign nation, the Kingdom of EnenKio. The two men drafted a constitution and tried to sell $1 billion in war bonds, using Wake Island's puzzling political status to run interference for their scam. But the Kingdom of EnenKio's leader had recently died, his associate told me, as had the sovereignty claim.

I called Christina Ponsa again, and a Harvard expert in territorial law, and peppered them with highly specific questions about particular Insular Cases and territorial history. They had some insights but both also, at times, confessed that they had not been to all the territories themselves and they didn't have answers for all of my questions. Perhaps no one did.

On Super Bowl Sunday, Carlos called me from Café Lucia. He was in the middle of the dinner rush—he had customers today, more than a few—but had decided to take a break and drink a shot and, what the hell, give me a call. Emanuel was taking care of things.

Business was fine, Carlos said. His family was doing well. He was rooting for the Seahawks—"Yeah, man, they're my team.

"Doug, did you write about us yet?" he said.

"Not yet," I replied apologetically. Still working on it.

"You're gonna tell people about us, though, right?"

"Of course."

"Good," Carlos said. He paused. "All right, man. Back to work."

As he signed off, he added—and I could picture his gaze, intense, but with a small smile—"Don't forget about us."

• • • •

THE TERRITORIES have made us who we are. They represent the USA's place in the world.

They've been a reflection of our national mood in nearly every period of American history, starting with the early 1800s era of Manifest Destiny, when a young country was trying to prove itself and started gathering up those tiny bird-covered islands. By the end of the century, the nation was even more eager to control the seas and become a true global power, like the other empires—the territories were integral to the military engagements and commercial enterprises that made the United States what it is today. In World Wars I and II, territory residents fought for the United States while their islands were literal battlegrounds, and were, in some cases, taken over by our enemies. And then, as the Cold War simmered and decolonization movements spread, the introduction of commonwealths and well-intentioned modernization efforts represented a softening of United States power, a showcase of our noble, egalitarian spirit. Today, in an ever more globalized world, they're a critical link to the rest of the planet, a place where we welcome tourists but also, out in the Pacific, where we keep watch on the world's newest superpower.

The territories weren't obstacles or afterthoughts on the journey toward American prosperity, they were fuel for the journey. And they continue to serve that role.

Christina Ponsa reminded me about one of the most recent territory-related Supreme Court cases, which, she said, seemed to offer insight into where things might be headed. It had to do with another recurring headline topic that kept piquing my interest: Guantánamo Bay.

The case was 2008's *Boumediene v. Bush.* In the post–September 11, 2001, era, the CIA practiced "deliberate offshoring of interrogation and detention," including at Guantánamo Bay, the naval base the United States has controlled since the Spanish-American War, thanks to the terms of the 1898 Teller Amendment, which assured Cuba of independence . . . *Except we're keeping this little part.* This arrangement means that Guantánamo Bay "has many unique attributes that render it virtually U.S. territory," Kal Raustiala notes in his 2009 book *Does the Constitution Follow the Flag?* For the Bush administration, Guantánamo's limbo status—not quite foreign, not quite domestic—was a feature, not a bug, seemingly allowing them to write their own rules, including suspending the rights of habeas corpus. But the Supreme Court ruled that these rights did apply in Guantánamo Bay (and therefore in all territories), even for foreign detainees.

Even more intriguing, Christina Ponsa said, were a pair of lines in Justice Anthony Kennedy's majority opinion. First: "It may well be that over time the ties between the United States and any of its territories strengthen in ways that are of constitutional significance." And second, Kennedy rejected the notion that "the political branches have the power to switch the Constitution on or off at will." These comments seemed to indicate that the Insular

Cases could be overturned, although it was, in legal terms, just an idle thought, to be taken up another day.

Neil Weare, of the We the People Project, told me that if the American Samoa citizenship case went to the Supreme Court, he hoped it would lead toward the overturning of other Insular Cases, and this would help empower people in the territories to fight for their own future, whatever it may be. Months later, after a setback in the District of Columbia appeals court, Weare and his team petitioned the Supreme Court to hear their case. Neil seemed confident they would do so. But in June 2016, the court declined, leaving American Samoa's antiquated citizenship laws in place.

The same day that the Supreme Court passed on Weare's case, it issued a ruling on another territory-related case, *Puerto Rico v. Sanchez Valle*, which revolved around a question of double jeopardy. The Constitution says that you can't be charged twice for the same crime *unless* the trials are in "separate sovereigns," by which it means the federal and state governments. Luis M. Sánchez Valle was convicted in federal court on firearms charges, and charged with similar crimes in Puerto Rico, but his lawyer argued that Puerto Rico, by virtue of its political status, was *not* a "separate sovereign," and these charges amounted to double jeopardy, in violation of the Fifth Amendment. *Slate* summarized the central question: "The Supreme Court Ponders Whether Puerto Rico Is a Real State or a Fake Colony." To say it is *legally* a separate sovereign is to effectively grant Puerto Rico more autonomy than it actually has under the current legal setup; to say it's *not* separate is to admit that the ELA is basically a sham, and Puerto Rico is a territory and, by the UN's measurement, a colony.

U.S. Solicitor General Donald Verrilli—the voice of the federal government before the Supreme Court—filed a brief stating that Puerto Rico is *not* a sovereign. "As a constitutional matter, Puerto Rico remains a territory subject to Congress's authority under the Territory Clause." The court, in a 6-2 ruling, agreed.

Alexis de Tocqueville wrote that "scarcely a political question arises in this country that does not sooner or later resolve itself into a legal question," and that was certainly true of the expansion debate, as the Imperial Moment led to the Insular Cases. But while the territories have largely been forgotten as a political matter, they remain an active concern in the courts.

These two recent cases were setbacks in the mission to overturn the Insular Cases, but at some point, the legal questions will bear enough weight to force the political questions back into broad debate. Add in Puerto Rico's next referendum, and it's clear that the territories may yet reenter the national conversation and may yet attain more self-determination.

Here's to hoping.

• • • • •

MEANWHILE, on the global scale, familiar issues of empire-building were repeating. Russia planted a titanium flag at the bottom of the Arctic Ocean, in an attempt to claim the North Pole (and any oil or other minerals in the seabed) and, more generally, to assert ownership over an icy region that was becoming increasingly accessible due to global warming. And the world's eyes were on the South China Sea, where China was not just colonizing specks of land but building them from scratch, in the Spratly Islands. The satellite images were stunning: new landmasses with bases and runways, where months earlier there had been the tiniest of islets or mere reefs, the transformations involving a sophisticated dredging system utilizing flotillas of ships. The largest island-building was at a place called Fiery Cross Reef, where a ten-thousand-foot runway now cut through the water. In nearby areas, Japan, Vietnam, the Philippines, Taiwan, and Malaysia were busy staking their own claims to various bits of land. The *New York Times* published a map of the region showing all these outposts, and there were so many highlighted dots that it looked like someone had spilled confetti. At stake: mineral resources, fishing, and control of one of the planet's busiest shipping regions, carrying $5 trillion worth of trade every year.

The U.S. Department of Defense said that China's "extensive land reclamation activities, particularly the prospect of further militarizing those outposts, are very concerning to us," and were part of the reason for the ongoing "Asia-Pacific shift," a key of which was the buildup of the bases on Guam. China, for its part, insisted that its activity was all for civilian purposes, including "aids for navigation, search and rescue, as well as marine meteorological forecasting services, fishery services and other administrative services." The same talking points that the United States used when it sent colonizers to Howland, Jarvis, and Baker Islands. *Nothing to see here, move along.*

Somewhere, Alfred Mahan, he of the Imperial Moment call-to-action *The Influence of Sea Power upon History,* was smiling.

• • • • •

What *should* the future hold, for Puerto Rico or any of the territories?

I've been grappling with that question since those first days of research, after the Quarters of Destiny, and the honest truth is, I'm still not sure. Statehood seems to make the most sense for Puerto Rico—count me as a Jaded Realist in that regard—but

I'm also sympathetic to the independence view. One suggestion I heard a few times is a referendum offering a straight, once-and-for-all choice between statehood and independence. To me, this makes a lot of sense.

But never mind what *I* think. It should be up to the citizens of the territories, both the long-standing ethnic groups and the newcomers who call these places home, to decide their own fate. Their affairs have been largely dictated by far-off and often indifferent administrators and local officials consumed with maintaining their own power. It's high time the people had more say in what happens to them—you know, all that *democracy* stuff—not just by repackaging the existing setup (this means you, commonwealth status) but in real, tangible ways.

And the issue of political status is, in the immediate term, not the right question. There are so many other underlying issues that can and should be addressed first, including the need for more investment in basic services and the creation of long-term economic opportunities beyond minimum-wage jobs and corporate tax breaks that could be repealed at any minute. In addition, American Samoa should be *organized* and all the territories *incorporated*, so that they're really, truly part of the country, not merely possessions, and have the full and unquestioned protections of the Constitution. Beyond that, it's high time they got true congressional representation and a presidential vote. Yes, it'll require a change to the Electoral College, but I trust that with a bit of all-American effort and ingenuity we can somehow make it work, as we did with the District of Columbia. It's a travesty for a country that claims to be a Magnanimous Exemplar of Democracy for the World to shut anyone—let alone millions—out of the political system purely because of the geographic coordinates of their home.

The last hundred-plus years have shown that, contrary to the Democrats' talking point in the 1900 election, a nation *can* endure half republic and half empire. But that doesn't mean it *should.* As the 1900 Democrats said a paragraph later, the territorial setup, as it stands, is "a colonial policy, inconsistent with republican institutions." To answer the question I'd been pondering since the earliest days of this project: Yes, the territories are, in fact, modern-day colonies. Of course they are. This fact has not changed since the Imperial Moment. And that's a problem, one that we, the United States of America, must resolve.

We need to talk about the territories again. We need to start listening to them, too. The people of these far-off islands are not "foreign aliens." They are us.

ACKNOWLEDGMENTS

My thanks, first of all, to the many people in each territory who shared their stories and perspectives and let me into their lives, if only for a moment. Time and again, complete strangers went out of their way to show me around their neighborhoods, their towns, their entire islands.

I've mentioned many of these people throughout the book, and in a few rare instances, I've changed names and other identifying details to protect their privacy, but every person is entirely, singularly real. I recorded formal interviews and many other conversations either with a digital recorder or through copious notes in real time. During some casual interactions, however, I did not actively take notes but wrote down as much as I could minutes or hours later; in doing so, I did my absolute best to stay true to the tone, content, and phrasing of the discussion. In assembling the narrative of the book, I also occasionally shifted the chronology of my experiences on each island.

Beyond the individuals who appear in the chapters, I'm grateful to everyone who helped me with my travels, either in the planning stages or during my travels on the ground. A few people deserve special mention for going above and beyond. In the U.S. Virgin Islands: Elizabeth Sudmeier Stevenson and Win-grove Lynton. In American Samoa: Celeste Brash and Michael Larson. On Guam: Catherine Kowal, Jamie Knapp, and Andy Wheeler. In the Northern Mariana Islands: Rellani Ogumoro. In the Marshall Islands: Jay Plasman and Scott Christensen. In Puerto Rico: Yaremis Felix, David Skeist, Julie Schwietert Collazo, Hal Bromm, and Doneley Meris. And Noelle Kahanu provided much-needed information about the Hui Panalä'au island-colonization project.

The many times I struggled to understand the legal matters relating to the territories, I sought out the patient explanations of Harvard Law Professor Gerald Neuman, and, most of all, Columbia Law Professor Christina Duffy Ponsa. Neil Weare also helped walk me through these issues and put me in touch with a number of people in the territories. Neil's organization, the We the People Project (www.equalrightsnow.org), is fighting the good fight and, even with minimal resources, making strides in gaining more rights for the territories.

This would all be simply a stack of notebooks, a not-quite book, if not for the support and hard work of my agents at the Jean V. Naggar Literary Agency, Alice Tasman and, especially, Elizabeth Evans, whose early encouragement helped propel me out the door and into the world. It was a joy working with my editor, Matt Weiland, whose insights, wisdom, and gentle critiques over the course of many months and more than a thousand(!) marked-up pages transformed a mass of ideas into the book you now hold in your hands. Thanks also to Remy Cawley and the whole team at Norton who worked tirelessly behind the scenes.

I'm grateful for the feedback on early drafts from Michael Cook, Leif Pettersen, Frank Bures, Jason Albert, Maggie Ryan Sanford, Lars Ostrom, Sara Aase, Dennis Cass, and Ashley Shelby. Their comments, commiseration, and arguments over word choice improved this book immeasurably. Thanks to Kirk Horsted for his ongoing encouragement and to Michael Blades, Kathy Kilroy, and everyone at the Key West Literary Seminar for their support.

My family and friends provided unending pep talks and, when needed, morale-boosting pastries. Special thanks to Elisabeth Munger, Shirley Sailors, Sebastian and Becky Celis, Hannah Kaplan, John Neely, and, especially, to my parents, who were my earliest boosters and continue to support me in so many ways. And a shout-out to Tiffany Loeb Schneider, who happened to tweet a story about the National Park of American Samoa, which Maren happened to see, setting this book in motion.

Finally and most of all, to my wife, Maren, and our daughter, Maja, who inspire me and keep me going every day. As I write this, it's the small hours of the morning and they're both in bed while I'm sprawled on the living room floor, the tight knots of the carpet etching my elbows as I stare at my laptop screen, searching for the right words—a familiar scene around here. But I know Maren's waiting up for me, ever-supportive of my writing career, and I can hear Maja starting to stir in the baby monitor, so it's time for me to return to them, with these words for posterity: I love you both so much. Thank you for everything.

FURTHER READING & NOTES ON SOURCES

These pages are not the final word on the territories but merely a starting point—I encourage readers to go to the territories, have conversations, read more, learn more. There's lots I had to leave out and, as I'll be the first to admit, a whole universe of perspectives and history that I still don't know, despite my best efforts.

Researching this book took me deep into government white papers, century-old texts in assorted libraries, and even a few offbeat YouTube videos, along with stacks and stacks of books and articles from newspapers and magazines. I've called out my sources throughout the book, but a few deserve special mention here, particularly for anyone interested in learning more about the territories.

For a general overview of the territories, their histories, and some of the high-level issues, I relied most heavily on Arnold H. Leibowitz's *Defining Status* (1989), along with the books *Foreign in a Domestic Sense* (2001), edited by Christina Duffy Burnett and Burke Marshall; *Colonial Constitutionalism* (2002), by E. Robert Statham, Jr.; *Does the Constitution Follow the Flag?* (2009), by Kal Raustiala; *Imperial Archipelago* (2010), by Lanny

Thompson; and *Reconsidering the Insular Cases* (2015), edited by Gerald L. Neuman and Tomiko Brown-Nagin.

Beyond these books, I relied on an assortment of works related to each specific territory. For the USVI, my key sources were *America's Virgin Islands* (2010 edition), by William W. Boyer; *A History of the Virgin Islands of the United States* (1974 edition), by Isaac Dookhan; and *St. Croix Under Seven Flags* (1970), by Florence Lewisohn. For American Samoa: *American Samoa: 100 Years Under the United States Flag* (2000), by J. Robert Shaffer, and I'd be remiss if I didn't also mention the delightful memoir *My Samoan Chief* (1977), by Fay G. Calkins, mother of Charles Ala'ilima and Marie Alailima. For Guam: *Destiny's Landfall* (1995), by Robert F. Rogers; the online resource Guampedia also provided useful insights on a variety of subjects. For the CNMI: *From Colonialism to Self-Government: The Northern Marianas Experience* (2010), by Jose S. Dela Cruz, along with the documentary *The Insular Empire* (2010) and, specific to the garment industry, *Nobodies* (2007), by John Bowe. For Puerto Rico: *Puerto Rico in the American Century* (2007), by César J. Ayala and Rafael Bernabe; *The Puerto Ricans: A Documentary History* (1999), edited by Kal Wagenheim and Olga Jimzenez De Wagenheim; and *Puerto Rico: The Trials of the Oldest Colony in the World* (1997), by José Trías Monge. And, finally, for the Minor Outlying Islands, *The Great Guano Rush: Entrepreneurs and American Overseas Expansion* (1994), by Jimmy M. Skaggs, and, for the Hui Panalā'au program, the documentary *Under a Jarvis Moon* (2010), along with the *Hui Panalā'au: Hawaiian Colonists in the Pacific, 1935–1942* oral histories compiled by the University of Hawaii at Manoa in the early 2000s.

In addition to the copious amounts of reading, I also conducted dozens of interviews, as discussed throughout the book and noted in the acknowledgments section.

Finally, I must give credit to two earlier travelogues that helped show me the way: Simon Winchester's *Outposts* (1985) and Harry Ritchie's *The Last Pink Bits* (1997), both of which traipse through the cultures, histories, and modern-day lives of the British colonies.

INDEX

Note: Page numbers in italics indicate maps; page numbers followed by "n" indicate notes.